# THE ARTS
# OF MANKIND

*EDITED BY ANDRÉ MALRAUX*
*AND GEORGES SALLES*

General Advisor
ANDRÉ PARROT

# *Byzantium*

## FROM THE DEATH OF THEODOSIUS
## TO THE RISE OF ISLAM

ANDRÉ GRABAR

# BYZANTIUM

## FROM THE DEATH OF THEODOSIUS
## TO THE RISE OF ISLAM

*TRANSLATED BY STUART GILBERT*

*AND JAMES EMMONS*

THAMES AND HUDSON

# Contents

*To my wife*

# Introduction

It was the fifth and sixth centuries that saw the flowering of the Christian art of Antiquity. However important the stimulus given to Christian art by Constantine, over half a century elapsed before the initial efforts and experiments of the pioneers resulted in a mature art of sufficient scope and power to meet the needs of the Christian community disseminated throughout the Roman Empire.

The necessary conditions for the rise and diffusion of a 'complete' Christian art were created by Theodosius I, who threw the weight of his great authority into the task of consolidating the Church and its unity by stamping out paganism and the Arian heresy, and making Christianity the sole religion of the Empire. It was in his time, moreover, and under his immediate successors, that the Fathers of the Church powerfully strengthened the authority of the Church and raised the prestige of Christianity. They laid the foundations of a 'Christian humanism'—a Christian culture which, instead of rejecting the heritage of classical antiquity, accepted it wherever this seemed feasible. On the lower levels of religious practice, a similar adaptation was made, if less explicitly, and took widespread effect as a result of the massive influx of pagans into the Church.

The same was true of Christian art. The great Doctors of the Church were quick to see the services art could render to the cult of the Cross and the martyrs. In Rome Pope Leo I was instrumental in the creation of a new, more elaborate iconography, for the decoration of the apses of the great basilicas. At the same time, local varieties of religious worship, more or less popular in character, led to a proliferation of devotional images, influencing both their content and their form.

Christian art of the fifth and sixth centuries had a field of action as extensive as the Empire itself as it then was, prior to its territorial losses and the division of the Roman State into an Empire of the West and an Empire of the East. And in fact it was just at this time, after the death of Theodosius (395), that the division took place. But to all intents and purposes the political unity of the Roman Empire was not yet a dead letter, and indeed it was temporarily restored under Justinian. So far as art is concerned, the situation was similar: on the one hand, the same art forms prevailed throughout

1

Christendom, from Mesopotamia to Great Britain and Morocco; on the other hand, the works produced over so vast an area naturally showed differences of emphasis and accent, more or less marked according to the time and the locality.

The most obvious differences, however, do not correspond to the political division between the Empires of the West and the East as constituted in the fifth and early sixth century. For many provinces, moreover, the number of extant works of this period is too meagre to warrant any attempt to distinguish between an 'eastern' and a 'western' tradition within the bounds of the Empire. Probably our safest course is to try to distinguish the traditions peculiar to a given province, and to assume that they were imposed by the art of its metropolis. For in the last analysis the originality of the art of a given province and the extent of its diffusion are found to depend on the quality and quantity of work produced in its chief city. In some cases (Milan, Salonica) we are fortunate in possessing both the monuments of the seminal centre and the copies of them made in the surrounding area. Oftener, however, we have only one of the two groups to go on. Thus in the case of Rome no monuments have survived in the inhabited area in the immediate neighbourhood of the city; in the case of Syria and North Africa, it is the monuments of their respective 'capitals' that have disappeared. Even more confused is the situation in Asia Minor and Egypt; Alexandria and the coastal towns of Asia Minor are known to have been great art centres, but far too few works have survived for us to form any clear idea of the kind of art produced there.

We are better placed to judge of Constantinople and the role it played in the sixth century, because there is a sufficiency of extant monuments and we can study both the prototypes in the capital and the copies made in the surrounding region. But Constantinople is a case apart, since it was the political centre of a vast Empire. Constantinopolitan influences were propagated in two different ways and had two destinations, some being transmitted by ordinary channels to the near-by provinces, others by directives issued from time to time by the central authority and taking effect in different parts of the Empire.

Similarly, the religious ascendancy of Rome was instrumental in disseminating the influence of Roman monuments throughout the Latin West, including Illyricum. But for the period under consideration the study of the influence exerted by Rome has not yet been carried very far, owing no doubt to the rarity of surviving monuments. Apart from Rome, Milan and Ravenna, Italy is very poor in monuments of the fifth and sixth centuries, and other countries of the West are even poorer. Too few remain for us to be able to determine the regional characteristics of the different art forms, country by country; but there are enough to show conclusively that all the art forms typical of Christian art in the fifth and sixth centuries were practised in every country of the Latin West.

The art style of the Latin West was essentially the same as that prevailing in all the lands around the Mediterranean. Harder to define, for the reasons already stated, are the regional characteristics which must have developed in the West just as they did in other provinces of the Roman and Christian world. Indeed, in view of the political autonomy of most countries of Western Europe in the fifth and sixth centuries, the original element in their arts must have been more pronounced than that of the provinces which still lay within the frontiers of the Empire. However, these indigenous features fore-shadowing the national traditions of Western art are little in evidence in the fifth- and sixth-century works dealt with in this volume.

Monastic architecture, which came as the latest development of Christian archi-tecture, made its appearance in the course of these two centuries. Needless to say it was not the monasticism of the anchorites that gave rise to it; it was due to the initiative of great nobles who installed monastic communities on their estates far from the towns, or to that of the founders of the communal (coenobitic) monasteries.

The art of these monastic centres, established in the 'wilderness' as a means of escape from society and the State, was, generally speaking, uninventive. It developed on the same lines as the other forms of contemporary Christian art and, like them, reflected regional practices and tastes. There are certain cases in which the influence of monastic art can be traced from one province to another (from Syria to Africa, from Egypt to Ireland), but as a rule it was the local tradition that prevailed. Monastic art must there-fore be studied, not in isolation, but in its natural relation to other works of architecture and painting.

# 1. Architecture

*Foreword*

A forest of Christian basilicas sprang up in the fifth century throughout the Roman Empire. True, there already existed a certain number of earlier churches, some of which we have described in the previous volume. But it was only from the end of the fourth century on that they were built in such large numbers in all the towns of every province, and very often in groups of two or more when located in a bishopric, a place of pilgrimage, a monastic community, or in the larger towns.

There was a tendency now to eliminate churches of an unusual design (which had been acceptable in the fourth century) and to replace them by regular basilicas. The town of Salona, on the Dalmatian coast, provides examples of an earlier church being rebuilt in the 'standard' form of a timber-roofed basilica, with the nave divided on each side from a lateral aisle by a row of arcaded columns, and with an apse at one end and an entrance at the other, facing the choir. Other elements—atrium, narthex, transepts of different types, and lateral apses—could be added; they were not obligatory and were included in the basilica in varying proportions depending on the region.

Further evidence of the gradual spread of this type of basilica is provided by the ruins of the early churches of southern Syria. The fourth-century churches here are only an adaptation of a local type of building whose characteristic forms and techniques are foreign to the normal basilica. In the fifth century Syrian church-builders overcame the difficulties of adaptation and succeeded—not without an effort—in producing exact imitations of the basilica adopted everywhere else in the Empire. The distinction between churches of northern and southern Syria, very pronounced in the fourth century, now tended to disappear. The basilica, with all its essential features, triumphed everywhere in the course of the fifth century, so completely that one might suppose it to have been imposed by the religious authorities. But as no text expressly calling for it has ever come to light, its adoption must have been due to a widespread spirit of conservatism, and initially, perhaps, to the prestige of the great basilicas founded by Constantine.

Thus throughout the Roman Empire the idea of a Christian church came to be closely associated with the basilical type of building, with the result that for over a

1. *Constantinople*, St Sophia. *Interior looking towards the Apse.*

5

century the general structural design of Christian churches evolved little if at all and, except for a few original features in some cases, and details peculiar to a given region, there was little to distinguish them from each other.

Therefore it seems best to study these monuments region by region. We shall deal in the following survey only with those (relatively few) edifices which are sufficiently well preserved to be regarded as veritable works of art.

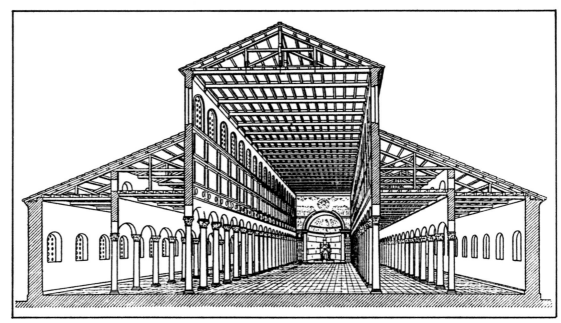

2. *Rome, San Paolo fuori le Mura. Section.*

*Rome and Italy*

It is the huge basilica of San Paolo fuori le Mura, at the gates of Rome, that today conveys the most impressive idea of the Early Christian churches of Imperial times. Begun in 386 by Valentinian II, it was not completed till about 440. The plan and elevation reproduce those of Old St Peter's founded by Constantine, and San Paolo is a signal example of the stability of the basilical type of church described above. Entirely reconstructed after the fire of 1823, this mighty building is remarkable for the sweep and splendour of its great nave with four identical colonnades. The illusion of spatial depth is created by the transept, which sets up a screen of light between the spectator and the altar in front of the apse. The present decorations imitate those that were destroyed, but their overall effect may not correspond exactly to that of the original decorations.

Hence our preference for Santa Maria Maggiore. Though the exterior of this basilica is Baroque, the interior has kept intact the chief features of the original edifice and of its mosaic decorations. All the older parts of the church date to the time of Pope

6

3. *Rome, San Paolo fuori le Mura.  View of the Nave looking towards the Apse.*

5. *Rome, Santa Sabina.  Exterior.*

Sixtus III (432-440), and it would seem that nothing now remains of the work of Pope Liberius (352-366), to whom until recently the main fabric and part of the decoration were still attributed. The nave is a splendid piece of architecture, with majestic colonnades whose grey shafts prepare the eye for the coloured revetment of the upper walls.  Between the windows, within monochrome frames (originally intended to represent tabernacles in side-view), panels of multicoloured mosaics stand out on a white ground; others cover the triumphal arch, scintillating against a gold ground.  The choir alone, remodelled in early times and encumbered with a huge Baroque altar, does not belong to the original fifth-century church, which must have been a masterpiece of tranquil power and stately beauty.  Here, better than anywhere else, we perceive the aristocratic element in the Christian art of Late Antiquity patronized by the Emperor and the Popes.

The same effect of harmonious equilibrium makes itself felt in the small basilica of Santa Pudenziana now that the columns of Pope Siricius (384-399) have been disengaged from the sixteenth-century pillars that had hidden them.  Like some of the other Roman basilicas (Santa Maria Maggiore, Santi Giovanni e Paolo and San Pietro in Vincoli), Santa Pudenziana had a triple bay in the wall facing the apse; this was a characteristic feature of the Roman basilicas of the fifth century.

4. *Rome, Santa Maria Maggiore. View of the Nave looking towards the Triumphal Arch.*

7. *Rome, Santa Sabina.   Polychrome Marble Revetment in the Nave.*

The church of Santa Sabina, built on the Aventine after the sack of Rome by Alaric (410), is one of the outstanding monuments of Early Christian Rome.  Nothing could be more perfect than the quiet grandeur and beautiful proportions of the nave and side-aisles, separated by two rows of columns.  The polychrome marbles lining the walls, remarkable for their sobriety, contribute to the harmony of the interior, whose most original feature is no doubt the abundance of light.

As well as the basilicas, which represent the main line of development of Christian architecture, other churches were built which kept to the traditional radiating or central plan: some were rotundas, some were polygonal, some were trefoils or quatrefoils, some were given the form of a cross or a square.

Dating to the time of Constantine, the rotunda of Santa Costanza was in the direct lineage of the monumental circular tombs of the Romans, for it was originally erected as the mausoleum of the Emperor's daughter Constance.  Her mother, St Helena, had a similar mausoleum.  The Theodosian dynasty built two circular mausolea near St Peter's for members of the imperial family; these have disappeared but drawings of them are extant.  With the triumph of the Christian ideal of humility, mausolea ceased to be built for ordinary mortals—only, on occasion, for princes (and then only in the West) and for saints.  The martyrium, built on a site hallowed by the memory of a saint or a relic, gave scope for various types of funerary architecture for centuries to come.

8. *Rome, Lateran Baptistery. Interior.*

It is in Rome that we find the oldest example of a baptistery on the central plan. As early as the reign of Constantine, when the Emperor installed the Bishop of Rome and the episcopal church in his Lateran palaces, a circular room was built to serve as a baptistery. The foundations of this early rotunda are still visible, but the building itself was entirely remodelled in the fifth century by Pope Sixtus III (432-440). The rotunda was replaced by an octagon; the interior was organized around the tall columns that divide the central area, containing a piscina, from the aisle around it. The eight columns must have supported a cupola, while the surrounding aisle was covered with barrel vaulting. In spite of later changes (notably a second row of colonnettes and the inner balustrade), this venerable monument, forerunner of so many octagonal baptisteries in Italy, retains its ancient aspect.

San Stefano Rotondo, founded by Pope Simplicius (468-483), keeps to the rotunda plan, but here the layout is far more complex. It includes a double circular aisle, and within it is inscribed a Greek cross. The building is a little too low for its size (which is comparable to that of the Holy Sepulchre), and the thick columns inside detract from the sense of space within the rotunda which, with its timber roof and the large number of light interior supports, had, even for its time, the aspect of an archaic edifice.

12                                        10. *Rome, San Stefano Rotondo. Interior.*

9. *Rome, San Stefano Rotondo.  Exterior.*

12. *Ravenna, Sant'Apollinare in Classe. Exterior.*

Outside Rome, the two imperial cities of Ravenna and Milan were flourishing centres of Christian life and culture in the fourth, fifth and sixth centuries. This is particularly true of Milan where, in the years since the Second World War, many new discoveries have thrown light on the Early Christian architecture of the city.

Sant'Ambrogio, the 'basilica of the martyrs,' was built by St Ambrose in 385-386 to house the bodies of St Gervasius and St Protasius, patrons of the city. But very little now remains of the original edifice, the church having been entirely rebuilt in the Middle Ages. It is flanked by an oratory-martyrium, roughly square in plan, preceded by an atrium; the latter is rare in many provinces of the Empire, but not in Northern Italy.

The most famous monument of ancient Milan is the magnificent octagonal church of San Lorenzo, which I would date to the fifth century rather than to about the year 400, as Italian scholars often do today. It is the largest known building of the type it represents: that of a domed quatrefoil church. Though its plan and its position outside the city walls suggest it may have originated as a martyrium, the initial purpose of the building remains an open question, for there is no martyr saint whose name can be connected with it. Nevertheless, in the light of the many martyria on the same plan in Syria and Armenia, some also of the fifth century, some of the sixth and seventh centuries, I think we may assume that San Lorenzo was originally founded as a martyrium. This would account for the presence of five other rooms, built on to the four apses. This layout, with the four-branched aisle and the gallery, produces a fine effect and it says much for

13. *Ravenna, Mausoleum of Galla Placidia. Exterior.*

the technical skill of the architects that they were able to increase the height of the building without unduly enlarging the supporting members. It is possible that the original design included a dome, but the piers seem too slender to bear the weight this would have represented. The aisles were certainly vaulted and smaller cupolas covered the oratories on the periphery; of these, the one on the right, Sant'Aquilino, served for a time as a baptistery *(plan p. 346, fig. 397)*.

As a result of air-raids during the Second World War the ancient walls of two other important martyria in Milan—San Nazzaro (formerly Santi Apostoli), dating to 382, and San Simpliciano, of the late fourth century—have been uncovered. And now that the early date of these walls has been firmly established, we can add to the repertory of Milanese architecture this type of cruciform building, large as a church, with a single nave some sixty-five feet high and a transversal hall projecting outward on either side like the transept of a medieval church. The outer walls, which rose up straight, without a break, were decorated with arcades and pierced with large windows. The general effect is similar to that of the famous secular basilica of Trier. Like the latter, the two Milanese martyria had timber roofs. These three monuments anticipate the great Rhenish and Lombard churches of the early Romanesque period *(plan p. 347, fig. 401)*.

The Ravennate branch of Early Christian architecture was an offshoot of Milan. But judging by the churches that are still standing, the architects confined themselves to imitating buildings of the established types. These are, for the most part, timber-roofed basilicas with two rows of arcaded columns and a projecting apse. The cathedral (Basilica Ursiana) has a nave and four aisles, the other churches a nave and two aisles (San Giovanni

16

14. *Ravenna, Sant'Apollinare Nuovo. Colonnade in the Nave, with Mosaics.*

Evangelista, 425; Sant'Apollinare Nuovo, 519; Sant'Apollinare in Classe, 549). The church of Santa Croce, now destroyed, may have been more original in design; it seems to have had a nave without aisles, preceded by a transverse narthex to which was joined the only element of the original building now remaining: the domed, cruciform tomb of Galla Placidia, daughter of Theodosius I, sister of Honorius and mother of Valentinian III.

The architecture of these basilicas differs only in a few details from that of the Roman basilicas and others of the same kind, and these details are unsystematically disposed. Thus the two small rooms, one on either side of the apse of San Giovanni Evangelista, are not to be found in the other Ravennate basilicas, which do not include any form of transept, narthex or atrium. The only feature that does recur several times is the apse ribbed on the outside; this may derive from Byzantine models.

15. *Ravenna, Mausoleum of Theodoric. Exterior.*

16. *Ravenna, San Giovanni Evangelista. Exterior showing the Apse.*

The Christian mausolea of Ravenna—the tomb of Galla Placidia in the form of a Latin cross, and the circular tomb of Theodoric before the gates of the city—keep to the design of Roman funerary monuments, although that of the Ostrogoth king (who died in 526) has certain features which make it virtually unique. The features I have in mind are not so much the use of dressed stone (whereas all other buildings of this period in Ravenna are of brick) as the dome, carved from a single block of stone, and the curious ornamental band running along its cornice. The influence of Germanic tradition has been read into this ornament; but, while such an influence is quite possible, its presence here remains conjectural for want of any monuments to which this tomb might be compared.

Apart from the mausoleum of Theodoric, architecture on the radiating plan is represented at Ravenna by two baptisteries whose mosaics have made them famous. The so-called Orthodox Baptistery or Baptistery of Neon (first quarter of the fifth century), adjacent to the cathedral, is a singularly tall, slender structure, much resembling a tower. This effect was originally tempered by the addition of a corridor running round the lower part of the octagon. The smooth surface of the façades is only faintly animated by a few lines of shadow cast by the very low pilasters and arches. Although the ground plan of the baptistery is that of a square with rounded corners, the four niches occupying these

19

17. *Ravenna, Orthodox Baptistery. Exterior.*

18. *Ravenna, Arian Baptistery. Exterior.*

corners are relatively low in elevation, thereby disengaging the octagon of the interior and enabling it to rise to a considerable height. Is this peculiarity to be accounted for by assuming that the height of the baptistery was increased as early as the fifth century? In that case we should have to assume that all that part of the interior which begins at the level of the stucco decorations was also a later addition. In my opinion there are no grounds for this assumption. On the other hand, the straight walls do seem to have been subsequently reinforced up to the base of the dome, which itself was built at the same time as the original octagon.

The second baptistery, the so-called Arian Baptistery, built about 500, is a similar edifice, except that it has not been raised to the same height. The weight of a dome was such that architects were compelled to support it with unbroken walls which more or less isolated the central hall with the baptismal font from the outer rooms around it. This was the case at Ravenna, where the first baptistery has been entirely deprived of the peripheral elements of the central octagon, while the second only retains part of them, and this part is in ruins. But the ground plan reveals their original extent: they consisted of a jointed corridor, octagonal in plan like the baptismal hall, this corridor being linked by arches and vaulting to the central core of the building, which is also octagonal in plan and has four apses. The remarkable extension of one of these apses reflects the growing influence of the liturgy on architecture, for hitherto no departure had been made from the strictly geometric regularity of a central plan.

San Vitale, begun in 532 and consecrated by Archbishop Maximian in 547, was the last Ravennate church to be built on a radiating plan. Again we have a domed octagon,

19. *Ravenna, Orthodox Baptistery. Interior.*

20. *Ravenna, San Vitale. Exterior.*

but this time the building is larger and its design more complex. A single hall within the outer walls is divided up by a system of supports rising between the central octagon and the ambulatory. A row of broad bays enables easy movement between these two parts of the building. A gallery encompasses the central hall, extending on either side of a choir which also has the form of a long hall ending in an apse. The width of the choir exceeds that of any one side of the central octagon, and this serves to emphasize the main axis of the building *(plan p. 347, fig. 400)*.

The architect took great care in designing the superimposed arches which occupy seven sides of the octagon, the eighth corresponding to the choir. Each of these seven sides opens out to form a concave exedra; the two pillars flanking each exedra, and linked by arches, here replace the continuous wall above. On the upper storey, a half cupola is supported by each pair of columns. The main central dome rests on all these supports together, taking its rise above a zone of eight pendentives, while transverse ribs lend support to the pillars which mark the corners of the central octagon, by transmitting to the corresponding corners of the outer walls a part of the thrust exerted by the dome. A narthex, flanked by two round towers and preceded by a small atrium, completes the building on the side containing the entrance doors. The choir is flanked by two small apses and two adjoining rooms, probably subsidiary martyry-chapels.

The dome is built in the Italic manner: it is made of pottery vessels, instead of bricks, in order to lighten the vaulting. This technical detail vouches for the local origin of the men who built San Vitale. The predominance of ascending lines in the general design of the building has been pointed to as a further confirmation of this origin. These considerations

21. *Ravenna, San Vitale. Side Wall of the Choir.*

22. *Perugia, Rotunda of Sant'Angelo. Interior.*

23. *Spoleto, San Salvatore. Façade.*

24

carry weight, but do they suffice to differentiate the aesthetic of San Vitale from that of similar, contemporary examples of Byzantine architecture? San Vitale is certainly the work of Ravennate builders, but they were obviously intent on imitating a Byzantine model.

In most Italian cities, despite the ravages of time, it is clear that the architects of the fifth and sixth centuries when planning groups of buildings aimed at an overall symmetry. Thus at Parenzo we find a basilica and a baptistery of central plan aligned along the same axis on either side of the atrium (plan p. 346, fig. 399).

Further south, at Perugia, is an admirable rotunda, the church of Sant'Angelo, standing on a hilltop. Dating to the late fourth century, this building reminds us of the Roman rotunda of Santa Costanza—with this difference, that far more care was taken with the proportions and decorations of the latter. The colonnade supporting the dome is intact, but the rectangular exedrae which formed a cross around the central rotunda were demolished long ago. This is much to be regretted, for this layout—a circular plan spanned by a cross—is rare and has a beauty of its own. The three arches through which the exedrae formerly opened into the ambulatory suggest that the parts of the building which now are lacking were designed with equal care.

The basilica of San Salvatore at Spoleto, whose transept does not project beyond the main body of the building and is traversed by the colonnades of the nave, is of interest as being one of the Early Christian churches which have best preserved their original features. This is particularly true of the entrance façade.

In Campania, two of the most remarkable examples of Early Christian architecture of the fifth century are the small chapel of Santa Maria Capua Vetere, near Naples, and, in Naples itself, the cathedral baptistery of San Giovanni in Fonte; both are decorated with mosaics. To these may be added the group of sanctuaries (three basilicas around an atrium) which St Paulinus, bishop, writer and art-lover, erected at Cimitile (ancient Nola), during the same period, in honour of St Felix. This was an art patronized and shaped by the great noblemen of the day, who imposed on the church their own taste for the lavish and spectacular. Unfortunately, in its present state Cimitile is but a pale reflection of its ancient splendour.

*Gaul*

However we interpret the descriptions of the lost churches of ancient Gaul handed down by the authors of the period (notably that of the famous decagonal church of La Daurade at Toulouse, with its mosaic decorations), the surviving monuments are too few to enable us to reconstruct the highly complex history of Early Christian architecture in this area. For the fifth century almost all we have to go on is the small underground basilica of the abbey of Saint-Victor at Marseilles and the two superimposed orders of marble columns flanking the side walls of the church of Saint-Pierre at Vienne (Isère). These serve to give us an idea of the layout and style of the original buildings, and of the Latin and Oriental influences that conditioned them.

Though nothing remains of the cathedral churches erected in Provence and the Rhone valley towards the beginning of the fifth century, a few of the baptisteries that stood beside them still survive. They belong to the same group as the baptisteries of northern

25. *Vienne, Saint-Pierre. View of the Nave with Arcade and Side Wall.*

Italy; despite individual particularities, all are of the same family. We do not know where the prototype of these buildings originated; imitations of it appear as far afield as Constantinople (St Sophia, c. 550) and Syria (Kalat Seman, c. 470). In any case its wide diffusion vouches for the unity of the tradition that pervaded Early Christian art throughout the Mediterranean area.

The octagonal baptistery makes its appearance at Marseilles at the end of the fourth century, with the one that was built near the episcopal church (now La Major). Its size was considerable, exceeding that of the Lateran baptistery in Rome. To the eight columns in the centre, supporting the dome, corresponded eight columns placed against the walls, which supported the vault of the ambulatory. The baptistery recently brought to light at Mariana, in Corsica, is of the same type and seemingly of about the same date (c. 400?).

Recent excavations have provided much information about other baptisteries in Provence deriving from that of Marseilles: those at Aix and Fréjus, of the early fifth century, and that of Riez, which is later and stands apart from the cathedral. But it is the Fréjus baptistery, located within a *temenos*, and in an almost unique state of preservation, on which our knowledge of Early Christian architecture in Gaul is chiefly based. Square on the outside, octagonal inside, with exedrae alternately flat and rounded, it is crowned with a dome (rebuilt) which, with its drum, rests on columns placed in the eight corners of the walls.

24. *Fréjus, Baptistery. Interior.*

26. *Riez, Baptistery. Interior.*

The baptistery recently excavated at Cimiez, near Nice, and datable to between 439 and 564, is of a different type. It belongs to the group of baptismal halls installed in one of the rooms of earlier Gallo-Roman edifices. At Cimiez it was a quite ordinary rectangular room in the public baths. A hexagonal font in the centre was surmounted by a vaulted ciborium. The baptistery of Poitiers, which preceded the Merovingian monument we see today, was of the same type; the foundations (fourth-fifth century) have been traced and the group of rectangular rooms which they reveal is highly characteristic. In Greece and elsewhere in the eastern Mediterranean, this type of baptistery often remained in use until the Arab invasion and even later.

Excavations carried out in 1956 at Portbail, in Normandy, brought to light the substructure of a hexagonal baptistery with a piscina. Two small apses stood at the north-west and south-west angles of the polygon. There were two doors, the larger of which, in the centre of the west side, was preceded by a vestibule *(plan p. 346, fig. 398)*. The early date of this baptistery (between the fourth and sixth century) and its location in northern France, near the Channel, make it a monument of prime importance in the history of the expansion of Early Christian architecture.

28

After the Arab invasion in the seventh century, the declining importance and prosperity of the countries extending along the north coast of Africa had the effect of preserving the Christian monuments there from complete destruction. To the testimony of their imposing ruins, the excavations of the last half-century have added that of the foundations of other monuments, some of key importance.

In most of the North African cities Christianity was adopted at the beginning of the third century. Galvanized by the Donatist heresy, against which St Augustine, Bishop of Hippo, led a crusade, the orthodox Christians triumphed at the Council of Carthage in 411, at the very time when the capture of Rome by Alaric and his barbarian hordes confronted them with a new adversary. In 430, having already overrun large parts of the Empire, in Gaul and Spain, the barbarians reached Africa. Despite the defeat inflicted on the Vandals by the Byzantines, the civilization created in North Africa by the Romans and the Christians began to crumble. With its ports open both to the West and to the East, Christian Africa was equally Mediterranean and Oriental. Its sphere of influence extended to Spain, where it can be traced even in the Visigothic period.

Donatists and Christians vied with each other in building churches in the fourth and fifth centuries. Most of the churches were erected in a rough-and-ready manner, often with makeshift materials taken from pagan temples. Hence they are of less interest for the history of art than for that of the liturgy, of funerary rites, and of the cult of relics which flourished intensively in Africa. Of all that has come down to us of the original decoration, the mosaic pavements have the highest aesthetic value. The best Christian examples are in Tunisia and date from the Byzantine reconquest in the sixth century.

Except for those with no side aisles (Batna, Tabia), the African churches designed on the basilical plan were timber-roofed. This type of building, fully developed as early as the time of Constantine (Orléansville), remained in favour until the Islamic invasion. The African architects had a predilection for spacious naves with several side aisles, and for columns as supporting members inside the church, sometimes coupled columns (Carthage-Dermesh, *plan p.* 347, *fig.* 402), or pillars carrying arches rather than an architrave (Henshir Goussa, *plan p.* 347, *fig.* 403). From the fact that churches with a central nave and four side aisles appeared very early at Orléansville and Carthage-Dermesh, one might be tempted to attribute them to the influence of the Constantinian basilicas of Rome; and this possibility cannot be ruled out. But it has been observed that in some basilicas—for example, St Salsa, near Tipasa *(plan p.* 348, *fig.* 405*)*—the number of aisles was increased from two to four, after a fire, by adding two more rows of piers to support the shortened beams of the timber roof. Something of the same sort may have been done in the case of the Great Basilica of Tipasa, where the nave was divided into seven aisles.

Some African churches had galleries (Tebessa). But the most striking features of these buildings are, on the one hand, the vestibule or narthex between the bases of two towers (Morsott, Tipasa) and, on the other, the 'counter-apse' at the opposite end of the nave from the choir, either recessed in a solid mass of masonry or flanked by two square rooms (Mididi, *plan p.* 348, *fig.* 407, and Feriana, *plan p.* 347, *fig.* 404). In this case the church was entered through doors in one of the side walls, on either side of the counter-apse.

27. *Jemila, Baptistery. Circular Gallery with Niches.*　　28. *Jemila, Baptistery. Ciborium over the Baptismal Font.*

These constructional details, which indicate a link with Oriental churches, reappear in the sixth century in Andalusia (Spain). The basilicas of Alcaracejos, San Pedro of Alcantara and Casa Herrera of Merida also have a counter-apse in the wall opposite the apse of the chevet.

Much of the Christian architecture of Africa consists of buildings on the central plan, which served as baptisteries and martyria. As elsewhere, these are vaulted edifices of small size which, though structurally independent of it, were built in conjunction with an adjacent basilica. Such is the case with the octagon of Tabarka *(plan p. 348, fig. 406)* and the square baptistery of Henshir Rhiria *(plan p. 349, fig. 408)* in Tunisia. The brick-built rotunda at Jemila still has its vaulting. This is an outstanding monument. Baptism took place in a round central room, where a ciborium on four columns stands over the baptismal font. Around this room extended a barrel-vaulted gallery adorned with thirty-six niches which served as seats and vestiaries for the neophytes.

30

29. *Damus-el-Karita (Carthage). Basilica.*

31. *Tebessa, Basilica.*

Of all the surviving examples of Early Christian architecture in Tunisia (Damus-el-Karita at Carthage) and in Algeria (Hippo, Tebessa, Timgad, Tipasa), most impressive is the great basilica of Tebessa. Surrounded on three sides by identical rooms (probably cells), it is preceded in front by a square atrium with two symmetrical staircases giving access to the upper storey of the atrium and the galleries of the church. The various units were built at different times in the fifth and sixth centuries. It was completed by a chapel and a surrounding wall with towers. In front of it stood another building of the basilical type (stables? *xenodochion?*), with an upper storey and no apse, which looked on to a great rectangular court bordered and traversed by porticoes. Beneath this group of buildings ran an elaborate system of underground rooms *(plan p. 349, fig. 410)*.

The orderly layout of the monastery of Tebessa and the no less careful—though different—arrangement of that of Ain Tamda *(plan p. 349, fig. 409)* justify us in comparing them with the early monasteries of Syria. Ain Tamda is related to the Syrian type of church with a cloister adjoining it on one side (a type that took root in Western Europe); whereas Tebessa follows the plan of the Byzantine 'Laura' in which the church is isolated in the middle of a court—a plan represented in Syria by Ruweiha. True, the features in common between these widely separated churches are limited in scope and such as might conceivably have originated at the same time in two different Roman provinces. But the priority of Syria over Africa can be defended in the present instance, since we are here concerned with monastic architecture and monasticism originated in the East.

33. *Sohag, White Monastery (Deir el-Abiad). View of the Exterior from the South-West*

## Egypt

If the Christian monuments of near-by Egypt had survived, they might have served to provide us with a more detailed and accurate knowledge of the architecture of Mediterranean Africa. Unfortunately the Early Christian remains at the mouth of the Nile are buried beneath the buildings of Alexandria, in ancient times a famous capital and a place of transit for eastward-bound pilgrims, who stopped there to see the cells of the anchorites and the monasteries of the coenobites. It is believed, not without good reason (but without material proof), that this Alexandrian art exerted an influence as far afield as Italy and Constantinople.

The abandoned temples of the Pharaohs were taken over by the Christians, just as they had been by the adepts of the cult of the Greek gods and later that of the emperors. Thus at Dendera, as late as the sixth century, a room in the temple of Hathor was carefully and completely re-equipped as a Christian sanctuary *(plan p. 350, fig. 412)*, in a style obviously inspired by an earlier type of building.

Founded by a Byzantine count, the two early fifth-century churches of the Red and White Monasteries, still standing in the desert at Sohag, anticipate the design of the church at Dendera, though they are appreciably larger than the latter. Here, as at Dendera, the triple apse of the chevet forms a massive, independent element, opening on the nave

34. *Sohag, Red Monastery (Deir el-Ahmar)*. *Upper Part of the South Apse*.

35. *Sohag, Red Monastery (Deir el-Ahmar)*. *Lower Part of the South Apse*.

36. *Sohag, White Monastery (Deirel-Abiad). North End of the Narthex.*

through a bay. The nave itself consists of a long hall surrounded on three sides by colonnades. Although this triple colonnade is similar to those of the Palestinian synagogues, it must have derived in this case from the porticoes of Pharaonic temples—an influence which also appears in the adjunction of a cumbrous transversal structure doing duty for a narthex *(plan p. 350, fig. 413)*. This structure recalls the pylons of Pharaonic temples, and the bareness and the slant of the very lofty outer walls increases the resemblance.

In contrast with these original features, which are peculiar to Egypt, the three apses of the choir and the decoration of the inner walls both of the apses and of the vestibule (polychrome marble facings, colonnettes and tabernacles) are undoubtedly of Hellenistic inspiration. As for the massive structure of the chevet, the effect it produces from the exterior is peculiarly Egyptian. But its plan and interior decoration link up with the tradition of the *cella trichora* of Greco-Roman funerary monuments, and it is probable that, when they installed this 'monument' in the chevet, the builders of the church were imitating the sanctuaries which had as their chevet a martyrium or a *memoria*, as at Ras Siaga (Mount Nebo), where the triple apse covered the alleged tomb of Moses. At Sohag, it was the tomb of the founder of the monastery, the great Coptic monk Shenudi, which justified the adoption of this architectural formula.

Recent excavations have revealed another great church of the fifth century (c. 430) which again displays some of the essential features of Sohag and its affiliates. This is the basilica of Hermopolis, which forms part of a complex of various buildings placed in a rectangle and containing an upper storey to which a staircase gives access. The narthex seems to have formed a transverse unit in front of the nave and aisles. The nave of the church, with its side aisles, is surrounded by columns on three sides; the chevet consists of a triple apse, not a transept, as stated by the excavator, A. H. S. Megaw. A crypt under the central apse served as the repository of a saint's body; as to his identity and the fate of his relics, we know nothing, but this very circumstance establishes another link with the triple-apsed basilicas referred to above. The trefoil chevet at Hermopolis is of a more classical type than that at Sohag: the exedrae on either side are provided with a turning aisle and the choir opens on the nave, whereas at Sohag it was separated from the nave by a wall specifically Coptic in character. In short, at Hermopolis Greek influence is more marked than at Sohag and Dendera, although certain Egyptian features are also present.

In other churches (Deir el Bucarah, Bâwit, St Simeon of Aswan), the chevet takes a peculiar form, but in each case a different one. These variants were probably due to very old local traditions, Pharaonic (closed cella and court surrounded by three narrow porticoes), Greco-Roman (church choirs designed in imitation of funerary architecture), or Hellenistic (basilical reminiscences and coloured marble facings).

The true basilica, as we find it everywhere exemplified in Christian churches from the fourth century on, must have been known in Egypt very early in the Christian era. The remains of the Christian edifices that sprang up among the Pharaonic ruins (at Philae, Karnak, etc.) are unquestionably of early date. The same is true of the churches of Hermonthis and Ibrihin, whose foundations show them to have been five-aisled basilicas—a plan which, in most countries, evokes the great churches built by Constantine and those of the late fourth century. Then there are the three basilicas of the monastery of St Menas, south of Alexandria, not far from Lake Mareotis, a famous place of pilgrimage in antiquity. Finest of them is an immense basilica with crypt, projecting apse and aisled transept, plausibly attributed by legend to the Emperor Arcadius. The plan, construction and capitals of this impressive building have nothing specifically Egyptian about them. The general design is clearly the work of foreign architects and it may even have been built by imported labour, so much does it have in common with basilicas erected in the first half of the fifth century at Constantinople, in Asia Minor and other parts of the Empire *(plan p. 350, fig. 411).*

The originality of the Coptic architects can be seen, even in their earliest buildings, in their frequent use of vaulting (barrel vaults and cupolas) to cover oratories and smaller churches. Notable examples are the mausolea of Bagawat and the domed chapel which, in the centre of the monastery of St Jeremiah at Sakkara, contained the founder's tomb. Such vaults were employed to cover not only oratories but also monastic cells. While the vaulting of mausolea was an established practice in the architecture of Roman times,

38

37. *Sakkara, Monastery of St Jeremiah. Partial View.*

one hesitates to assign a definite origin to the vaulting of private houses. Was it an adaptation of the secular vaulted architecture of Roman Egypt (private and public buildings at Karanis discovered by the University of Michigan excavators) or an extension of the architecture of mausolea? The first explanation would appear the more plausible in view of the variety of vaulted rooms in the Coptic monasteries and other architectural characteristics of these monastic agglomerations. For at Sakkara, Bawit, Aswan and elsewhere, the Coptic monasteries formed ˙an irregular complex of buildings large and small, conforming to no general plan (*plan p.* 351, *fig.* 414*)*. This serried mass of rather low buildings brings to mind the cities of the East as they have been in all ages and sharply contrasts with the harmonious layout of the contemporary monasteries of Roman Syria.

38. *Kfer, Apse of the Church.  Exterior.*

39. *Kalat Kalota, East Church.  South Façade.*

40. *Simkhar, Chapel beside the Basilica. Façade.*

*Syria*

More fifth- and sixth-century churches have been found in Syria than in any other province of the Roman Empire, but all are in ruins. It has therefore become impossible to pass any direct judgment on Syrian architecture from the aesthetic point of view, except with respect to isolated details that have survived on fragments. The overall effect of a building can only be gauged by means of careful reconstructions which, however helpful they may be to the historian, are but a poor substitute for the original monument.

The exceptional prosperity which Syria enjoyed in the fifth and sixth centuries led to an increased activity in all domains. New buildings were erected, and churches founded in many cities, towns and villages. Produced in the same period and under similar conditions, these churches closely resemble each other and, with a few exceptions, conform to the same type of basilical plan, the one which was introduced into Syria at the end of the fourth century.

Northern Syria was first to adopt the basilical plan. Southern Syria followed suit somewhat later, since it had to adapt its traditional building methods to the requirements of the new type of edifice. But by the fifth century this formative period was over and some uniformity of plan and construction had been achieved. This is not to say that other types of religious edifices wholly disappeared, but they were few in number and their liturgical function was limited, since they were usually martyria.

41

The beauty of certain Syrian monuments of early Christian times lies in the precision of the stereotomy (vaulted apse of the church of Kfer) and in the construction of the walls with their fine ashlar masonry (Ruweiha I, South Church). The beautiful proportions of the Ruweiha church contribute to the harmony of a very plain façade, whose decoration, in flat relief, is limited to the lintels of the three doors. Preceded by an atrium, the façade of the church of St Mary at Sheikh Sleman forms a transverse portico. The presence of a terrace above this portico accounts for the use of an horizontal architrave instead of arches. A few very simple geometric designs in low relief decorate the parapet which rises just above the architrave. The church of Kharab Shems is tall and narrow. Its façade is more attractive, owing to the greater number of windows patterning the wall, whose masonry again is particularly fine.

The type of church found at El-Bara (El-Hosn I, *plan p*. 352, *fig*. 415)—a long narrow basilica with interior colonnades and, on either side of both the apse and the main entrance, two rooms connected by porticoes—was later imitated in Armenia (Ereruk).

Not until the sixth century do we find an amplification of the decoration of the façades (sometimes, too, of the inner walls of churches), imparting to them something of the plastic opulence of antique façades (El-Bara). In the chapel added in the sixth century to the church of Simkhar we have an excellent example of a façade designed with an eye to aesthetic effect. The doorway in particular is one of the handsomest in Syria; the festoons running round it have an almost Baroque luxuriance.

In addition to these individual churches, there are also several groups of buildings in Syria which were planned to compose an organic whole (Bakirha). A study of these architectural complexes is rewarding, for their rarity in other lands lends a special interest to certain features of the layout (leaving aside local peculiarities) which are found throughout the Mediterranean area in the period we are considering.

The ground plans of these complexes show how the different buildings were disposed. In some cases the layout was governed by the lie of the land, and no particular geometric pattern emerges (Dar Kita, *plan p*. 352, *fig*. 416). Elsewhere the edifices are confined to an area which evidently corresponded to a demarcated tract of land allotted to the founders. Thus the two monasteries built in the sixth century on the outskirts of Deir Seman are located in a well-defined rectangle, though not completely filling it. Further constructions on one side make the central courtyard asymmetrical; to the porticoes surrounding the court correspond the porticoes enclosing the main buildings and the *xenodochion* *(plan p*. 352, *fig. 418)*.

The transition from the fifth to the sixth century was marked by a growing concern for regularity. There now developed a tendency to isolate the church, to set it apart as a 'monument,' as was formerly done in the case of the pagan temples. At Ir-Ruhaiyeh, three almost identical churches were erected successively in the sixth century on three sides of a square porticoed courtyard *(plan p*. 352, *fig*. 417*)*. Ed Deir (sixth century) shows an equally well-ordered plan, but here a single church is symmetrically flanked by two small annexes; this church faces the entrance of an atrium, of which it forms one side, while the three other sides, flanked by porticoes, house the dependencies *(plan p*. 353, *fig*. 419*)*. Finally, at El-Anderin, the church stands alone within a fortified enclosure which entirely surrounds it *(plan p*. 353, *fig*. 420*)*.

41. *Kalat Kalota, East Church. West Façade.*

42. *Bakirha, Baptistery of the West Church. Exterior.*

43. *Kalb Lauzeh, Basilica. West Façade.*

The ground plans make it clear that all these churches had a similar layout: a tripartite choir and a nave with two side aisles. There are, nevertheless, some differences in their shapes. The oldest basilicas are long and narrow and the supporting columns stand fairly close to each other. At Ruweiha I, for example, the columns are linked by semicircular arches and carry a very simple clerestory. In the more highly developed basilicas on the other hand, columns are replaced by T-shaped pillars (here only four in number), which extend the span between the supports from three to seven or even nine metres. Thus the Bizzos church, at Ruweiha II *(plan p. 353, fig. 421)*, and that of Kalb Lauzeh may be correlated to the Byzantine churches of the same period with a dome carried by four pillars rising in the middle of the nave. But domes are lacking in these sixth-century Syrian churches, and their naves are longer and narrower than those of the Byzantine churches. Nevertheless the prestige of the Byzantine capital must have exercised an influence on the Syrian architects, for we can trace a definite connection between the two groups of monuments.

Thus Kalb Lauzeh has two features in common with contemporary Byzantine churches: a single projecting apse and a narthex. The latter does not form part of the main structure of the church (which does not mean that it was built later); above the narthex

44

44. *Kalb Lauzeh, Basilica.  Exterior from the South-East.*

45. *Kalb Lauzeh, Basilica.  Exterior showing the Apse.*

46. *Kalb Lauzeh, Basilica. North Arcade of the Nave.*

46

47. *Kalb Lauzeh, Basilica. Exterior from the North-East.*

48. *Kalb Lauzeh, Basilica. Interior showing the Apse.*

rise two square, rather squat towers with a terrace extending between them. Seen from in front, the church has something of the appearance of the future Romanesque and Gothic basilicas. But the masterpiece of this group of churches must have been the basilica of Turmanin, which was visited and studied just a century ago by the Comte de Vogüé (it is no longer extant). Despite the resemblances between these buildings—styled 'cathedrals' by Jean Lassus—and Romanesque and Gothic churches, there is nothing to substantiate the view that they were imitated in the West and in Gaul in particular.

In the desert area of North Syria, the putative cathedral of Resafa, centre of the cult of St Sergius, belongs to the same group of churches. The design of the façade, with its five doorways, is modelled on that of the Roman triumphal arch, and the great arcades of the nave rest on columns. We here find the system of superimposed arches (two small ones under a large one, *plan p. 354, fig. 425*) which was employed in contemporary Byzantine architecture. The Resafa builders could have learned this procedure in Syria itself, for the architects from Constantinople (or Syrians emulating them) employed it in the church of Kasr Ibn Wardan, at the level of the galleries *(plan p. 353, fig. 422)*.

There is nothing surprising in the fact that echoes of Byzantine architecture can be found in sixth-century Syria. Constantinopolitan architects are known to have worked in Syria in the time of Justinian, notably Isidoros the Younger, one of the builders of

49. *Kalat Seman and Deir Seman. Aerial View.*

St Sophia; and architects and craftsmen are said to have been sent by the Emperor Zeno from Constantinople to the Syrian monastery of Kartamin and, even earlier, to the most important sanctuary in Syria, that of Kalat Seman, which was built round the pillar on which St Simeon Stylites spent so many years of his life.

Founded about 480, the great sanctuary of St Simeon consisted of a martyrium-church, two other churches, a baptistery, dependencies and *xenodochia*, all of them adapted to the lie of a vast stretch of hilly ground and protected by an enclosure wall *(plan p. 354, fig. 423)*. The main entrance was through a 'triumphal gateway' of particularly fine construction. The idea of an immense cruciform martyrium, composed of basilicas converging on a shrine in the centre, probably originated in Constantinople, for the most likely prototype of this form of cult sanctuary, the church of St John the Evangelist at Ephesus, was built in the fifth century by Constantinopolitan architects. At Kalat Seman the central shrine, where the thirty-foot pillar of St Simeon stood, forms a tall, graceful octagon, each side of which is pierced by a semicircular arch and embellished by decorative columns which seem to carry the arches. The dome covering this octagon must have been

51. *Kalat Seman, Monastery of St Simeon Stylites. Central Shrine with the Base of the Saint's Pillar.*

50. *Kalat Seman, Monastery of St Simeon Stylites. Apse on the East Side.*

52. *Turmanin, Basilica. Reconstruction by M. de Vogüé.* 53. *Kalat Seman, Monastery of St Simeon Stylites. Apses on the East Side.*

55. *Kalat Seman, Monastery of St Simeon Stylites. South Façade.*

of wood. But the small exedrae annexed to four of the eight sides (at the exact point where similar but vaulted rooms create a niche-buttress) show that this octagon derives from vaulted octagonal edifices (mausolea, baptisteries). In fact it is an imitation in lighter materials of a traditional octagonal building, only the skeleton of which it has retained.

This transposition must have been made deliberately at Kalat Seman, for reasons unknown to us. But it was certainly not due to ignorance of vaulting techniques, for the baptistery that stands beside the great basilica had a central octagonal hall with a stone-vaulted dome *(plan p. 354, fig. 424)*. The basilicas themselves keep to the earliest form of this type of building, with rows of columns set close to each other. The sculptured decoration of the apses anticipates that of Kalb Lauzeh and the Syrian 'cathedrals' of the sixth century, which show the same signs of a return to façades of a classical type. At Kalat Seman the finest surviving fragment, apart from the west façade, is the main apse with its superimposed columns engaged in the wall and carrying a cornice of small arches and modillions. This might almost be taken for a piece of Roman architecture of the first or second century, or a Romanesque façade of south-western France. Yet, for all the abundance of ancient churches in Syria, it must not be forgotten that we know almost nothing of the ones built in the larger cities of that province.

It was at Antioch, first metropolis of the new religion, that Constantine erected the 'Golden Church,' an octagonal, vaulted edifice. Nothing is visible today of the ruins of ancient Antioch, which have been completely submerged by the modern city. Thus we would have no idea what the monuments of this great artistic and religious centre were like, were it not for the foundations of a late fourth-century martyrium dedicated to St Babylas which have come to light outside its walls, at a place called Kaoussieh. Though of considerable size, this is an archaic structure, in the form of a cross with arms of equal length. Theoretically it is an ancestor of the church of St Simeon, which also served as a shrine but was given a far more highly developed structure.

54. *Kalat Seman, Monastery of St Simeon Stylites. Main Portal of the South Façade.*

56. *Kalat Seman, Monastery of St Simeon Stylites. North Side.*

On the other side of Antioch, in the outlying town of Daphne, the foundations of another martyrium, dating to the fifth century, have been cleared; they show it to have been a fine quatrefoil building with an ambulatory and a projecting choir. At Resafa there is a somewhat similar building, slightly extended to the south-west. These Syrian quatrefoil churches were never vaulted. At first sight the fifth-century quatrefoil martyrium at Apamea excavated by a Belgian expedition (results as yet unpublished) might seem to be an exception to the rule. But what look at first like large piers intended to support the dome are actually the walls of a small rectangular edifice enclosed within the quatrefoil and undoubtedly of earlier construction; it may have been a reliquary shrine around which the quatrefoil martyrium was built.

Further south, in the direction of Palestine, the sixth-century martyria in the towns of Ezra, Bosra and Shagra were all built on the radial plan, with either an octagon or a rotunda enclosed in a square; but each time the plan is varied *(plans p.* 355, *fig.* 426-429). Ezra has preserved part of its dome, which was supported by eight interior piers, while at Bosra the dome (destroyed) rested on four piers, between each pair of which were several columns. This latter dome, in view of its slender supports, must have been of wood. Both plans, especially that of Bosra, are remarkable for the harmonious regularity of their design and the way in which all the elements are linked together, including the tripartite chevet (of the Syrian type) which, at Bosra, is flanked by side chapels. The central-planned church at Resafa is related to these urban sanctuaries of the sixth century but—as is often the case at this later period—the liturgical function of the edifice is less certain; if in the fifth century these rotundas and cruciform churches served only as martyria, in the sixth they were adapted to a more generalized type of worship.

Judging by the Christian monuments at Gerasa, a city in near-by Palestine, the sanctuary on a central plan would appear to have been an urban rather than a rural or monastic edifice. This is explicable in view of the purposes which buildings of this type were intended to serve. If baptisteries, they were built beside cathedrals; if mausolea or martyria, they usually stood just outside the city walls; as for the domed churches, they were still being built in the sixth century chiefly in cities (for it was in the cities that the influence of Byzantium was most strongly felt), although we also find them beside the residences of imperial governors, as at Kasr Ibn Wardan, and in the large monastic centres which the emperors endowed with churches adapted to their personal taste.

Imperial patronage seems also to account for the Byzantinizing style we find at Resafa and Kalat Seman, including perhaps the form given the martyrium: an octagon combined with a cross. The country churches, on the other hand, had no need of baptisteries and special martyria; relics of martyrs were simply placed in small, sarcophagus-shaped receptacles which were deposited in one of the rooms beside the chevet of the church, or in some similar place undistinguished by any particular architectural features.

This practice of locating martyrs' chapels beside the choir originated in Syrian churches (Brad, Kalat Kalota), and it spread to neighbouring lands, notably to Cyprus, but the structure of the church as a whole was little affected by it. Nor was it affected by the installation in the nave, facing the altar, of a monumental pulpit from which the Holy Scriptures were read to the congregation. This massive reading desk, the ambo, must have obstructed the view in many Syrian churches, but it led to no changes in the architectural layout of the nave. It may be noted, however, that both in the central-planned churches (Antioch-Kaoussieh, Antioch-Daphne, Resafa-Sergiopolis) and in the 'cathedral' basilicas of the sixth century (Kalb Lauzeh, Resafa) the monumental ambo stood immediately beneath the dome or the high-pitched roof replacing it, or else between the four central piers (which seem to imitate the Byzantine dome-supporting piers). Thus the ambo, by its position in these churches, may perhaps be taken as further evidence that the Syrian architects used a domed edifice as their model.

## Palestine

The 'New Jerusalem' created by Constantine and adorned with Christian edifices in the imperial style, impressed all the travellers of antiquity. At the end of the fourth century and during the fifth, the empresses of the Theodosian line patronized the arts as Constantine and St Helena did before them. Thanks to them and to other donors, many new churches were founded in the Holy City and its neighbourhood. Moreover the zeal of Constantine, whose activities ranged far beyond Jerusalem itself (he founded the memorial church beside the sacred oak of Mamre), gave a lead to the Christian communities of the fifth century, and they erected many memorial churches in all parts of the country, including Transjordania and Samaria. Justinian and his contemporaries continued the work begun by Constantine. The great emperor himself restored the Church of the Nativity at Bethlehem, and at Jerusalem erected a large church dedicated to the Virgin.

During the period covered by this volume the Christian art of Jerusalem must have exerted a widespread influence. This can be gathered from a study of such information as we possess, both factual and legendary, concerning the origin of the churches and relics of fifth-century Constantinople. And in Italy, too, we find tokens of the influence exerted by the church architecture of Christian Palestine. But with the exception of the Bethlehem basilica, our knowledge of large-scale architecture in Palestine at this time is very scanty, and the sources yield only a few references to buildings of smaller dimensions. These include *memoriae*, the memorial churches and oratories which were the glory of the Holy Land. Unfortunately they have nearly all disappeared, and with them the types of architecture which might have been expected to reveal most originality.

Exceptionally, excavations have brought to light the octagonal plan of the *memoria* of the Ascension (c. 378) on the Mount of Olives; that, also octagonal but with a large apse, of the *memoria* erected over the tomb of the Virgin *(plan p. 356, fig. 430)*; and the unusual octagon, surrounded by four chapels, of the Church of the Virgin on Mount Garizim *(plan p. 356, fig. 431)*. This last *memoria*, founded by the Emperor Zeno, stood on a mountain-top on the site of an ancient temple of the Samaritans. All these sanctuaries fall into the same category as the martyria housing a saint's relics and keep to a central plan, sometimes with variants. The *memoria* of St John the Baptist, in Jerusalem, belongs to this group, despite the fact that it has a trefoil plan *(plan p. 356, fig. 432)*.

South of the Holy Land, on Mount Sinai, a venerable sixth-century *memoria* still retains its original basilical plan, with two rows of thick columns dividing the nave from the aisles, and the arches and a clerestory supported by these columns. The basilica is timber-roofed and still has both its original ceiling, on which the names of its imperial founders, Justinian and Theodora, are inscribed, and its carved wooden doors. It is impossible to say how old the narthex is, but mention may be made of the rooms running along the outer side of the aisles—chapels and sacristies separated by transverse partitions.

Here again we have a large agglomerate of building units, like the ones in North Africa (Tebessa) and above all in Christian Egypt (Sohag, St Menas); we shall encounter them again in Northern Mesopotamia. But though the Palestinian architects were evidently familiar with a layout of this kind, they reproduced it on a somewhat smaller scale. In the sanctuary of Mount Nebo it was adapted to a basilica and in the Church of the Virgin (Theotokos) on Mount Garizim in Samaria (late fifth century) a chapel or a portico is built on to each of the eight sides of the octagon.

The arrangement of the chevet also affiliates the Mount Sinai church to those of the surrounding countries. While the two small domed rooms, on either side, are chapels, the one in the centre is a *memoria* of the Burning Bush. We can see the idea behind the choice of this location for the *memoria*: here, as at Bethlehem, the chevet enclosed a 'holy place' that had been venerated before the founding of the church.

At Ras Siaga, in Transjordania, the 'holy place' of the tomb of Moses is a trefoil building which certainly dates back to the time when the tomb had been the object of a Jewish cult. To the original building, which stood alone, like the *memoria* of St John the Baptist in Jerusalem, the Christians added on a basilica with a triapsidal choir. At Portogruaro, between Venice and Aquileia, and Kerbet Bou Addoufan, in Algeria, a basilical hall with three apses was also added to an earlier building.

54

57. *Gerasa, Cathedral. Main Doorway and Flight of Steps.* 55

58. *Gerasa, Cathedral. Columns with Part of the Architrave.*

56

The basilica of El Tabga, on the Sea of Galilee, was built around the stone of the Multiplication of Loaves and Fishes. Brought to light by the excavators, this stone was embedded in the pavement in front of the altar, at the entrance to the apsidal choir of the church. But in front of the back wall and around the relic stone, a transept, not projecting beyond the sides of the main building, was subsequently added, probably with a view to enlarging the space available to worshippers around the stone *(plan p. 356, fig. 434)*.

The cathedral of Gerasa (Jerash) was founded in the fourth century in the immediate vicinity of the pagan acropolis. Though it is now in ruins, some fragments still testify to the pristine magnificence of the building. This is evidenced by the main doorway, whose frame is still *in situ*, and by the flight of steps leading up to the cathedral. The general effect must have resembled that of an ancient Roman edifice, an effect enhanced by the two columns still carrying part of the architrave (here employed instead of arches). At all points where it remains in place the masonry is excellent and says much for the competence of Palestinian masons in the late fourth century.

The church of Sts Peter and Paul at Gerasa, built about 540, stands out from the common run of the basilicas of Palestine, which are unoriginal and very much alike. The three apses recessed in the massive wall of the chevet (which is flat viewed from the outside) foreshadow the layout of Carolingian churches three centuries later *(plan p. 357, fig. 435)*. Again at Gerasa, the later church of Genesius (611) has a rudimentary transept in front of the apse. A new feature here is the transverse screen dividing the choir from the nave; out of this the iconostasis was later to grow up, on the lines of a *scenae frons*.

A question arises in connection with these Palestinian basilicas: what do they owe, if anything, to the local synagogues which, as early as the third century, were also given the form of basilicas? These basilical synagogues, as already mentioned, had been founded under the auspices of the Severus dynasty.

In studying the art of Palestine in this period, we must never lose sight of the fact that churches and synagogues were erected in roughly equal numbers. After the closing of the pagan temples, the only religious art to maintain itself alongside that of triumphant Christianity was Jewish art. It would be surprising indeed if, thus existing side by side, the two cultures did not exert some influence on each other. Unfortunately, in both of the two great centres of Eastern Mediterranean civilization, Alexandria and Antioch, where the Jewish community was exceptionally numerous and active, the monuments have either disappeared or come down to us in insufficient numbers.

Entirely unknown half a century ago, the architecture of the ancient synagogues can now be studied thanks to the survival of some ruined edifices and of the foundations of several others in Palestine itself and in Galilee. Many of these monuments cannot be dated, but it is safe to say that all of them lie between the third century A.D. (Capernaum) and the sixth or seventh century (Beit Alpha, *plan p. 356, fig. 433*, and Jericho). To this group can be added the synagogue of Dura Europos (early third century) and those of Gerasa in Palestine and Apamea in Syria, which were converted into Christian churches under Justinian (c. 530).

A comparative study of these Jewish and Christian edifices makes it quite clear that, at the time when the Christians were erecting their first basilicas in the Holy Land, there already existed a good many synagogues of basilical design in the cities and villages

59. *Gerasa, Church of Genesius. Apse and Rudimentary Transept.*

of Palestine. Although we cannot tell with any certainty whether, as early as the fourth century, these synagogue-basilicas already included a clerestory above the nave, or an apse, whether projecting or not (the projecting apse appears at El Hammeh, *plan p*. 357, *fig*. 436, Beit Alpha and Jericho only at the end of this period), we do know that they included all the other features of the Christian basilica: a long rectangular hall divided by rows of columns into nave and side aisles, galleries above the aisles, a pediment crowning the façade, and sometimes a porticoed courtyard on one side of the building.

Actually the Jewish architects did no more than take over the Hellenistic basilical hall and adapt it to their needs. But the fact that the latter building served as a model for the synagogues of Palestine as early as the beginning of the third century suggests that these synagogue-basilicas were, in their turn, the models on which the Christian churches of Palestine were subsequently based.

Certain devices used in the decoration of the Palestinian synagogues lend support to this view. For in these synagogues we find a Jewish symbol inscribed at the top of the capitals and on the lintel over the doors—the very places where, in Christian churches, a cross or some other symbol of Christ was commonly inscribed. Whatever the symbols displayed (seven-branched candlestick, crown or arch), the fact that they invariably figured on capitals and lintels in both Jewish and Christian places of worship can hardly be accidental: the builders of Christian basilicas must have been familiar with Jewish basilicas and borrowed certain elements of their art.

58

What is true of the basilical churches of Palestine, where the normal services were held, is also true of the commemorative edifices. Of those of the Jews, we have only the tombs of patriarchs and prophets; these continued to be venerated by Christians (Mount Nebo and the tomb of Moses at Ras Siaga). Other Jewish holy places can be traced by material remains left by the Jews themselves, before they were taken over by the Christians, who established their own places of worship on these sites associated with Jewish cults (the sacred oak of Mamre and the spot where Joshua crossed the Jordan). Here again, then, Jewish traditions may have contributed something to the architecture of the Christian *memoriae*.

But Jewish antecedents were excluded from the most important Christian memorial sanctuaries, those in Jerusalem and the surrounding area, founded to commemorate the birth, death, resurrection and ascension of Christ (sanctuaries of Golgotha, the Mount of Olives and Bethlehem). These great Christian monuments, erected in the fourth century, reflected local traditions only in so far as they conformed to the usual basilical plan.

### Mesopotamia

In studying the history of Early Christian architecture in Mesopotamia, we must distinguish between the work of two widely separated regions, Middle and Northern Mesopotamia. Middle Mesopotamia, round about Baghdad, was then the central province of Persia, and it was here that the kings of the Sassanid dynasty had established their capital, Ctesiphon. The Christian community of Persia was at that time a large one, and some of their churches have come to light in recent excavations at Ctesiphon and at Al Hirah. No date can be assigned to these buildings, but they are certainly anterior to the Arab conquest of Zoroastrian Persia (c. 640).

The churches erected at Ctesiphon and Al Hirah both conform to the general plan of a basilica (an elongated rectangle). But the other elements of the basilical edifice —two rows of columns parallel to the side walls, and the juxtaposition of a three-aisled nave and a tripartite chevet reserved for the altar and the clergy—were handled by the local builders in such manner as to make these Christian churches resemble Sassanian palaces. To the art of these palaces the Christian architects of Mesopotamia owed far more than to the architects of Roman Syria, their immediate neighbours to the west.

How great was this debt is proved by the plans of Sassanian palaces and upper-class houses *(p. 357, fig. 437-438)*. The reception halls of these Sassanian residences derive in turn from the architecture of the secular basilicas, which had become more or less standardized throughout the Roman Empire. Even so, however, it was not the design of these halls that was imitated by the Christian architects of Mesopotamia, but the way in which they were roofed. All were covered with barrel vaults, half-domes and full domes. A reconstruction of the vaulting in a hall of the palace of Sarvistan gives us a good idea of what the inside of an Early Christian basilica built by Mesopotamian masons must have looked like.

Far to the north-west, in that part of Northern Mesopotamia which was under Roman domination (Nisibis, Edessa, Amida, Melitene), Persian traditions no longer exerted any appreciable influence, but on the other hand the proximity of Syria and

Palestine made itself felt. Here again, however, it must be emphasized that the number of surviving monuments is exceedingly small, and some of these have clearly been rebuilt. In a region which for centuries was a battlefield where Persians, Arabs, Turks and Byzantines confronted each other, it is no wonder that so little remains. Under these conditions it is impossible to draw any general conclusions concerning Early Christian architecture in Northern Mesopotamia. This is particularly regrettable in the case of Edessa which, as the capital of the Kings of Osrhoene (bearing the name of Abgar) was the oldest Christian metropolis of the world, preceding Constantinople. According to a very old tradition (no later than the fourth century), the kings of this dynasty were converted to Christianity in Christ's lifetime, and one of the Abgars is said to have been in touch with Jesus, possibly his disciple.

But nothing remains at Edessa of either the ancient churches or the palace of the Abgars, which at the end of the fourth century was visited by the female pilgrim Etheria. Nisibis has only a single Early Christian monument, but it is a particularly interesting one. A cubical edifice which must originally have been vaulted, it was founded as a baptistery in 539 (the date is given in an inscription). A little later it was converted into a martyrium in honour of a local saint, James of Nisibis, and a crypt was then added to it. A projecting apse and a porticoed antechamber *in antis* went to complete this small building, whose profiled cornices and door- and window-frames, and openings in a degenerate classical style, gave it a more articulated design than was common at the time *(plan p. 358, fig. 439)*. The church of the same period which once stood to the left of the baptistery was replaced in the eighth century by a rudimentary edifice of no artistic merit.

At Behnam a small edifice, similar in type, communicated by an underground passage with a mausoleum hewn out of the rock; this consists of an octagonal room with arcosolia, alternately large and small, recessed into each side of it *(plan p. 358, fig. 440)*. It keeps to the standard plan of Roman sepulchral chambers. Two similar rooms exist at Kartamin in the great Monophysite monastery of Northern Mesopotamia founded at the end of the fourth century but rebuilt in 512 by Anastasius, Emperor of Constantinople *(plan p. 358, fig. 443)*. As far as their type form is concerned, all these round or octagonal halls enclosed within a square building might date to any time in the period running from Constantine to Justinian. The sixth century would appear to be the likeliest date.

It is doubtful if the churches of the Kartamin monastery have retained any vestiges of the early period at which the monastery was founded. The main one is a good specimen of a type of church which, from an undetermined period on (late sixth century?), was often imitated in Northern Mesopotamia and particularly in the Tur Abdin district *(plan p. 358, fig. 442)*. Two features distinguish these edifices from the bulk of Early Christian churches: the part reserved for the congregation was developed breadthwise instead of lengthwise, and it was vaulted like all the other parts of the building. There would be no point here in going into the antecedents of the first of these particularities, which has been wrongly assumed to derive from Babylonian or Hittite art, and therefore to be of fabulous antiquity. It is, rather, the churches of Middle Mesopotamia which follow ancient Oriental models. Those at Kartamin and Salah, on the other hand, derive from memorial churches of the type of St John the Baptist at Jerusalem (fifth century); in the former, as in the latter, we find a tripartite choir preceded by a nave, consisting

60

of a single bay, and a narthex. The church of the Virgin (al Hadra) at Hah keeps to the elevation of the triapsidal choir and also to the system of transverse ribs dividing the roof of the nave into three separate vaults, i.e. a dome and two half-domes *(plan p. 358, fig. 441)*; whereas at Salah and Kartamin the side apses and the division into three vaults have been done away with and the transverse bay with its barrel vault is unbroken by any subdivision.

From these general characteristics we may infer that the architects of Tur Abdin took for their models some of the famous martyria or *memoriae* of the day, located either in the same neighbourhood or in some important religious centre like Jerusalem or Antioch. And this is a legitimate inference, since in near-by Transcaucasia, at the end of the sixth century, it was from the martyria that the earliest churches drew their essential features, notably their plan and vaulting.

It must be remembered, moreover, that the ancient churches of Northern Mesopotamia have never been excavated. This is probably the only reason why no basilicas of the usual type are known here. Since they existed in Transcaucasia, we may certainly expect to find traces of them in the region of Edessa and Melitene, for this was the starting point of the Christian missions that converted Transcaucasia. It is true that certain churches of the Tur Abdin district approximate in some ways to the basilical type, but their version of it seems to derive rather from basilicas of the Ctesiphon region; this would account not only for their all-over vaulting but also for their tendency to reduce the external form of a highly complex edifice to a massive parallelepiped.

Some insignificant vestiges at Amida have made it possible to reconstruct a rough plan of a large quatrefoil building of the same type as the martyria at Antioch-Daphne and Apamea. This is a further indication of the importance attached to these martyria in the eastern provinces of the Empire, and of the role they may well have played in Transcaucasia in the early fourth century.

The cathedral of the Holy Wisdom at Edessa (present-day Urfa), erected towards the end of the sixth century, is known only by a written description of it. With its central plan and dome, it was undoubtedly modelled on St Sophia at Constantinople. This is yet another example of the influence exerted by the contemporary architecture of the Byzantine capital; we have noted similar influences at Kartamin and at several places in Syria.

*Asia Minor*

The capital importance of this province for the history of Early Christian and medieval architecture is recognized by all scholars. But until more extensive and systematic excavations can be carried out, we must refrain from drawing any definitive conclusions from such monuments as have survived or have been excavated up to now. Since they fall into several distinct groups, there is as yet no justification for assuming them to be offshoots of a single parent art indigenous to Asia Minor.

The first group of ruined churches is to be found in the ancient provinces of Cilicia and Isauria; to these may be added the foundations of several churches uncovered at Korykos and Meriamlik (Seleucia). A good many other ruins have been recorded further north, beyond the Kara Dagh range, in neighbouring Cappadocia.

The 'cathedral' of Korykos (Isauria) is an excellent specimen of the commonest type of basilica. The nave, with its side aisles divided off by two rows of columns carrying arcades, is preceded by a narthex; the apse is polygonal on the outside, as at Constantinople. A second basilica at Korykos, *extra muros*, has a transept and two small apses flanking the main apse *(plan p. 359, fig. 444)*.

The apse of a martyrium-church which stood just outside Korykos shows how the local masons constructed a vault in the fifth century. The half-barrel vault was built up of superimposed courses of stones hewn with such precision that each course could safely project a little beyond the one beneath it, the wooden centring being needed only to support the stones of the upper courses while they were being placed in position. The layout of this church is of a very peculiar type *(plan p. 359, fig. 445)*. To begin with, the chevet departs from the norm, two long narrow rooms being added alongside the usual triple apse. Also, the longitudinal aisled nave is replaced by a quite unusual arrangement. In front of the choir stands a square aedicula with an exedra recessed into at least one side (possibly into three sides); probably a martyrium (since two tombs were discovered inside it), the aedicula is surrounded by three rooms forming an ambulatory, the room on the west side being divided into two aisles by a transverse colonnade at right angles to the axis of the church. This edifice shows how freely the architects of the fifth century could vary the standard elements of church design when called upon to meet particular requirements.

At Hieropolis, in Phrygia, are two basilicas attributed to the fifth century and an octagonal martyrium. At Meriamlik (Seleucia of Isauria), the remains of several churches and of the underground basilica of St Euphemia, can still be seen. The edifice that concerns us here is a short broad basilica, preceded by a narthex and atrium and ending in a pentagonal apse (standing between two rectangular rooms) of a rather peculiar plan *(p. 359, fig. 447)*; it appeared at first to be an early example of what is known as a domed basilica. Since the latter is a typically Byzantine type of building, the excavators of the Meriamlik church, Herzfeld and Guyer, proposed to identify it with one, mentioned in an ancient text, which was founded by the Emperor Zeno (474-491). This tentative identification supplied a date for the building and accordingly made it an important piece of evidence for the early history of Byzantine architecture. Recently, however, G. M. Forsyth has questioned whether a dome really existed over the nave, and his observations carry the more weight since the Meriamlik church in other respects has no resemblance to any other church within the zone of Byzantine architecture. Its internal arrangement, moreover, is related to that of the martyrium-church in the neighbouring town of Korykos, described above; it has the same square aedicula in front of the choir, which, as at Korykos, may be taken to be a martyrium. Whatever the type of covering over this aedicula, the church cannot have been a domed basilica; there are thus no grounds for its supposed connection with the Emperor Zeno and the art of Constantinople.

Early in this century, Miss Gertrude Bell called attention to other monuments in Cilicia belonging to the same architectural tradition (Anazarab, Budrum, Kanytelideis) Some fine fifth-century ruins at Ak Kala show a vaulting technique peculiar to this region. A facing of carefully fitted masonry was used to conceal the body of the vaulting, which was composed of a rubble of stones and mortar. A subsequent development of this building technique in the sixth century can be seen at Dag Pazarli.

60. *Dag Pazarli, Church. Interior of the Apse.*

61. *Dag Pazarli, Church. Exterior of the Apse.*

62. *Alahan (Alahan Monastir)*, *Main Church of the Monastery*. *Exterior from the South-East*.

But the finest and, historically, the most interesting of the Christian monuments of Cilicia is the one which goes today by the Turkish name of Alahan Monastir (or Khodja Kalessi). The ruins are those of a monastery, with a courtyard, three churches, and funerary monuments. The core of this building complex must date back to about 450. Most noteworthy of the churches is a basilica with a tripartite choir of the Syrian type, the central apse invisible on the outside. The choir is preceded by a central rectangle, each side of which is extended by two rows of arcades. As in the Korykos martyrium, the space between this central rectangle and the entrance wall is intercepted by a transversal element consisting of one large and two small arches. This church is so well preserved that for once we can study the elevation. The corner squinches of the tower that stands over the central rectangle are of particular interest. The covering of the tower has disappeared, but it may be safely assumed to have been a timber roof with four slopes. In view of what we see at Alahan, we may infer that the churches at Korykos and Meriamlik had similar square towers, and that this was a regional characteristic. The Alahan type of edifice may have originated in this part of Asia Minor, either for the housing of martyria or for some more general purpose. On the other hand, it may have made its first appearance at Antioch, the religious capital.

63. *Alahan (Alahan Monastir)*, *Main Church of the Monastery*. *The Nave, looking towards the Apse*.

60. *Dag Pazarli, Church. Interior of the Apse.*

61. *Dag Pazarli, Church. Exterior of the Apse.*

62. *Alahan (Alahan Monastir), Main Church of the Monastery. Exterior from the South-East.*

But the finest and, historically, the most interesting of the Christian monuments of Cilicia is the one which goes today by the Turkish name of Alahan Monastir (or Khodja Kalessi). The ruins are those of a monastery, with a courtyard, three churches, and funerary monuments. The core of this building complex must date back to about 450. Most noteworthy of the churches is a basilica with a tripartite choir of the Syrian type, the central apse invisible on the outside. The choir is preceded by a central rectangle, each side of which is extended by two rows of arcades. As in the Korykos martyrium, the space between this central rectangle and the entrance wall is intercepted by a transversal element consisting of one large and two small arches. This church is so well preserved that for once we can study the elevation. The corner squinches of the tower that stands over the central rectangle are of particular interest. The covering of the tower has disappeared, but it may be safely assumed to have been a timber roof with four slopes. In view of what we see at Alahan, we may infer that the churches at Korykos and Meriamlik had similar square towers, and that this was a regional characteristic. The Alahan type of edifice may have originated in this part of Asia Minor, either for the housing of martyria or for some more general purpose. On the other hand, it may have made its first appearance at Antioch, the religious capital.

64          63. *Alahan (Alahan Monastir), Main Church of the Monastery. The Nave, looking towards the Apse.*

64. *Aspendos, Basilica. Forepart. Watercolour of 1885.*

It is important to note how early (450) these modifications were made in the design of the basilica which, at that time, had never yet departed from the long, rectangular, colonnaded nave, its only variations being in the form of the choir. The innovations made at Alahan, and in the churches affiliated to it, clearly point the way to sixth-century Byzantine architecture in Constantinople. The techniques used at Alahan, however, are quite different from those used at Constantinople: at the first, ashlar masonry, in the second bricks; at the first a timber roof, in the second a brick dome. For the prototypes of the Alahan basilica we must look not to Constantinople but to North Syria. This holds good particularly for the corner squinches at the base of the tower, which reappear in the chevet towers of the basilica of Resafa-Sergiopolis. The carved ornamentation (cornices, brackets, pilaster capitals, etc.) is also similar.

The Christian architecture that arose along the southern coast of Asia Minor, west of Isauria, in Pisidia and Pamphylia, cannot have been very different from that outlined above. No systematic study of the monuments of this region has yet been made, but timber-roofed basilicas have been reported at many places. The plan of an immense basilica at Aspendos, with projecting apse, is an extremely simple one *(p. 360, fig. 451)*. Count Lanckoronski, in 1890, published a watercolour and a sectional drawing of the front part of this basilica (an early form of *Westwerk*), whose function is not clear.

In several of these monuments, at Perga for example *(plan p. 360, fig. 448)*, the size and prominence of the projecting transept is a distinctive feature. The variety of the ground plans is no less characteristic. The architects of these wealthy towns of southern Asia Minor were evidently more inventive, readier to innovate, than their Syrian contemporaries. Technically too, these were remarkable buildings. Witness the ruined basilica with transept at Sagalassos in Pisidia: the walls consist of large, well-fitting blocks

66

64. *Aspendos, Basilica. Forepart. Watercolour of 1885.*

It is important to note how early (450) these modifications were made in the design of the basilica which, at that time, had never yet departed from the long, rectangular, colonnaded nave, its only variations being in the form of the choir. The innovations made at Alahan, and in the churches affiliated to it, clearly point the way to sixth-century Byzantine architecture in Constantinople. The techniques used at Alahan, however, are quite different from those used at Constantinople: at the first, ashlar masonry, in the second bricks; at the first a timber roof, in the second a brick dome. For the prototypes of the Alahan basilica we must look not to Constantinople but to North Syria. This holds good particularly for the corner squinches at the base of the tower, which reappear in the chevet towers of the basilica of Resafa-Sergiopolis. The carved ornamentation (cornices, brackets, pilaster capitals, etc.) is also similar.

The Christian architecture that arose along the southern coast of Asia Minor, west of Isauria, in Pisidia and Pamphylia, cannot have been very different from that outlined above. No systematic study of the monuments of this region has yet been made, but timber-roofed basilicas have been reported at many places. The plan of an immense basilica at Aspendos, with projecting apse, is an extremely simple one *(p. 360, fig. 451)*. Count Lanckoronski, in 1890, published a watercolour and a sectional drawing of the front part of this basilica (an early form of *Westwerk*), whose function is not clear.

In several of these monuments, at Perga for example *(plan p. 360, fig. 448)*, the size and prominence of the projecting transept is a distinctive feature. The variety of the ground plans is no less characteristic. The architects of these wealthy towns of southern Asia Minor were evidently more inventive, readier to innovate, than their Syrian contemporaries. Technically too, these were remarkable buildings. Witness the ruined basilica with transept at Sagalassos in Pisidia: the walls consist of large, well-fitting blocks

66

65. *Bin Bir Kilisseh, Church I. Side Aisle.*

of carefully squared stone, and under the moulded cornice is a row of masks taken over from classical architecture.

Turkish excavations now in progress at Side, in Pamphylia, have brought to light further Christian churches of the basilical type, some martyria, and buildings forming part of an episcopal residence of the fifth century. Among them is a baptistery of the highest interest as showing a ciborium—usually no more than a symbolic baldachin placed above the baptismal font—which here joins up with the central vault of the baptistery, itself entirely vaulted *(plan p. 359, fig. 446)*.

The inland provinces of Asia Minor have lost all their Christian monuments. But the depopulation of the upper plateaux, stretching northwards from the Kara Dagh, has preserved a few groups of impressive ruins from disappearing altogether. Some are scattered over a site known to the natives as Bin Bir Kilisseh ('The Thousand and One Churches'); the others are located a few miles away, at Daouleh. Together they form a group of over twenty churches. We have no way of knowing what town or community they belonged to.

66. *Bin Bir Kilisseh, Church VI. Apse.*

67. *Bin Bir Kilisseh, Two Ruined Buildings. From a Drawing by L. de Laborde.*

65. *Bin Bir Kilisseh, Church I. Side Aisle.*

of carefully squared stone, and under the moulded cornice is a row of masks taken over from classical architecture.

Turkish excavations now in progress at Side, in Pamphylia, have brought to light further Christian churches of the basilical type, some martyria, and buildings forming part of an episcopal residence of the fifth century. Among them is a baptistery of the highest interest as showing a ciborium—usually no more than a symbolic baldachin placed above the baptismal font—which here joins up with the central vault of the baptistery, itself entirely vaulted *(plan p. 359, fig. 446)*.

The inland provinces of Asia Minor have lost all their Christian monuments. But the depopulation of the upper plateaux, stretching northwards from the Kara Dagh, has preserved a few groups of impressive ruins from disappearing altogether. Some are scattered over a site known to the natives as Bin Bir Kilisseh ('The Thousand and One Churches'); the others are located a few miles away, at Daouleh. Together they form a group of over twenty churches. We have no way of knowing what town or community they belonged to.

66. *Bin Bir Kilisseh, Church VI. Apse.*

67. *Bin Bir Kilisseh, Two Ruined Buildings. From a Drawing by L. de Laborde.*

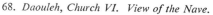
68. *Daouleh, Church VI. View of the Nave.*        69. *Daouleh, Church VI. Exterior showing the Apse.*

While some of these churches may go as far back as the fourth and fifth centuries, most of them date only to the eighth or ninth. Much emphasis was given them many years ago by Strzygowski and Guyer, two scholars who, though they agreed on little else, were at one in believing that from this group of ancient churches in Asia Minor developed the Romanesque churches of the Latin West; for characteristic of many of them is the cruciform plan and a square tower in front of the choir.

The distance and the length of time separating these monuments from those of Western Europe are such that few scholars today would share this view, and it has been further discredited by the recent discovery in Milan of Early Christian churches on the cruciform plan. The latter, dating to the sixth century, have demonstrated that the cruciform Romanesque churches had early antecedents in the West itself. Similar churches in Asia Minor are but distant relatives of these, all of them presumably deriving from the mausolea-martyria of the Antioch-Kaoussieh type.

It may be that the earliest basilicas in Asia Minor were more elongated *(plan p. 360, fig. 449)*, while in later basilicas a shorter nave was adopted, making them seem broader *(plan p. 360, fig. 450)*. But all of them, strangely enough, combine features which elsewhere belong to churches of different periods. Thus, as in all the very early basilicas, the choir is devoid of any architectural elaboration: there are no rooms on the sides and no transept, while the two rows of arches in the nave extend to the back wall, flanking a single project-ing apse. But the nave and side aisles are vaulted and, in order to support the springers of the barrel vaults, columns are replaced by piers of a special shape. Elongated in a direction at right angles to the axis of the basilicas, the piers incorporate two embedded columns which carry the thrust of the transverse arches. These arches help to support

69

70. *Bin Bir Kilisseh, Church I. Exterior showing the Apse.*

70

71. *Korykos, Church 'extra muros'. Double Bay.*

68. *Daouleh, Church VI. View of the Nave.*

69. *Daouleh, Church VI. Exterior showing the Apse.*

While some of these churches may go as far back as the fourth and fifth centuries, most of them date only to the eighth or ninth. Much emphasis was given them many years ago by Strzygowski and Guyer, two scholars who, though they agreed on little else, were at one in believing that from this group of ancient churches in Asia Minor developed the Romanesque churches of the Latin West; for characteristic of many of them is the cruciform plan and a square tower in front of the choir.

The distance and the length of time separating these monuments from those of Western Europe are such that few scholars today would share this view, and it has been further discredited by the recent discovery in Milan of Early Christian churches on the cruciform plan. The latter, dating to the sixth century, have demonstrated that the cruciform Romanesque churches had early antecedents in the West itself. Similar churches in Asia Minor are but distant relatives of these, all of them presumably deriving from the mausolea-martyria of the Antioch-Kaoussieh type.

It may be that the earliest basilicas in Asia Minor were more elongated *(plan p. 360, fig. 449)*, while in later basilicas a shorter nave was adopted, making them seem broader *(plan p. 360, fig. 450)*. But all of them, strangely enough, combine features which elsewhere belong to churches of different periods. Thus, as in all the very early basilicas, the choir is devoid of any architectural elaboration: there are no rooms on the sides and no transept, while the two rows of arches in the nave extend to the back wall, flanking a single projecting apse. But the nave and side aisles are vaulted and, in order to support the springers of the barrel vaults, columns are replaced by piers of a special shape. Elongated in a direction at right angles to the axis of the basilicas, the piers incorporate two embedded columns which carry the thrust of the transverse arches. These arches help to support

70. *Bin Bir Kilisseh, Church I. Exterior showing the Apse.*

70

71. *Korykos, Church 'extra muros'. Double Bay.*

the parallel series of barrel vaults above the nave and side aisles. For greater strength all three series of vaults are built at the same height, there being no clerestory in these basilicas; they are therefore badly lighted and this is their chief defect. Some churches at Bin Bir Kilisseh had galleries and a narthex, but these were not obligatory.

However, apart from the overall vaulting of these churches (whose masonry is not so carefully constructed as in most Oriental buildings of this period), their most striking feature is the pair of symmetrical towers flanking the entrance and dominating the vestibule of several of them. Here again we are reminded of the future Romanesque churches of the distant West. But while there is probably no authentic link behind this curious similarity, there does seem to be some connection between these towers and those of sixth-century Syrian churches. Whence we may infer that the basilicas of Bin Bir Kilisseh are either contemporary with the Syrian churches or subsequent to them, for as a rule influences flowed from Syria to central Asia Minor rather than in the opposite direction.

As things stand, the relations between the two regions are not yet adequately documented, and may have been more complex than is commonly supposed. To those who are undeterred by the gulf of centuries from seeking parallels, the church towers of central Asia Minor may seem but a new version of the Hittite *hilani*.

## The Aegean Region and Constantinople

Early Christian architecture developed on much the same lines in the lands around the Aegean Sea and in the Greek islands. And the monuments of Constantinople belong to the same area. This being so, we propose to group together in a single section the buildings of the fourth, fifth and sixth centuries in Greece, the northern Balkans, western Asia Minor and Constantinople. True, this was not the general practice in the past. But since the researches of Strzygowski, Wulff, Diehl and Dalton, who grouped together all the monuments of Asia Minor, the documentation at our disposal has been much increased by the excavations on the southern and western coasts of Asia Minor, on the Greek islands and in mainland Greece, Yugoslavia and Bulgaria.

As a result the hundred or so monuments recorded in Greece and the Balkan provinces of the Roman Empire are now seen to be more closely related to similar buildings on the Aegean coast of Asia Minor than to those of eastern Anatolia. Moreover, excavations carried out at Ephesus, Philippi, Constantinople and elsewhere have demonstrated that the origins of Byzantine architecture properly so called, whose seminal centre from the fourth century on was Constantinople, may be traced to a tradition current in and peculiar to the Aegean region.

We have already mentioned several basilicas in Pamphylia (Perga, Side) whose design differs considerably from that of the churches on the central plateau of Anatolia and even from those in the coastal cities of Cilicia and Isauria. On the other hand, basilicas akin to those of Perga and Side are to be found further west, notably on the Aegean coast of Asia Minor, in the Greek islands and in mainland Greece. These are timber-roofed basilicas with three aisles and a semicircular apse usually projecting beyond the main structure. The Pergamum excavations have revealed a typical example, completed by a narthex and an atrium.

72. *Ephesus, Church of the Virgin.  Detail of the Ruins.*

73. *Ephesus, Church of the Virgin.  Detail of the Ruins.*

 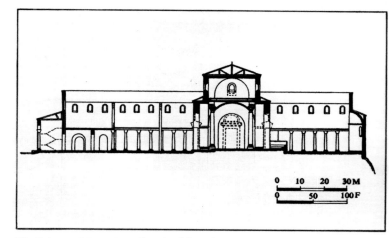

74. *Ephesus, Martyrium Church of St John (1st state). Reconstruction.*     75. *Ephesus, Martyrium Church of St John (1st state). Section.*

In another Hellenistic city, Miletus, a similar basilica has a semicircular ambulatory running around the apse, reminiscent of San Sebastiano in Rome. We now know that in Roman cemeteries of the fourth century buildings of this type were more numerous than was once supposed. The same funerary function, and perhaps the same date, should therefore be assigned to the basilica of Miletus, beside which, moreover, stood a curious mausoleum or martyrium, a round vaulted structure with five deep niches. This massive edifice seems as archaic in design as the chevet of the basilica beside it.

At Ephesus the episcopal cathedral was installed in the fourth century in a gymnasium of the second century. Utilizing its porticoes, the Christians converted it into a three-aisled basilica with a timber roof. The subsequent modifications of this famous edifice reflect the revolutionary changes in church architecture effected in the Aegean area during the sixth century under the leadership of Constantinople *(plans and section p. 361, fig. 452-454).*

There were, however, two other large churches at Ephesus which, though contemporary with the cathedral basilica, have no resemblance to it. Owing to their renown as cult centres and the ascendancy of the city of Ephesus in the ancient world, they were buildings of considerable size, but they owed their peculiar features to the fact that they were designed as memorial monuments.

The first is the martyrium of St John, built over the 'empty tomb' of the saint. This cruciform edifice, in its fifth-century form (as reconstructed by the excavators), resembled the great Syrian sanctuary of St Simeon Stylites, with which it was contemporaneous. Like the latter, it consisted of four intersecting basilicas, the saint's relics being enshrined in the central square of the crossing. Only this central square was vaulted. The four basilicas conform to the usual plan. The fact that the number of aisles varies from one to another shows that the different parts of St John of Ephesus were built up piecemeal, not in accordance with any pre-determined plan.

The second martyrium commemorated the miracle of the Seven Sleepers of Ephesus, who awoke after two centuries in 451. This was a vaulted basilica with a single aisle, corresponding to a type of cemeterial church which in the Byzantine world lasted until

73

76. *Ephesus, Church of the Seven Sleepers. Interior of the Lower Basilica.*

the Middle Ages. The actual vaulting has nothing distinctive and resembles that of other mausolea. But the brick vaults of the Seven Sleepers seem to me to reflect the architecture of the domed churches built in Constantinople in the sixth century; and if this is so the vaulting of the Seven Sleepers need not be explained as stemming solely from an established tradition of cemeterial architecture (e.g. the church of St Sophia in Sofia).

Its sepulchral purpose, however, accounts for other features of its design: the crypt under the nave, the superimposed arcosolia recessed into the walls, the large vaulted hall which takes the place of an atrium and served as another collective mausoleum extending all round the church *(plans p.* 362, *fig.* 455). For centuries innumerable Christians chose this as their last resting place, there to await a resurrection like that of the Seven Sleepers to whom the martyrium owed its peculiar sanctity.

On the European coast of the Aegean Sea the oldest basilicas may go back to the end of the fourth century (Corinth, Epidaurus). In the fifth century basilicas large and small sprang up all over Greece and the Aegean islands, and many of their features vary little from place to place: a nave divided into three aisles by two rows of arches; a projecting semicircular apse; a narthex; and a timber roof. But their most characteristic feature (increasingly apparent as more of them are excavated) is the variety of the designs adopted for certain structural details, notably in the layout of the chevet, by builders who were guided by both practical and aesthetic considerations.

Epidaurus shows a transept with no lateral projection and no side aisles; at Philippi (Church A) we find a variant, a slight projection and a turning aisle *(plan p.* 363, *fig.* 459), which in St Demetrios at Salonica is developed and improved on *(plan p.* 362, *fig.* 456).

74

77. *Salonica, Basilica of the Virgin Acheiropoietos. Interior before Restoration.*

78. *Salonica, Basilica of the Virgin Acheiropoietos. Interior after Restoration.*

79. *Salonica, Basilica of St Demetrios. Façade after Restoration.*

In the Doumetios basilica at Nicopolis the transept projects well beyond the sides of the nave. In the basilica of Dodona, in Epirus, the projecting arms of the transept end in apses; this, together with the apse of the choir, gives the chevet a trefoil plan *(p. 363, fig. 458)*. Here, moreover, the colonnades of the nave extend beyond the triumphal arch, crossing the transept and ending at the wall of the chevet. Outside Greece, this formula was also applied in Milan (Santa Tecla) and Rome (San Pietro in Vincoli).

A square demarcated by four large piers marks the spot where a kind of monumental ciborium stood in front of the apse of the Ilissos basilica in Athens; here, moreover, the chevet was widened by the addition of two narrow wings, which produce the effect of a kind of rudimentary transept *(p. 362, fig. 457)*. Though the apse generally projects beyond the main fabric, it was sometimes enclosed in a flat chevet and flanked in consequence by two rectangular rooms (island of Lesbos). In the large basilica-martyrium of St Demetrios at Salonica we have another example of this type of chevet, but its details

76

cannot be clearly ascertained owing to extensive reconstructions at various periods. Still we may be thankful that this building, elaborately restored after the fire of 1917, is still standing.

The church of St Demetrios and the so-called Acheiropoietos basilica (renamed Eski Juma, or Old Mosque, by the Turks), both at Salonica, compel our admiration, such is the impression of majestic calm produced by the spacious naves lined with columns and piers. The lighting effects are particularly intense in the Acheiropoietos, thanks to the many large windows both on the ground floor and the upper storey. At the level of the galleries the side walls are almost entirely filled with windows.

Most striking in the interior of St Demetrios are the facings of coloured marble and the sculptured capitals. The Acheiropoietos basilica has some equally fine capitals. Another notable feature in St Demetrios is the disposition of the supports, alternately massive and slender (several columns between each pair of piers)—a device which was used to fine effect in the West in Romanesque architecture. Curious but less successful is the arrangement of the side aisles, where the columns are only half the height of those in the nave (exactly the opposite of what we see, for example, in San Paolo fuori le Mura in Rome). In both St Demetrios and the Acheiropoietos the galleries extend round three

80. *Salonica, Basilica of St Demetrios. Nave after Restoration.*

81. *Salonica, Church of St George. Exterior.*

sides of the nave, and the building is entered through a triple arcade, reduplicated in front of and behind the narthex, the atrium having been destroyed. The narthex also had its gallery and was flanked by two flights of steps.

At Salonica as elsewhere, there were sanctuaries designed for special purposes, built on a central plan and vaulted. One of them, the church of St George, is famous.

78

82. *Salonica, Church of St George.  Dome Mosaics, detail: Martyrs in a Symbolic Architectural Setting.*

83. *Salonica, Church of St George.  Dome Mosaics, detail: Martyr in the Orant Attitude.*

84. *Constantinople, Church of Sts Sergius and Bacchus. Exterior.*

This rotunda, originally a *heroon* or mausoleum built by the pagan emperor Galerius, was later converted to Christian worship. It is thus a special case, and neither its plan nor its decoration had any influence on Christian architecture *(plan p. 364, fig. 461)*.

The oratory of Christ Latomos (also called Hosios David) has on the contrary a special interest for the historian of Byzantine architecture. For with its square plan with an inscribed cross and its barrel vaults symmetrically disposed round an exceptionally lofty central vault, this modest edifice points the way to the typical Byzantine churches of the Middle Ages *(plan p. 363, fig. 460)*.

Excavations on the island of Thasos have brought to light the foundations of a large cruciform church, a basilica with a rather short nave and a transept of the same width as the nave. The side aisles extended all round the building, which had a timber roof and whose walls cannot have risen above the intersection of the arms of the cross. Earlier than the sixth century, this building foreshadows the cruciform Justinianian churches such as the Holy Apostles in Constantinople and St John at Ephesus (in its sixth-century form), where the method of vaulting with a series of domes makes its first appearance *(plan p. 364, fig. 462)*.

Before Justinian's reign, the churches of Constantinople were similar to the basilicas of the Aegean area. Examples are the basilica of Top Kabu Serai and the group of basilicas with short broad naves whose foundations were unearthed in the Bayazid Square. But the most famous is that of the monastery of St John of Studion (471), part of which is still standing *(plan p. 365, fig. 464)*. We can still admire the columns and carved entablature in white marble of the entrance portico, the columns of grey-green marble in the nave (which also carried an entablature) and the fine proportions of the three broad aisles composing the nave. A vast apse, polygonal on the outside, formed the chevet of the church, which was lighted by large windows placed beneath a timber roof. There was neither diaconicon nor prothesis. Galleries overlooked the side aisles and narthex.

The great churches of the capital, founded by Constantine and completed under Constantius II (St Sophia, St Irene, Holy Apostles), and other great imperial foundations such as the churches of the Blachernae and the Chalcoprateia, dedicated to the Mother of God, were also basilicas. Probably there was little to distinguish them from each other apart from secondary features. The Blachernae church seems to have had apses in the side walls, like the basilica of Dodona in Epirus.

Of the basilica of St Sophia which preceded the domed church erected in the sixth century, excavations have revealed a façade with a portico surmounted by a pediment, in the style of a classical temple. Though at Constantinople, as in all the Mediterranean lands at that time (fifth-sixth century), the basilicas predominated both numerically and in size, there were also smaller edifices on the central plan, round, square or cruciform,

85. *Ephesus, Church of St John (2nd state). Exterior (reconstruction).*
86. *Ephesus, Church of St John (2nd state). Interior (reconstruction).*

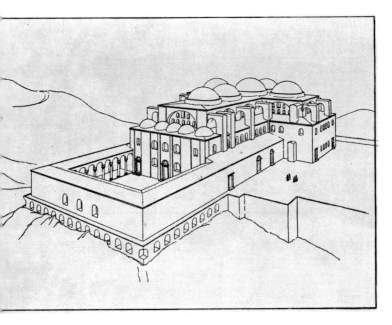

87. *Constantinople, Basilica of St Sophia. Theodosian Façade with Portico (reconstruction).*

which served as baptisteries, imperial mausolea and shrines for relics. The foundations of but a single martyrium have come down to us, that of Sts Carpos and Babylas. It consisted of a central rotunda surrounded by a circular aisle and an asymmetrical chevet with two (instead of three) apses *(plan p.* 364, *fig.* 463*)*. The whole was vaulted over, and the brick cupola of the central room is not only one of the best examples known of a fifth-century dome but ranks beside the magnificent vaults of the church of the Seven Sleepers at Ephesus and St Sophia at Sofia. On the whole, these religious edifices of the fifth century belong to the family of similar monuments widely diffused in the Aegean area, and in other Mediterranean lands as well. But henceforth, now that the city had been elevated to the rank of capital of the Empire, a number of civil edifices were erected in Constantinople and these gave a new, distinctive character to its architecture, which became still more pronounced in the next century.

The city's new status as a capital called for the construction of an imperial palace, a senate house, administrative buildings, residences for imperial dignitaries, porticoed markets and streets, and also public works of various kinds: aqueducts, cisterns, fortifications. The vast scope of these building and engineering operations made Constantinople, from the fourth century on, but particularly in the fifth and sixth centuries, an unrivalled centre of artistic and architectural activity, all the more outstanding as the other cities of the Empire were incapable of any such enterprises, with the sole exception of Ravenna where, however, all such work was necessarily on a restricted scale.

The imperial palace (Great Palace) no longer exists and excavations have revealed only a few vestiges, notably the porticoed courtyard and its mosaic pavement, which I would prefer to date to the mid-fifth rather than the sixth century. The Hippodrome built under Septimus Severus on the model of the Circus Maximus in Rome, and embellished by Constantine and Justinian, did not survive the fall of the Empire. Recently when portions of the tiered rows of seats and the entrance stairways were cleared of

82

88. *Constantinople, Walls of Theodosius II, detail.*

the later constructions built over them, it became apparent not only that the masonry had been cut and fitted with extreme precision, but also that the proportions were harmonious and the decorative motifs (of which but few had survived) were finely carved. Near the Hippodrome are the ruins of a large palace which appears to go back to the fifth century. Symmetrically grouped along two large semicircular porticoes was a series of round, square and polygonal rooms; in the very early Middle Ages, one of them was converted into a martyrium dedicated to St Euphemia *(plan p. 365, fig. 465)*.

Utilitarian architecture on a monumental scale is represented by large fragments of the aqueduct of Valens (364-378). The underground cisterns, though partially hidden from view, are sometimes impressive. The most remarkable, those of Yeri Batan Serai *(plan p. 365, fig. 466)* and Bin Bir Derek (528), are divided into a series of bays by hundreds of slender columns supporting arches and vaults. The architect of the Bin Bir Derek cistern, drawing on the greater resources put at his disposal by Justinian, built two tiers of superimposed columns like those of the Alexandrian cisterns.

83

It was probably in consequence of the sack of Rome by Alaric in 410 that Theodosius II resolved to surround the eastern capital with a new line of defensive walls stouter than the old ramparts of Constantine. The defensive works constructed by the Byzantine engineers (c. 413-440), which revolutionized the art of pre-medieval fortification, enabled Constantinople to withstand all attacks for eight centuries to come.

A brief description of these fortifications will suffice for our present purposes. They consisted of two parallel walls, protected on the outer side by a moat and secondary defences. The breadth of these defensive works varied from 190 to 207 feet: the vertical distance from the bottom of the moat to the top of the outer wall (the higher of the two) was over 110 feet. The landward walls were flanked by 192 towers, those of the seaward defences by 110 towers. By the use of alternating courses of masonry and bricks, walls and towers were given not only structural coherence but a fine aesthetic effect. Arches, niches, and vaults were constructed exclusively of brick and executed without centring. The bricks were laid in vertical or slightly tilted courses, so that while the first rested against the wall, each successive layer rested on the one below. Barrel vaults, groined vaults and domes covering the rooms inside the towers were constructed in this manner.

From the mid-fifth century on, the experience they had gained in the building of the defensive wall, far more than in that of the cisterns, enabled the Byzantine architects to outclass all rivals. This great enterprise, carried on actively over a period of many decades, provided a training school for specialized craftsmen in every branch of the builder's trade. The skills thus acquired admirably qualified them for other architectural tasks, notably the construction of the great vaulted churches which were built in all parts of the city during the sixth century.

89. *Constantinople, Defensive Wall (reconstruction).* 90. *Constantinople, Interior of a Tower on the Wall (reconstruction).*

91. *Constantinople, St Sophia. Overall View from the South-West.*

That the secular and religious arts were then undifferentiated, at least as regards architecture, is proved by the fact that all these technical procedures were common to both. We know, moreover, thanks to the researches of Choisy and more recently those of Ward Perkins and Deichmann, that all the elements of this technical expertise had long been common knowledge in the Aegean region. At Miletus, Ephesus, Pergamum and Salonica, fragments of Roman buildings dating to the first centuries of our era have survived in which we find very similar constructional methods. It is well to emphasize the fact that, in the civil architecture of Constantinople in the fifth century and in the Byzantine churches of a slightly later date, the vaulting techniques employed had been handed down by an uninterrupted tradition. For while it is true that the vaulting of medieval churches in the West was perfected only after long and arduous experimentation, it was not so in Byzantium, where the early medieval architects benefited by the experience of their immediate predecessors in the Aegean region.

It must be remembered, nevertheless, that in Constantinople, in the period when the Theodosian fortifications and their vaulted towers were being built, churches on the basilical plan were always covered with a timber roof, vaults being used only in small sanctuaries on the central plan. This holds good not only for Constantinople but for all Mediterranean lands, from Mesopotamia to Spain, including Greece and Italy. But while the sixth century saw no new developments in church-building in these countries, the reign of

85

Justinian (527-565) brought radical changes in religious architecture both at Constantinople itself and in the area under its direct influence.

This new architecture forms an essential part of Byzantine art properly so called, and if it is to be understood it must be studied first of all in Constantinople itself, where it made its appearance in the sixth century. Further examples of it subsequently appeared in the cities of the Aegean area. But everywhere the architecture of the largest of the new churches must be studied when possible in the light of the edifices that immediately preceded them.

St Sophia, cathedral of Constantinople and the glory of Byzantine art, dominates all these creations. An earlier church on the site was destroyed by fire in the Nika riot of 532. Justinian ordered a new church to be built and five years later it was solemnly inaugurated. The emperor spared no expense, and the finest materials were brought from all the regions of the Empire. The workmen employed, whether native or foreign, were selected and conscripted on the basis of a system resembling the 'liturgies' (or contributions in kind) of ancient Greece. They were organized in corporations and placed under the orders of two engineers, Anthemios of Tralles and Isidoros of Miletus. It is sometimes assumed that, in view of their cities of origin, it should be possible to trace influences stemming from Asia Minor in the work of the two architects. But in fact there is no justification for this assumption. Not only are both cities located in a part of Asia Minor that is quite near Constantinople, but Procopius, who speaks of Anthemios of Tralles, does not state that he had come directly from his native town; he simply records the fact that, because of his high reputation as an 'artificer,' he was put in charge of building operations on the new cathedral. The chances are that he was trained in Constantinople itself, where large-scale construction work was constantly in progress throughout this period.

The ground plan of St Sophia is nearly square, except for the small projecting apse of the choir. It seems curiously archaic for the period, having neither a diaconicon nor a prothesis. Excavations carried out in front of the façade suggest that Justinian's church may have taken over not only the single small apse but also the length of the nave from the basilica that had previously existed on the site. The fact that the proportions of St Sophia correspond so closely with those of St John of Studion (471), as regards both length and width, makes it all the more likely that the plan of the sixth-century cathedral reflects certain aspects of fifth-century church architecture.

The ground plan of St Sophia, however, is not of prime importance. The essential features of this architecture are the great central dome and the piers, arches and subsidiary vaults upholding it. The rest only serves to delimit the space occupied by the edifice and to define its volume. The subordinate character of the enclosing walls becomes evident when it is realized that the eye cannot take in their continuous extent either from the interior, where no overall view is possible, or from the exterior, where bulky projecting pillars break up the otherwise uninterrupted surfaces. Although when seen from the outside, particularly from the east, the great church rises up harmoniously from level to level, to the very top of the central dome, its soaring lines are by no means free from a somewhat excessive ponderousness, even a certain gaucherie. The curves of the arches and domes, for example, seem ill-adjusted to the verticals of the heavy projecting buttresses. Inside, on the other hand, everything conspires to produce the impression of an immense

92. *Constantinople, St Sophia. Interior, detail.*

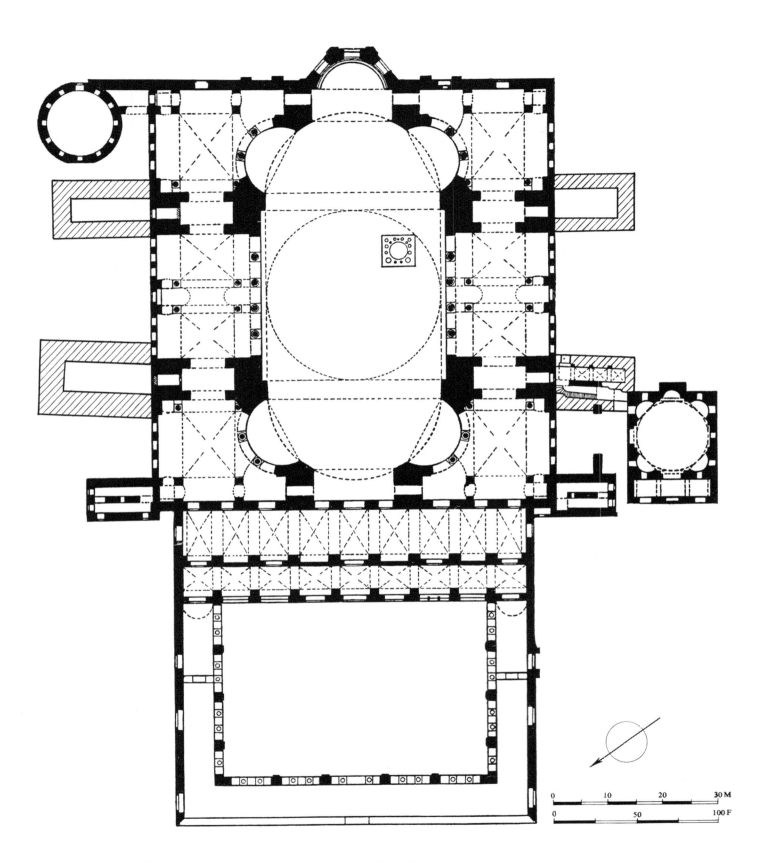

93. *Constantinople, St Sophia. Plan.*

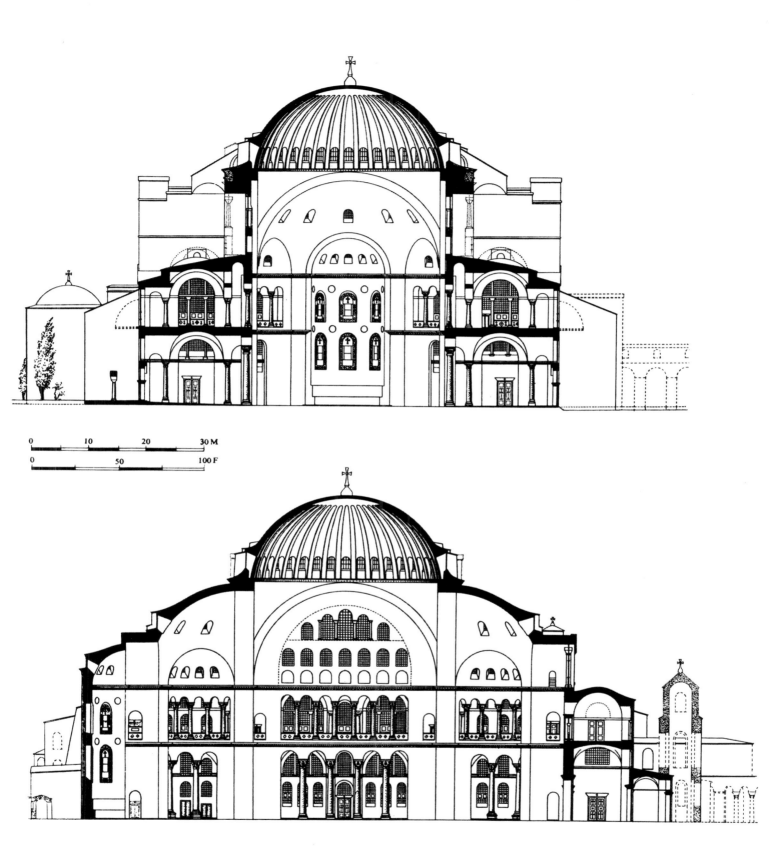

94. *Constantinople, St Sophia. Cross-Section (east-west axis).*
95. *Constantinople, St Sophia. Cross-Section (north-south axis).*

89

0  10  20  30 M
0      50      100 F

90    96. *Constantinople, St Sophia. Exterior from the East.*

97. *Constantinople, St Sophia. Aerial View.*

98. *Constantinople, St Sophia. West Façade.*

92

99. *Constantinople, St Sophia. Interior, detail.*

space ideally organized. From the main door of the nave, looking along the axis of the church towards the apse, the beholder can appreciate the noble sweep and majestic proportions of the vast interior, with its supporting columns and walls covered with polychrome marbles. His gaze is drawn towards the mighty vaults overhead which—apparently so cumbrous when seen from the outside—seem to float in air, released from the pull of gravity, the moment one has entered the church.

This effect, noted by Procopius as early as the reign of Justinian, derives from the exquisite proportioning of all the structural elements and the skill with which the massive bulk of the four great piers and their lateral buttresses is concealed from the eye. Finally, the illuminated zone set up at the base of the dome and the many windows with which it is pierced, create an impression of soaring lightness that makes us forget that this exceptionally wide vault, representing a tremendous weight, is upborne only by means of the great piers and arches on which it rests.

No praise is too high for the skill with which the architects of St Sophia exploited all the possibilities of sunlight. Each hour of the day has its own pattern of light; entering by different windows, the rays are focused on this or that point, or, crisscrossing at different levels, glance along the walls and flow across the pavements. The play of light is continually changing, and its shifting patterns enhance the strangely unreal effect of this gigantic 'fabric of a vision.'

Light effects are at once subtler and more constructive when the light is evenly disseminated, not canalized in independent rays, and one of the characteristics of St Sophia, and of all religious architecture of its time at Byzantium, is this use of light. The central area under the dome is much better illuminated than the portions of the church around it, and this illuminated area is also the most spacious. In elevation it rises to the summit of the vaulting, whereas the rooms around it are divided into superimposed storeys, some of them framed by secondary columns and piers. The central aisle moreover forms a single unbroken unit extending from the entrance to the apse, while the side aisles are divided into three distinct sections. For it is only here, in the side aisles, that one becomes conscious of the massiveness—not apparent from the central aisle—both of the four great piers supporting the dome and of the four others buttressing them, two on each side of the building.

That concessions were made here to the basilical type of church is evidenced in the upper levels of St Sophia by the disparate treatment of the semidomes of the great cupola: on either side, behind the columns, the great piers are buttressed by further piers, while over these columns rises a wall pierced with large windows. Colonnades and sheer walls help to emphasize the longitudinal axis of the central aisle. The vaulting of the nave, on the other hand, was not inspired by the basilica but by the design of central-planned churches. Instead of having a uniform roof extending the whole length of the nave, as in a basilica, St Sophia is dominated by a central dome symmetrically flanked to east and west (i.e. towards the apse and towards the entrance) by two identical semidomes, each of them supported by two columned exedrae.

Although—probably for reasons of practical convenience—some elements of the traditional basilica were incorporated in St Sophia, they did nothing to solve the essential problem: how to support the great central dome. The original dome having collapsed a

100. *Constantinople, St Sophia. Interior looking towards the Apse.*

101. *Constantinople, St Sophia. Central Dome, exterior.*

few years after the church was built, it was replaced by another which, having a shorter radius and being thus more convex and compact, has lasted to the present day. Made of brick, it was given additional strength by being erected over a ribbed shell (the ribs being reinforced) with a casing of masonry which, externally, consolidates the base of the vault. The dome rests on four brick-built arches carried by four piers, a spherical triangle known as a pendentive being inserted between the base of the dome and the foot of these arches, which are supported by enormous piers rectangular in section. The use of the pendentive (instead of corner squinches) gives the vaulting a special elegance. From now on the pendentive became the most constant and most characteristic feature of the domed edifices erected by Byzantine architects down to the fall of the Empire and even after.

Unlike the vaults and arches of brick, the piers are built with large hewn stones perfectly fitting together and strongly bonded with molten lead. The same painstaking care was given to the construction of the lateral pier-buttresses, linked to the central piers by brick arches on both the ground-floor and the gallery levels. It is at these points, on the north and south sides of the nave, that St Sophia has best resisted the ravages of time (though not without some consolidation in the Turkish period), while on the east and west sides the great dome has not been so effectively buttressed as might at first sight

96

102. *Constantinople, St Sophia. Central Dome and Semidomes,* **interior.**

103. *Constantinople, St Sophia. Semidome,* **exterior.**

he supposed. True, nothing could seem better suited to support the dome than a semidome of the same diameter adjusted to the great arches which carry the dome. In practice, however, this procedure proved less successful in St Sophia than the system of buttresses which is employed on the north and south sides of the dome.

As for the rest of the church, groined vaults were skilfully adapted—both on the ground floor and on the level of the galleries—to the layout of the rooms grouped round the great central nave, to the narthex, and to the east portico of the atrium (the rest of it has not survived).

Under Justinian several other Constantinopolitan churches were rebuilt on the same principles as those determining the architecture of St Sophia. One of them was the famous church of the Holy Apostles which was entirely destroyed by the Turks; its design was copied, however, in St John's church at Ephesus, which thus gives us a good idea of what it was like. The Holy Apostles, like St John's, was a cruciform church. But the architects divided it into six sections, each on a square plan and each surmounted by a dome, that of the central square being loftier than the others. From the constructional point of view, this was a juxtaposition of similar elements which, taken separately, had affinities with the central portion of St Sophia. A third church, Sts Sergius and Bacchus *(plan p. 366, fig. 467)*, a rectangular edifice crowned by a brick dome, viewed from outside, resembles St Sophia. But the similarities of external design conceal a very different arrangement of the interior. Here too the building is dominated by the dome, which, however, rests on eight instead of four piers. As a result the nave is octagonal instead of rectangular. Here, better than elsewhere, we can see the priority assigned in Justinianian architecture to the dome and its supports; the domical canopy was the prime and constant element, while the layout of the church which it crowned could be varied at will.

Originally St Irene must have resembled a church at Philippi, in Macedonia, which was built in all probability by architects summoned from Constantinople. A dome rose over the square section preceding the apse, while the nave, a short and wide one, was covered with a vault of whose exact form nothing is known *(plan p. 366, fig. 468)*. For, inadequately buttressed on the choir side, the dome collapsed, it seems, during the construction of the church, and this accident, like the similar one at St Sophia, suggests that the dome was a new structural element overhastily introduced before the necessary techniques had been fully mastered.

The structural disposition at Philippi is particularly instructive. Here, side by side, are two churches on very much the same plan, one of the fifth century with a timber roof, the other of the sixth century crowned by a dome, and this similarity of plan enables us to trace the development from the earlier type of basilica to the later domed church.

Even more revealing is the church of Pirdop, in Bulgaria, where at some time in the sixth century the choir of the ancient basilica was demolished and replaced by a brick dome with its appropriate system of supports, also of brick. There could be no more eloquent testimony to the prevailing desire to endow churches with a central dome, even though, as at Pirdop, no change was made in the other parts of the traditional timber-roofed basilica *(plan p. 366, fig. 469)*.

It is impossible to fix the exact limits of the area where, under the lead of Constantinople, domed churches were now erected or domes added to existing churches. On the

European mainland they can be traced as far as southern Serbia (Konjuh) and, in Greece, to the region around Salonica (St Sophia); another example has been found on the island of Paros. But in the remoter provinces of Yugoslavia and Dalmatia this new type of architecture seems to have been unknown.

It was, however, adopted on the Asiatic coast of the Aegean at Ephesus, where St John's church and the cathedral dedicated to the Mother of God provide two fine examples of edifices crowned with domes.

The originality of sixth-century Byzantine architecture is plain to see. This originality was not a matter of technique, for, as we have indicated, the materials and vaulting techniques used by Justinian's architects were not new in themselves. But when in the great seaport towns of the Aegean (Ephesus, Miletus, Salonica) we observe the far-reaching changes that took place from the fifth to the sixth century in the design and construction of churches we cannot fail to realize how great was the innovation these betokened—an innovation by which, however, all the other provinces of the Mediterranean world remained almost completely unaffected.

For outside the strictly Byzantine area we find only a small number of churches which, in one way or another, can be related to the Justinianian monuments. Even when their design shows the influence of the capital, the actual construction in many cases must have been entrusted to local builders, for it reveals unmistakable departures from the Byzantine practice and affinities with other local monuments. This is the case with the octagonal church of San Vitale at Ravenna, whose dome was built of light materials and which shows traces of a tendency towards the verticalism traditional in the East. The trefoil apse of the Church of the Nativity at Bethlehem is another example of non-Byzantine inspiration, remarkable in this case since the edifice is believed to be one of Justinian's foundations. This apse, like the dome at Pirdop in the Balkans, was substituted for the choir of the original basilica. But while adopting the central plan characteristic of Justinianian churches, the Palestinian architects did not venture to cover the building with a dome; they kept to a type of roofing traditional in the East. We have spoken of attempts that were made to imitate features of Byzantine design in Syrian basilicas and the churches of northern Mesopotamia and eastern Asia Minor. But actually only a single one of these edifices, the church at Kasr Ibn Wardan (564) in Syria, can be described as being of Byzantine inspiration.

To sum up, the originality and splendour of the church architecture, Byzantine in the strict sense of the term, which flourished in Constantinople and the Aegean area in the sixth century, are incontestable. None the less the diffusion of this art patronized by the emperors was somewhat limited. In the domain of architecture local and regional practices prevailed over the directives of Constantinople. This much is clear, though there are no means of knowing just how far these directives went, and indeed it may well be that the Imperial government of that age never had any idea of applying its influence to the promotion of any specific type of church architecture.

# 2. Painting

*Foreword*

The fifth and sixth centuries were the great age of antique Christian painting, that of the masterpieces—mosaics, wall paintings and illuminated manuscripts—whose outstanding aesthetic qualities are so highly appreciated today.

The beginnings of Byzantine painting, like those of architecture, may conveniently be situated in the Theodosian period. Some early texts mention wall paintings in the churches of Asia Minor and even describe the subjects treated by the artists—e. g. the life and martyrdom of Sts Barlaam, Theodore and Euphemia. Though these references (in the sermons of Sts Basil, Gregory of Nyssa and Asterius of Amasia) give no detailed accounts of the basic iconographic cycles, we learn from other texts that paintings of many kinds already figured on the walls of basilicas.

About 400, in a letter to the Eparch Olympiodorus in Constantinople, St Nilus expressly charges him to have the Cross represented in the apse of the church, and Old and New Testament scenes in the nave, and rejects the Eparch's proposal to introduce hunting and fishing scenes and images of animals into these parts of the church.

Biblical scenes, we may be sure, already figured on the walls of Old St Peter's in the Vatican. These frescoes have perished but we can get an idea of their appearance from paintings in later Roman basilicas, notably those in Santa Maria in Via Lata and also the drawings made from paintings by Pietro Cavallini who (at the end of the thirteenth century) touched up, or imitated, many of the ancient frescoes in San Paolo fuori le Mura.

Despite the all but total destruction of the apse paintings in fifth-century basilicas, there are good reasons for believing that the revival of large-scale painting was due to the influence of Pope Leo I (440-461). It has been shown by Wilhelm Koehler that, in all probability, Carolingian manuscript illuminations contain reminiscences of these lost works of the fifth century. The rare surviving examples do not encourage us to generalize the information given by contemporary writers, for the remains of these decorations differ considerably from what they tell us. The unique example of an early apse mosaic that has survived (at Salonica) does not contain the cross which, according to St Nilus's letter, was indispensable. At Salonica, again, the martyrs in the dome of St George's are quite unlike the paintings of the same period in the martyria of Asia Minor, as described by the Greek Fathers of that region. Finally, both in Rome (triumphal arch and nave of Santa Maria Maggiore) and at Milan (vestibule of the rotunda of Sant'Aquilino) the mosaics entirely differ from the descriptions of wall decorations in the works of contemporary writers. While going to prove the great variety of works of art produced during this period, these anomalies also make us realize the gaps in our knowledge and the impossibility of forming any estimate of the frequency of figure paintings in fifth- and sixth-century churches, and, *a fortiori*, of basing any conclusions on the silence of our sources.

*Mosaics*

Pavement and wall mosaics had been in vogue in the Roman empire long before the coming of Christian art. They provided a decoration that was both stable and impervious to damp. Indeed the effect of the mosaics adorning fountains and pools was enhanced by the flow of water, and the colours shone with an intensity far exceeding that of ordinary painting. Moreover, the use of small juxtaposed tesserae made it possible to clothe the curves of arches and vaulted ceilings with a wealth of scintillating colours. For flat walls slabs of marble and inlays forming decorative patterns were commonly employed.

But very soon the mosaic was adapted to more ambitious programmes and came to rank as one of the most highly esteemed techniques of large-scale figural art. It was at this stage of its development (before the time of Constantine) that it came to be used for figure subjects of a Christian order. Neither then, however, nor in the first half of the fourth century, did the mosaicists bring to fruition all its possibilities in the field of monumental art—and it was not until the Theodosian period that the Christian mosaic got into its stride. Thereafter it made rapid progress, culminating in the masterpieces of the fifth and sixth centuries, marked with the imprint of the young school of Constantinople.

For the mosaic pavements, which needed not only to be watertight but also to resist rough usage, trodden on as they were by surging crowds, only stone tesserae were used. By varying their colours, size and layout, many different effects were achieved, enhanced by a rich diversity of themes.

In the wall mosaics tesserae of tinted or gilt glass were employed; for the latter, gold leaf was affixed to the undersides of the cubes. These mosaics owe their compelling power to the brilliancy of the gold grounds, their two-dimensional figurations and the majesty (often combined with a certain rigidity) of the figures. That no painter could link up so effectively his images with the walls acting as their support was due to the fact that walls and mosaics were made of the same material, solid in both cases. Once the mosaic-workers had realized the possibilities this opened up—and the Constantinopolitan artists were, it seems, first in the field—some of the finest mosaics that the world has seen came into production, from the fifth century on.

At Byzantium, this stylistic evolution can best be studied if we begin by an examination of more traditional works, first of all the floor mosaics, produced in large numbers throughout the Mediterranean world in the fifth and sixth centuries. Finest of these is the group of pavements that have been uncovered in an arcaded courtyard on the site of the Great Palace at Constantinople. Their dating is conjectural, but for stylistic,

105. *Constantinople, Great Palace.  Mosaic Pavement: Water Mill.*

106. *Constantinople, Great Palace. Mosaic Pavement: Eagle and Snake.*

107. *Constantinople, Great Palace. Mosaic Pavement, detail: Man's Head.*

iconographic and topographical reasons we can safely assign them to the middle of the fifth or, at latest, to the early sixth century. Set out on a white ground, a great number of independent scenes form coherent compositions, however wide the gaps between the motifs. These are extremely varied. To begin with there are the idyllic scenes so much in favour in Late Antiquity: shepherds and shepherdesses, flocks, trees, rocks and water mills. Akin to these 'idylls' are the scenes of children's games so frequently depicted by Roman decorators, even on the walls of mausolea.

From scenes of hunting hares or big game we pass on to others of a more and more spectacular order: fights between elephants and beasts of prey, snakes and eagles or mythical monsters of the types current in ancient Ionian art. This juxtaposition of two kinds of scene, pastoral and dramatic, was obviously intentional, and, to the best of my belief, unique in the art of this period. The scenes are framed in acanthus scrolls, interspersed with birds, animals and fruit, and alternating with human heads.

Most of the floor mosaics found at Antioch are in public buildings or private houses. Their themes resemble those of the contemporary pavement of the Great Palace at Constantinople and their style reflects the sophisticated tastes prevailing in the eastern capital

105

108. *Constantinople, Great Palace. Mosaic Pavement: Two Children riding a Camel.*

from the fourth century on. Already apparent in the reliefs on the triumphal columns at Constantinople, this style persisted there throughout the Middle Ages. In this figural art faces are ennobled but also standardized; the drawing is precise, the composition rhythmic, each face has an air of studied dignity appropriate to ceremonial occasions.

The same is true of the large heroic (and moralizing) hunting scene of the *Megalopsychia*, in which we see huntsmen congregated round a personification of Magnanimity. The surrounding frieze, however, is in a different spirit. Crowded with scenes of life in the streets of Antioch, it gives a panoramic view of the great Syrian city. Here we have a wholly realistic art devoid (so far as can be judged) of any abstract connotation.

At Antioch we find again a taste for animal, particularly wild animal, motifs. But here there are traces of Sassanian influence, absent in the art of the Great Palace at Constantinople. In the mosaic representing a nimbused phoenix and a lion passant framed in a frieze of ibexes we have an imitation of the designs of the textiles which were then being manufactured at Antioch for near-by Persia. These textiles also found their way to purely Byzantine cities and their influence can be seen in some mosaic decorations (secondary vaults at St George's, Salonica).

106

109. *Antioch.    Megalopsychia Hunt, detail: Figure personifying Magnanimity.    Antioch.*

110. *Antioch.    Megalopsychia Hunt, detail of the frieze: Street Scene in Antioch.    Museum of Antiquities, Antioch.*

111. *Antioch.* *Megalopsychia Hunt, detail: Lion Hunt.* *Museum of Antiquities, Antioch.*

112-114. *Antioch.* *Megalopsychia Hunt, detail of the frieze: View of Antioch with its Buildings.* *Museum of Antiquities, Antioch.*

113. *Antioch.    Mosaic Pavement, detail of a frieze: Ibexes. Louvre, Paris.*

116. *Kabr Hiram. Mosaic of the Months, Seasons and Winds, detail. Paris.*

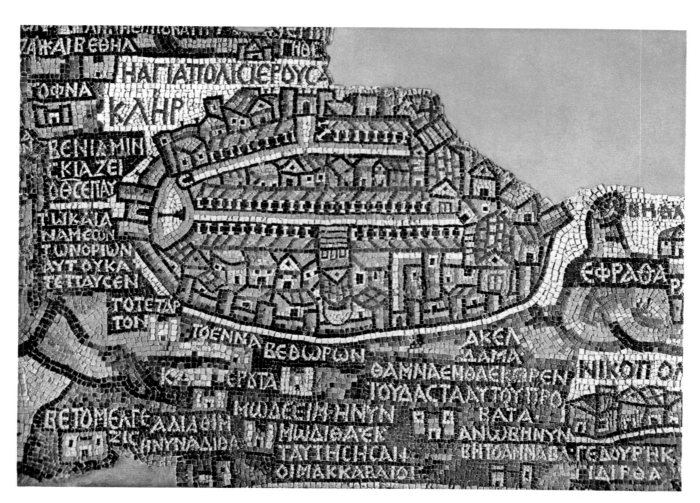

117. *Madaba. Mosaic Pavement: Map of the Holy Land, detail: Plan of Jerusalem.*

111

115. *Antioch. Mosaic Pavement: Nimbused Phœnix on a Flower-patterned Ground. Louvre, Paris.*

118. *Aquileia, 'Fondo Tullio' Church. Mosaic Pavement, detail: Lamb lying in the Shade of a Vine. Museo Paleocristiano, Aquileia.*

Mosaic pavements were also laid in churches, but in them figural motifs were rarely used. The largest ones date no earlier than to the sixth century and the abstinence from this type of decoration was probably due to a feeling that it was unseemly that sacred scenes should be displayed at ground level, for all to tread on. The decorations of floor mosaics were usually of a pagan character: the months of the year at Kabr Hiram in Phoenicia (Louvre) and in the church of St John the Baptist at Gerasa in Palestine; the Cosmos at Nicopolis in Greece; a map of the Holy Land at Madaba in Transjordania; hunting and fishing scenes, plants and flowers in many churches in all the Mediterranean provinces.

When Christian subjects were employed they were usually treated as allegories, as in the choir of the 'Fondo Tullio' church at Aquileia (late fifth century), at El Mouassat (sixth century, Tunisia), on Mount Nebo (Palestine) and at Madaba. Sometimes we see the Lamb or sheep lying in the shadow of a vine, crosses, and a paradise garden. A mosaic from a sepulchral oratory at Jerusalem, now in Istanbul, represents a 'Christian Orpheus'. In the floor mosaic of the choir at El Tabgha, near the sea of Galilee, the Miracle of the Loaves and Fishes has a special appositeness, since it was here that the miracle took place.

119. *Jerusalem. Mosaic Pavement: Christian Orpheus with Animals. Archaeological Museum, Istanbul.*

120. *Madaba.    Mosaic Pavement: Tamed Animals in Paradise, detail.*

114

121. *El Tabgha, Church of the Multiplication of Loaves and Fishes. Loaves and Fishes.* — 122. *Beit Alpha, Synagogue. Hen with Chicks.*

Often a floor mosaic containing an allegorical representation of the conversion of the whole world to the Christian faith figured in the nave. This grandiose conception was conveyed in various ways; by images of souls ravished by chants and music, by figurations of domesticated animals and birds, or again by scenes of harvest and the gathering of grapes or other fruits of the earth. At Mount Nebo, at Madaba and at Iunca (in Tunisia) the temple of Jerusalem is shown surrounded by tamed animals.

In this imagery of the world-wide triumph of the 'peace of God' we can detect the influence of the Jewish eschatological legend of universal peace. It was but natural that this influence should be most noticeable in Palestine and at Antioch; there we find pavements depicting the animals at peace among themselves, as prophesied by Isaiah (XI, 6-9, LXV, 25). These images also figure in the pavement mosaics of some contemporary synagogues discovered in Palestine, at Tiberias (c. 350), at Gerasa (c. 450) and at Beit Alpha (sixth century).

In many cases the repertory of the floor mosaics must have been identical with that of the mosaics on vaults and ceilings. That this parallelism is so rarely apparent is due to the fact that, given the present condition of the edifices, the number of extant mosaics of the latter kind is seldom adequate for a comparison. Still, it seems clear that the general effect of the decorations in a fifth- or sixth-century church was largely based on a harmony between the decoration of the floor and that of the vault and ceiling.

115

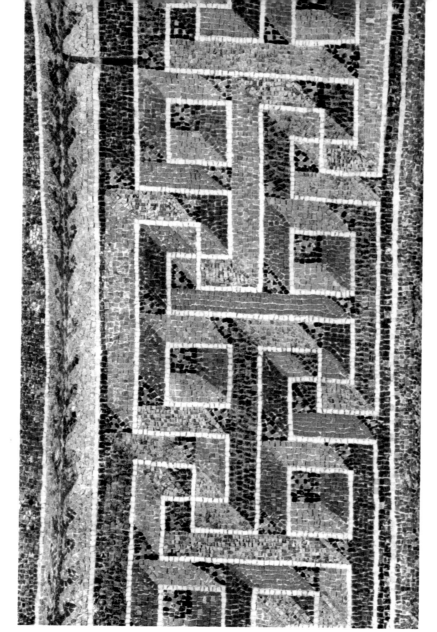

124. *Ravenna, Mausoleum of Galla Placidia. Decorative Mosaic with Geometric Designs, detail.*

Few examples of vault mosaics have survived. Most of them consist of garlands, scrolls and geometric motifs, sometimes with the addition of a Christian image, such as the Lamb or a Cross on a ground of stars. Except for the stars (obviously out of place on a pavement) the motifs of the mosaic pavements reappear in the few surviving vault decorations. The most striking are those in the vestibule of the Lateran baptistery at Rome (fifth century); of the Santa Matrona oratory at San Prisco near Capua (fifth century); of the large exedrae in the church of St George, Salonica (fifth century); of the mausoleum of Galla Placidia (fifth century) and the choir of San Vitale at Ravenna (sixth century).

The mosaics on the soffits of the arcades between nave and side aisles have counterparts in the ornaments of similar proportions that are often grouped around the mosaic of the main pavement (in, for example, the Acheiropoietos church at Salonica). As for the

123. *Ravenna, San Vitale. Vault Mosaic: Nimbused Lamb upheld by Four Angels.*

125. *Ravenna, Mausoleum of Galla Placidia. Lunette Mosaic, detail: Stag drinking at the Fountain of Life.*

friezes of continuous scenes surrounding certain floor mosaics (like the frieze from a private house at Antioch, described above, which represents a panoramic view of the main street of the city), these were presumably devised to match the paintings on the upper walls of basilicas, in particular those on cornices just below the ceiling (none of which, unfortunately, has survived).

118

126. *Rome, Lateran Baptistery, Chapel of St John the Evangelist. Vault Mosaic, detail: Nimbused Lamb.*

127. *San Prisco, Oratory of Santa Matrona. Vault Mosaic, detail: Vase with Vine Shoots and Birds.* 119

128. *Milan, Sant'Ambrogio, San Vittore Chapel. Dome Mosaic, detail : Bust of St Victor within a Wreath.*

129-130. *Naples, Baptistery of San Giovanni in Fonte. Dome Mosaic, details: Martyr standing beside a Cippus and The Wedding at Cana.*

The half-length portraits in floor mosaics at Aquileia and elsewhere are reproductions of those in the vaults and ceilings. In the chapel of San Vittore in Ciel d'Oro, in the basilica of Sant'Ambrogio at Milan, a portrait of St Victor enclosed in a wreath occupies the summit of a dome entirely lined with gold, evoking the light of heaven, brighter than earthly sunlight.

We have already spoken of the pavements adorned with figures of the Months; these were sometimes isolated from each other by decorative frames (Antioch), sometimes represented as a line of women carrying offerings (Carthage). The layout of the mid-fifth-century mosaics in the dome of the Early Christian Baptistery at Naples, divided up by ornamental frames, corresponds to that of the Antioch pavement, and the procession of apostles carrying crowns in the Orthodox Baptistery at Ravenna resembles that of the Carthage pavement (lost soon after its discovery).

Some of Christ's miracles and a *Traditio Legis* figure in the dome of the Naples baptistery. That the motif of simulated materials hung at the summit of the vault and the blue grounds derive from pre-Christian Roman mosaics is confirmed by the rather cumbrous renderings of figures and garments. These mosaics are more successful than those of Santa Costanza in associating the figures with the vault; this they do by increasing their scale and also by adding to the scenes in the top of the dome eight monumental figures of martyrs or prophets standing beside a cippus on which lies a victor's crown.

121

131. *Ravenna, Orthodox Baptistery.   Dome Mosaic, detail: Jude the Apostle.*

The art of the mosaics in the Orthodox Baptistery and the Mausoleum of Galla Placidia at Ravenna, while still keeping to the classical tradition, is of a higher order. But we can often detect a certain unsureness in the technique, especially when attempts are made to instill more vigour into the antique type of modelling and to locate the figures in space.  Marked in Italian fifth-century mosaics, this unsureness is less apparent in the Greek, Syrian and Egyptian works.

132. *Ravenna, Orthodox Baptistery.   Dome Mosaic: Baptism of Christ with Apostles.*

126      135. *Ravenna, Mausoleum of Galla Placidia. Lunette Mosaic, detail: An Apostle.*
136. *Ravenna, Mausoleum of Galla Placidia. View of some of the Mosaics.* ▶

133. *Ravenna, Mausoleum of Galla Placidia. Vault Mosaic, detail: Starry Sky.*
◀ 134. *Ravenna, Mausoleum of Galla Placidia. Lunette Mosaic, detail: The Good Shepherd.*

137. *Salonica, St George. Dome Mosaic, detail: Young Martyr. (Copy by Father Lefakis)*

The vision of the Heavenly Jerusalem in the drum of the dome of St George's church at Salonica resembles the one in the Ravenna Baptistery. But here two or three martyrs, making the *orans* gesture, stand in front of the aediculae in each compartment. Above

128

138-139. *Salonica, St George. Dome Mosaic, details: Two Martyrs. (Copies by Father Lefakis)*

them, only the feet of twenty-two figures—a larger version of the apostles in the Orthodox Baptistery of Ravenna—have survived. At the top, inscribed in the terminal medallion, was the figure of Christ (not a scene of baptism) holding a sceptre-cross.

Here we have an 'abstract' composition whose exact purport is hard to determine. What, one wonders, was the point of the twenty-two persons who seem to be keeping guard at the foot of the great dome? The fact that there are inscriptions beside these figures giving the months of their commemorations suggests a connection with the ecclesiastical calendar. The frieze of seven buildings may well have been inspired by an earlier pagan decoration that had figured at this spot before the conversion of the mausoleum of Galerius into a Christian church. By displaying Christ on the pediments, crosses, and a book of the scriptures, these pagan edifices were 'christianized'. There is much in common between these mosaics and the pavements in the Great Palace at Constantinople and private houses at Antioch. The faces and the drawing of the figures show how closely the early fifth-century Greeks kept to the forms and conventions of classical art. The heads of martyrs, for example, still retain many characteristics of the idealized portrait which was *de rigueur* in Greece in the Roman period, and the retention of this formula by the mosaicist throws light on the beginnings of the Byzantine branch of Christian art.

129

141. *Salonica, Oratory of Christ Latomos.  Apse Mosaic: The Vision of Ezekiel and Habakkuk.*

The superb fifth-century mosaic in the so-called oratory of Christ Latomos, a humble edifice located in a squalid suburb of Salonica, comes as a surprise.  Along with that in the chapel of Sant'Aquilino in the church of San Lorenzo at Milan, this is the earliest known apse mosaic. It is in much better condition than the Milan mosaic and of very high quality, not only technically but also as regards its style, which resembles that of the mosaics in St George's, Salonica.

Here the adolescent, beardless Christ, throned in a luminous cloud and surrounded by the four evangelist symbols, reminds us of the Good Shepherd of the Mausoleum of Galla Placidia at Ravenna.  But in the Salonica mosaic two figures (identified by the Byzantines of the Middle Ages as Ezekiel and Habakkuk) are gazing fixedly at him.  From a hilltop at his feet flow the four rivers of Paradise and above them is a personification of the river Jordan worshipping Him who was baptized in its waters.  An inscription at the bottom of the mosaic explains the imagery: Emmanuel is 'the spring of living water' at which the Faithful quench their thirst.

140. *Salonica, Oratory of Christ Latomos.  Apse Mosaic, detail: The Prophet Ezekiel.*

131

142. *Mount Sinai, Monastery of St Catherine. Apse Mosaic: The Transfiguration.*

The curious votive mosaics in the basilica of St Demetrios at Salonica date to the last years of the period we are dealing with. Each panel is an independent scene, usually representing the sainted patron of the church and city surrounded by persons soliciting his aid. Of varying artistic merit, all reveal a touching candour and a fervent faith in the saint's power to help in time of need.

In the apse of the monastery of St Catherine on Mount Sinai, associated with the cult of Moses, the very fine mosaics (c. 600) representing the Transfiguration are only now receiving the attention they merit. Their makers were probably expert mosaicists hailing from some great Hellenic city.

The design and modelling of faces in the Mount Sinai mosaics, the strongly accentuated features, the forms of the figures in movement, the handling of their cloaks, and the elegant colour orchestration set off by the uniform gold ground, testify to a technical competence of the highest order.

132          143. *Salonica, St Demetrios. Nave Mosaic: St Demetrios between a Bishop and a High Dignitary.*

144. *Kiti (Cyprus), Church of the Mother of God. Apse Mosaic, detail: Angeloktistos Virgin.*

145. *Rome, Santa Pudenziana. Apse Mosaic: Christ surrounded by Apostles and **Personifications of the Two Churches.***

Effigies of the Virgin and Child seem to have been particularly appreciated in Cyprus. Usually the Virgin is escorted by two angels. Those on either side of the 'Angeloktistos' Madonna, at Kiti, carry the terrestrial globe, symbol of the world-wide power of Jesus. The handling of the Kanakaria Virgin is less refined, but such is its expressive power that it must not be written off as merely 'rustic.'

In the West only a few apse mosaics have survived. Those in Santa Pudenziana, though 'trimmed' in the sixteenth century, give a good idea of the evolution of Christian art in Rome under the pontificate of Siricius (384-399). Here we see Christ enthroned between two groups of apostles and female personifications of the Ecclesia ex Circumcisione and the Ecclesia ex Gentilibus. The prototypes of these two figures, representing the Church of the Jews and that of the Gentiles, were seemingly the 'Victories' which were depicted in Imperial art bestowing garlands on the victors. The *collegium* of Christ and the disciples figuring in an exedra remind us of the Hellenistic and Roman figurations of gatherings of 'Sages.' Though the walls are low, space is made above this group for the cross on Golgotha, symbols of the Evangelists, and a view of Jerusalem and its Christian churches. These buildings, not represented in any other apse, remind us of the sixth-century floor mosaics, with views of sacred edifices in the Holy Land in some Palestinian churches.

135

146. *Rome, Santi Cosma e Damiano. Apse Mosaic: Christ surrounded by Saints.*

Three justly famous sixth-century apse mosaics are those of Sts Cosmas and Damian in Rome and those of San Vitale and Sant'Apollinare in Classe at Ravenna. Though in Sts Cosmas and Damian and in San Vitale the iconographic themes derive from Roman imperial art, they are handled in a hybrid manner, due to their adaptation to Constantinopolitan conventions. And whereas in the Roman works the essentially 'human' aspect of the figures, borne out by the gestures of the saints and their celestial patrons, is counteracted by the supernatural manifestation of Christ walking on the clouds, all the personages in the Ravenna mosaics, without exception, are shown standing on the ground and massed together almost as if they were taking part in some state function in the palace. Furthermore, when the Roman mosaicist departs from the traditional type of beauty incarnated in the youthful Christ of Ravenna, he does this deliberately. He reproduces, and stresses, the features of the Santa Pudenziana Christ, and there is a touch of sculptural, typically Roman massiveness in all his figures. In many of its particularities—including the sumptuous garment worn by St Theodore and giving him the air of a participant in some official ceremony—the apse mosaic of Santi Cosma e Damiano ranks as the most Roman of all the apse decorations of the period.

In the apse mosaic of Sant'Apollinare in Classe three sheep symbolize the three eye-witnesses of the Transfiguration, while twelve others escort the titular saint, who is

148. *Ravenna, Sant'Apollinare in Classe. Apse Mosaic: The Transfiguration and St Apollinaris as an Orant.*

147. *Ravenna, San Vitale. Apse Mosaic: Christ between Two Archangels with St Vitalis and Bishop Ecclesius*

149. *Rome, Santi Cosma e Damiano. Apse Mosaic, detail: Christ walking on the Clouds.* 150. *Ravenna, San Vitale. Apse Mosaic, detail: Christ handing the Martyr's Crown to St Vitalis.*

✝ SANCTVS     APOLENARIS

152. *Ravenna, Sant'Apollinare in Classe. Apse Mosaic: Bishop Ursicinus.*

shown raising his arms heavenwards beneath the cross in the main axis of the apse. An anachronism in the sixth century, this allegorical theme must have been the product of a local tradition, while the portrayal of the saint as an Orant derives from an earlier tradition, that of the funerary portraits. But St Apollinaris was also the archbishop of Ravenna. Thus in this basilica in which the bishops of that see were buried his portrait appears again among those of prelates and Byzantine emperors which occupy the lowest register of the curved wall of the apse.

The presentation of these figures is typically 'official'; they are modelled on the commemorative portraits of high dignitaries of the Empire which were placed in the offices assigned to them.

151. *Ravenna, Sant'Apollinare in Classe. Apse Mosaic, detail: St Apollinaris as an Orant.*

154. *Ravenna, Sant'Apollinare in Classe.   Apse Mosaic: Detail of the Prophet Elijah.*

153. *Ravenna, Sant'Apollinare in Classe.   Apse Mosaic: Detail of the Transfiguration.*

156. *Rome, Santa Maria Maggiore. Nave Mosaic, detail: The Parting of Abraham and Lot.*

Apart from these apses only two other examples give us an idea of the mosaic cycles in the fifth- and sixth-century churches.

The finest of these, commissioned by Pope Sixtus III (432-440), is in the basilica of Santa Maria Maggiore in Rome. Though the style of the mosaics on the triumphal arch differs slightly from that of the nave mosaics, this difference need not be taken to mean a difference of date.

Forty-four panels on the nave walls illustrate scenes from the first books of the Old Testament: incidents in the lives of Abraham, Jacob, Moses and Joshua. They are

155. *Rome, Santa Maria Maggiore. Nave Mosaic, detail: The Sacrifice of Melchizedek.*

157. *Rome, Santa Maria Maggiore.   Nave Mosaic, detail: Abraham entertaining the Three Angels.*

presented on the lines of an heroic saga, like the reliefs on the great Roman triumphal monuments, prominence being given to battles and crowds in movement.   Though the presence of Christ and angels in events taking place on earth strikes a Christian note, these pictures conform to the methods of classical antiquity.   Plastic values are strongly indicated by juxtaposed cubes of varied, often vivid colours, and little stress is laid on outlines.   There are also representations of clouds drifting across the sky and attempts to suggest the space in which the figures move, in settings composed of buildings and furniture.

That this is a transitional work is proved by the difficulties the artist has evidently experienced in representing the processional movement of the bearers of the Ark around the walls of Jericho.   His substitution of a gold ground for a realistic depiction of a cloudy sky, and his rendering of some of the hills in gold, have, so far as can be judged, no iconographic significance.

Possibly we have in the Santa Maria Maggiore mosaics an early manifestation of a Byzantine aesthetic then in process of formation, but in the absence of any means of comparison there can be no knowing.   Similarly the lack of any extant monuments makes it impossible to say if the lavishly ornate scenes with figures clad in sumptuous garments were inspired by Constantinopolitan prototypes.   This view seems plausible, but we

146

158. *Rome, Santa Maria Maggiore. Nave Mosaic, detail: The Crossing of the Red Sea.*

159. *Rome, Santa Maria Maggiore.    Nave Mosaic, detail: The Lord protecting Moses and his Companions.*

cannot accept it without reservations, whether for the mosaics in the nave or for the more elaborate ones on the triumphal arch.

Set out in four superimposed registers, these latter illustrate the childhood of Christ, from the Annunciation to the Massacre of the Innocents.  At the summit of the arch is an inscription in gold letters on a blue ground: *Xystus Episcopus Plebi Dei*.  The throne of God is placed in a central medallion, flanked by the symbols of the Evangelists and the figures of St Paul and St Peter.

The imagery in all the scenes here has obviously been influenced by that of the triumphal monuments of Roman emperors, and the youthful Saviour, the Virgin and her companions are shown in the attitudes and attire of princes and princesses.  The figures of their friends (the Magi, King Aphrodisios) and enemies (e. g. King Herod) are treated on the same lines. Aphrodisios is even dressed as an emperor and represented as if welcoming a foreign prince to his kingdom.

Since these mosaics date from shortly after the Council of Ephesus (431), it is often assumed that their iconography was intended to exalt the Virgin as the Mother of God; actually it serves rather to proclaim the triumph of Christ the King.  In fact the art of the Santa Maria Maggiore mosaics is a Christian and ecclesiastical counterpart of that of the triumphal reliefs which Theodosius the Great and his sons had revived at Constantinople a generation earlier.

148

160. *Rome, Santa Maria Maggiore. Nave Mosaic, details: The Fall of Jericho and Priests bearing the Ark of the Covenant.*

161. *Rome, Santa Maria Maggiore. Mosaic on the Triumphal Arch, detail: The Annunciation.*

162. *Rome, Santa Maria Maggiore. Mosaic on the Triumphal Arch, detail: Scenes of Christ's Childhood.*

163-164. *Ravenna, Sant'Apollinare Nuovo. Nave Mosaics: The Pharisee and the Publican and The Holy Women at the Tomb.*

At Ravenna, less than a century later (before 526), the Gothic king Theodoric commissioned the mosaics on the nave walls of the basilica which he founded alongside his palace and which is known today as Sant'Apollinare Nuovo.

This grandiose decoration is laid out in three superimposed tiers. In the top register twenty-six successive scenes illustrate Christ's miracles and Passion. Confined to human figures and some indispensable accessories, these scenes give the impression of being imitations of painted bas-reliefs. Essentially decorative, they ring the changes on a wide range of colours. In this range, patches of the 'imperial' colour, purplish violet, strike a distinctive note.

Presumably these artists became acquainted with the art of Constantinople by way of portable works, miniatures and icons. But in their interpretations of them they exercised their personal taste for clear-cut outlines and touches of vivid colour. They show much less feeling, however, than their Greek contemporaries for rendering plastic values and effects of modelling by juxtaposed tones.

In the middle register large, stately figures stand out on panels with gold grounds, level with the windows. Their layout seems to have been inspired by that of statues placed in niches like those of high officials which have been brought to light at Ephesus and Athens. One of their characteristics is the special type of idealization common to so many Constantinopolitan works.

152

In the original version of the lowest register (previous to the modifications made by Justinian) were portraits of Theodoric, his family and his court dignitaries, advancing towards the images of Christ in Majesty and Mary in Majesty, that figure in the apse. Also, appropriately in the context, there were views of the palace of Ravenna and its port, Classis, whence the procession started. The sixth-century mosaicists substituted for the figures originally represented two processions of male and female saints, some moving towards Christ and the others towards the Virgin. This changed the purport though not the aesthetic effect of the mosaic, whose major qualities have happily survived the misdirected zeal of modern restorers.

Such as they are today, the Sant'Apollinare Nuovo mosaics, enriched with a wealth of colours, gold, white, emerald-green, and spangled with broken gleams, rank justly as one of the masterworks of Byzantine art. Here we have a superb example of the processional frieze which had figured to such fine effect in earlier days not only in the Parthenon but also on the walls of palaces in Assyria and Persia.

165. *Ravenna, Sant'Apollinare Nuovo. Nave Mosaic: The Judgement of the Nations.*

ABEL                                    MELCHISEDEC

168. *Ravenna, San Vitale. Lunette Mosaic: The Sacrifices of Abel and Melchizedek.*

The mosaics of Sant'Apollinare Nuovo are complementary to the architectural frame of the basilica and leave the columns and ceilings to make their full effect undecorated. It is otherwise in San Vitale (consecrated in 547); here the whole surface of the choir, from ground level to the summit of the vault, is lined with mosaics and our gaze moves so freely and smoothly over flat surfaces and ridges, planes and curves that it accepts the vision of a well-defined, self-contained space created by this polychrome revetment.

Adorned with scroll-work, the vaults, tympana and floor form a coherent decorative whole. The Lamb occupies the summit of the vault and, below, under the horizontal line spanning the base of the vault, the walls are entirely covered with figurative motifs : angels upholding the Cross, symbol of Christ's victory, Moses gazing at the Burning Bush and receiving the Tables of the Law, prophets and evangelists, reminding the spectator of the concordance between the Old Dispensation and the New. On the tympana are prefigurations of the rite of Communion: the sacrifices of Abel and Melchizedek, the sacrifice of Isaac, and Abraham entertaining the three angels under the oak in the Plain of Mamre.

156

169. *Ravenna, San Vitale.  Lunette Mosaic.  Abraham entertaining the Three Angels.*

This self-contained cycle is supplemented by two separate panels showing the basileus and basilissa, Justinian and Theodora, bringing offerings to the church.  That these two famous pictures produce such an overwhelming effect of splendour is due not only to the sumptuousness of the garments but also to the artist's highly skilful handling of a great variety of colours.  The excellence of the portraits has often been commented on, as has the curious convention of slewing the heads round so as to face directly the spectator.  And whereas the heads are wonderfully lifelike, the bodies seem curiously weightless, as if hovering in the air.  All the figures in the retinue, devoid of volume and of exactly the same height and breadth, exist in a supramundane space of their own making.  There can be no question that they reflect the art of Constantinople; models of the portraits of Justinian and Theodora must have been brought to Ravenna after the Emperor's victory over Theodoric in 526.

It is harder to decide how much the mosaics dealing with scriptural subjects owe to the contemporary art of the Byzantine capital, for these subjects have nothing specific about them.  Nor, in the absence of any corresponding works in Byzantium, have we any means of comparison as regards the style and design of the San Vitale mosaics.

157

170. *Ravenna, San Vitale. Choir Mosaic, detail: The Emperor Justinian.*

171. *Ravenna, San Vitale.  Choir Mosaic: The Emperor Justinian and his Retinue.* ▶
172. *Ravenna, San Vitale.  Choir Mosaic: The Empress Theodora and her Retinue.*

173. *Ravenna, San Vitale. Choir Mosaic, detail: The Empress Theodora.*

174. *Milan, San Lorenzo, Sant'Aquilino Chapel.   Apse Mosaic: Chariot of Christ and Shepherd in a Rocky Landscape.*

175. *Milan, Sant'Ambrogio, San Vittore Chapel. Dome Mosaic, detail: St Ambrose.*

The fifth-century mosaics in churches at Milan, which constitute the western version of this art of the early period, are much less well known than those at Ravenna. The first group figures in the octagonal chapel of Sant'Aquilino, an annex of the church of San Lorenzo. One of the two apses (that on the right) contains a representation of Christ with the apostles; in the other are shepherds seated or standing among rocks bathed in streams of living water, while above them we see crossing the sky the chariot of Christ, 'True Sun.' Some fragments of the mosaics in the vestibule of Sant'Aquilino which have recently been cleaned contain representations, on several zones, of the patriarchs of the Old Covenant and of apostles and martyrs personifying the Church of the Saints. This cycle of images was paralleled by the contemporary cycle in the decagonal church of La Daurade, Toulouse, which was destroyed in the eighteenth century.

The mosaics in Sant'Aquilino link up with the traditions of Roman mural painting in the fourth century. The same is true of those in the San Vittore chapel in the basilica of Sant'Ambrogio where, in the vault (*in coelo aureo*), we see a half-length effigy of the patron saint towering above the saints escorting him in the lower part of the dome. The delineation of these figures standing out on a vivid blue ground, if somewhat rustic, has a singular expressive power. The justly famous head of St Ambrose, with its large, melancholy eyes, long nose and fleshy lips, gives the impression of a real likeness. Dating to about 470, this mosaic was composed only some seventy-three years after the death of this great bishop and Father of the Church. In the saint's 'official' portrait of a later date we do not find the same intensity of life.

176. *Rome, Catacomb of Commodilla. Fresco: Virgin and Child enthroned between St Felix and St Adauctus with the Donatrix Turtura.*

166

*Wall Paintings*

During the fifth and sixth centuries wall paintings served the same purposes and kept to the same programmes as the mosaics. But being inexpensive, speedier and simpler, the art of the fresco was of a more democratic order. Hence the disparities of style and execution, and also the depictions of daily life, even of popular superstitions, that we find in the wall painting of the period.

Very few fifth- and sixth-century frescoes have survived in Italy; apart from some insignificant fragments, practically the only ones are in Rome and at Naples. The most striking fresco in the latter town has been removed from the wall and is now on view in San Gennaro. It contains elegant draped figures bearing the imprint of Greek painting, an influence often visible in Neapolitan wall paintings of the sixth century, and even of the iconoclast period.

In Rome the earliest *imagines clipeatae* of the Popes (at San Paolo fuori le Mura) prove that the 'impressionist' style of the mosaics in Santa Maria Maggiore was adopted in wall painting. It seems that the art of the fresco evolved more rapidly than that of the mosaics. Whereas the mid-sixth-century mosaics in Santi Cosma e Damiano remained extremely classical in spirit, we find in some sixth-century painted portraits a change of style taking place in the direction of abstraction and a linearism resembling that of the mosaics in San Lorenzo fuori le Mura (578-590).

Roman paintings of the period show two trends: one towards a continuation of the sophisticated art of the imperial epoch, the other towards the creation of schematic, popularized versions of the traditional classical figurations. And it is these latter frescoes, on a more rustic level, that most clearly illustrate the evolution of wall painting in the sixth and seventh centuries and even later, up to the tenth.

True, in many cases only fragments of these ancient paintings remain which, once they are exposed to daylight, rapidly grow pale and are soon irreparably lost. Only in the catacombs do darkness and an even temperature ensure the preservation of the colours, which are often remarkably bright and fresh.

The cult of St Felix and St Adauctus practised in the cubiculum of that name in the Catacomb of Commodilla accounts for the presence there of several *ex voto* paintings. Most famous is the very fine fresco representing the donatrix Turtura before the throne of the Virgin and Child (528). Another votive painting, dated by an inscription to the seventh century, represents St Luke, standing by himself, in a rectangular frame. Like the figures on the walls of the subterranean oratory these are icons and they have the schematic style, emphatic outlines and surfaces in flat colours characteristic of all votive paintings.

In the ruins of the diaconicon of Santa Maria Antiqua in the Forum many frescoes with Greek and Latin inscriptions have been uncovered; some of the latest (ninth-eleventh centuries) cover up earlier ones dating to the sixth and seventh centuries. The discovery in 1900 of these paintings, much damaged though they are, was an event of prime importance for the history of Early Christian art.

Here more clearly than anywhere else we see the cleavage between the works keeping to the classical tradition and those, more numerous, in which its procedures and forms

177. *Rome, Catacomb of Commodilla. St Luke.*        178. *Rome, Santa Maria Antiqua. St Demetrios.*

were modified and schematized. Catering for the taste of the masses, these latter imitate the portable wooden icons, some specimens of which have been recently found in Roman seventh- and eighth-century churches.

Of particular interest is the fresco portrait, set in a niche, of the sainted physician Abbacyr who is shown with his spatula and medicine box. The handling here closely resembles that of the Coptic paintings at Bawit and Sakkara; indeed they may have had a common source, since the centre of the cult of St Abbacyr, before it spread to Rome

179. *Rome, Santa Maria Antiqua. St Abbacyr the Physician.*

180. *Rome, Santa Maria Antiqua. The Three Holy Mothers: The Virgin between St Elizabeth and St Anne.*

in the seventh century, was at Alexandria. Also in Santa Maria Antiqua are two pictures, likewise in small niches, in which we find the traditions of Byzantine icon-painting combined with Roman traditions: one is a half-length Virgin pointing to the small figure of the haloed Child; the other represents the three Holy Mothers, the Virgin with St Elizabeth and St Anne.

Among the works in the classical vein a slightly bent angel's head is remarkable for its beauty and charming colours. But the face does not reflect any real inner life, and keeps to the classical norm of late antiquity.

In North Africa practically all the Early Christian wall paintings were destroyed by the Moslem invaders. Only some fragments in underground shrines have survived, among them the figure at Carthage of a handsome young saint wearing a Persian cap.

181. *Rome, Santa Maria Antiqua. Fragment of an Annunciation: The Archangel Gabriel.*

182. *Rome, Santa Maria Antiqua. Virgin and Child.*

171

183. *Carthage, Underground Baptistery. Bust of a Young Saint.*    184. *Bawit, Monastery of St Apollo. Medallion with the Head of a Woman*

Whom this represents is hard to say; possibly Daniel, one of the three Holy Children in the fiery furnace, or one of the three Magi.

In Syria, Palestine and Asia Minor, too, the Early Christian frescoes have perished, and the same fate has befallen those of Constantinople and Ephesus.

Egypt has fared better, for here some frescoes, buried for centuries under accumulations of dry sand, have been uncovered by recent excavations at Antinoe and in the ruined monasteries at Bawit and Sakkara.

Though some of these frescoes were painted on the columns of basilicas (a practice by no means surprising for it was already current in the Egypt of the Pharaohs) and though they contain some *cruces ansatae* inspired by the ankhs on hieroglyphs, it does not follow that we have here a survival of Pharaonic art. Actually, unlike the sculpture, and even Coptic architecture, Christian wall painting in Egypt kept in line with the practices current in other Mediterranean lands.

The frescoes at Bawit and Sakkara adorned the walls of the many small chapels around which the monks in Coptic monasteries grouped their cells. Whatever the precise liturgic function of these oratory chapels may have been, the fact that each had an apse and also the themes of the frescoes suggest that mass was celebrated and the monks held services in them. Limited though they were by lack of space, the figurations, particularly those in the apse, focal point of the chapel, where the altar stood, must have resembled those of the large contemporary churches. The decorative motifs in these apses derive from those in the niches of temples of Roman the period (where, however, they are carved, not painted) in Asia Minor, Syria and Egypt itself.

172

185. *Antinoe. Theodosia between St Colluthus and St Mary.*

The dating of these monastic paintings of Coptic Egypt is highly uncertain, and even to establish a rough chronological sequence is no easy task. Contrary to what once was thought, it is now clear that the Christian monasteries of Bawit and Sakkara were not abandoned when the region was overrun by the victorious Arabs, for some of the paintings date to the Islamic period. One is tempted to draw up a chronological chart indicating the gradual supersession of the most classical by schematic paintings. But the unreliability of all such 'absolute' chronologies is common knowledge. In Egypt itself we have a striking example of this in the so-called Fayum funerary paintings: these include both classical and schematic portraits which in some cases are not only contemporaneous but even figure in the same tomb.

While assigning to the Sakkara frescoes a slightly later date than to those at Bawit, and after eliminating certain elements undoubtedly belonging to a later period, we can assign the majority of these painted decorations to a period covering two or three centuries. This cannot begin before 400, *terminus a quo* of the rise of monumental Christian art in the Empire. For there can be no question that the Bawit and Sakkara painters imitated the apse decorations of great contemporary basilicas. By how long these rustic imitations postdated the originals, which may go back to 400 (mosaics in Christ Latomos, Salonica) or else date much later (sixth- and seventh-century mosaics of Mount Sinai and Cyprus), remains to be determined.

However, without pausing to describe them one by one, an examination of the most characteristic paintings in the chapels at Bawit and Sakkara may help to a solution of this chronological problem.

173

186. *Bawit, Monastery of St Apollo. Christ in Majesty and Virgin and Child with Apostles. Coptic Museum, Old Cairo.*

In most of the apses of the chapels Christ is represented in Majesty, between the four animal symbols of the evangelists. Below this theophany we see the Virgin in the *orans* position or enthroned between two angels, with the apostles on either side. In some cases Mary is suckling the Divine Babe, flanked by two angels, while the arch encircling her is adorned with half-length personifications of her virtues. Elsewhere she is shown in a medallion with the Child on her knees.

More abstract in conception, but deeply impressive, is a group of three medallions aligned at the base of an apse. The central medallion encloses a bust of the Virgin, seen frontally without the Child; on each side is the bust of an angel. Here for once Mary seems to have been depicted for her own sake, and not as the Mother of God, as is the case in the other chapels of Bawit and Sakkara.

174          187. *Bawit, Monastery of St Apollo. Virgin and Child with Apostles, detail. Coptic Museum, Old Cairo.*

ΑΗΛ
ΩΜΑΣ ✝ΒΑΡΘΟΛΟΜΑ ✝ΦΙΛΙΠΠΟΣ ✝ΑΝΔΡΕΑΣ ✝ ΠΕΤΡΟΣ
ΙΟΣ

188. *Sakkara, Monastery of St Jeremiah.  Head of the Virgin.*

176      189. *Bawit, Monastery of St Apollo.  Orant Virgin with Apostles, detail.*

190. *Karanis. Isis suckling Harpocrates. (Cf. List of Illustrations.)*

191. *Sakkara, Monastery of St Jeremiah. Sainted Monks with Kneeling Donor. Coptic Museum, Old Cairo.*

All these paintings, including the portraits of saints, enclosed in circles or ovals, which sometimes encircle the base of the apsidal arch, are assignable to a group of works produced in many parts of the Christian world in the sixth and first half of the seventh century. We have specially in mind the Palestinian ampullae, the mosaics of Mount Sinai and Cyprus and those in San Venanzio in Rome. Thus there are in our opinion good reasons for dating the Bawit and Sakkara frescoes to some time in the period 400-640.

This dating seems to be confirmed by the mural paintings elsewhere than in apses. Negatively, on one hand, by the absence or near absence of Biblical scenes; positively by the numerous portraits of saints and monks, presumably likenesses of deceased members of the monastery, made after their death. Some of the frescoes in the naves were, it seems, commemorative, while others were of an *ex voto* or apotropaic order. Among the latter a depiction of the Holy Knight Sisinnios slaying a female demon is accompanied by a classical image of the 'evil eye' together with beings or objects averting its pernicious influence.

192. *Bawit, Monastery of St Apollo.  St Sisinnios on Horseback transfixing a Female Demon.*

193. *Bawit, Monastery of St Apollo.* *The Virgin enthroned presenting the Christ Child in a Medallion.*

Both as regards their purpose and functions and in their technique these works are at a far remove from the major, more or less official pictorial art of the time. They have a scale of values of their own, based on the efficacy of their popular appeal, but they clearly had no immediate influence outside Egypt. None the less some of them herald the Romanesque art of the future and indeed point to one of its sources.

Traces of Coptic art have been detected in several western countries—in Spain, Gaul, Ireland and England—but the actual presence of Coptic works of a monumental nature in the west has not, so far, been established. It is quite possible, moreover, that such apparent analogies as exist are the products of a common stock of motifs and traditions. This, as things stand today, seems the most plausible view regarding the two distinctive features of the Bawit and Sakkara frescoes which bring to mind Romanesque monuments : the iconographic programme and layout of the apsidal paintings, and the repertory of ornaments and decorative elements in their frames. Both were to be taken over by Romanesque art.

194. *Sakkara, Monastery of St Jeremiah.* *The Virgin suckling the Child.* *Coptic Museum, Old Cairo.*

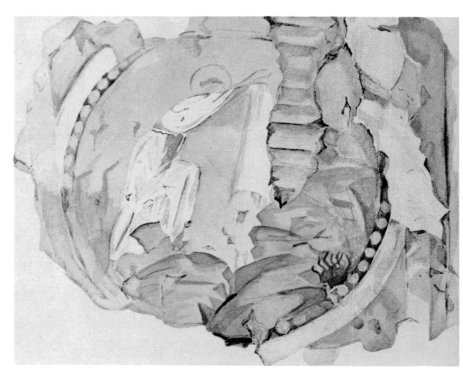

195-196. *Perushtitsa, Red Church. Angel Caryatid holding up the Lamb and Moses receiving the Law (copies). Sofia.*

The frescoes in a ruined sanctuary known as the 'Red Church' at Perushtitsa near Philippopolis in Thrace are the only ones giving an idea of the nature of the Constantinopolitan type of Byzantine painting in the century of Justinian.

On a fragment of the north wall of the nave scenes of the childhood of Christ are set forth in continuous friezes, without vertical separations, on several registers. Thus it is proved that this compositional arrangement, which was regarded, on the strength of some examples extant in Egypt and Cappadocia, as peculiar to the Christian arts of Asia, was current from the sixth century on in the Constantinopolitan area. Nor should we forget that the iconographic cycle depicting the childhood of Christ was held to be of eastern provenance. Damaged though they are, the Perushtitsa frescoes prove that the Byzantines of the pre-iconoclast period had a habit of juxtaposing scenes from both Testaments. A sequence of Old Testament scenes, in medallions, is placed below scenes from the Gospels in the vaults of the passages between the central hall and the north wing of the church. Here we have a reminiscence of the small paintings in round frames which had figured in arcosolia in the Catacombs two or three centuries earlier.

Equalling in interest the medallions with half-length angels on the soffits of the enormous arch which forms a link between two of the pendentives of the dome, are two

182

197. *Stobi, Cathedral Church. Fragment of a Head. National Museum Belgrade.* — 198. *Salonica, St Demetrios. An Emperor entering Salonica.*

angel-caryatids upholding the Mystic Lamb on one of the intermediate vaults. Forbidden in 692 by the Quinisext Council, this allegory of Christ proves that the Perushtitsa frescoes antedate the end of the seventh century. Some frescoes of the same period were uncovered when a church at Stobi on the Vardar was excavated. Unfortunately only a few isolated heads remain, not easily assimilable to any of the paintings found elsewhere, nor can we even be sure that they are of Byzantine inspiration.

In 1917 a large part of the basilica of St Demetrios at Salonica was burnt down and several frescoes which had just been brought to light in the outer side-aisles perished in the fire. The copies on view in the Byzantine museum at Athens are poor substitutes for the lost originals. They depict large historical scenes such as the triumphal entry of an emperor, and the panic-stricken populace of Salonica taking refuge in the basilica from a Slav invasion. Iconographical counterparts of the written *Miracles of St Demetrios*, these paintings belong to the hagiographic genre of decoration that came into vogue in churches dedicated to saints during the fourth century. The earliest extant examples, however, are of a much later period. Most typical are the seventh-century illustrations of the lives of the two patron saints in the chapel of Santi Quirico e Giulitta in the church of Santa Maria Antiqua at Rome.

200. *Sinai, Monastery of St Catherine. Abraham's Sacrifice, detail.*

*Icons*

To the cult of beneficent or thaumaturgic saints may be ascribed the popularity of the movable images painted on wood (more rarely on marble or metal) known as icons. They were set up in churches and bishops' palaces, in private houses, in public edifices, even in shops. There were also small icons in metal; these were worn as pendants round the neck.

The earliest surviving icons date back no earlier than the sixth or seventh century, and even these are very scarce. Two were preserved in Rome, but most were found in Egypt or on Mount Sinai. Some (notably the Sinai icons) have remained *in situ;* others found their way to museums in Kiev and Berlin in the nineteenth century.

All these paintings are executed in the encaustic technique currently used in Antiquity for mural decorations and portable pictures. The pigment was mixed into melted wax which while still warm was applied to a thin wooden panel, after which the surface was smoothed down as far as possible with a metal instrument.

Only a single example of encaustic painting applied to a wall has been discovered up to now: a scene representing Abraham's Sacrifice in the apse of the monastery church of St Catherine on Mount Sinai. It was uncovered by Professor Kurt Weitzmann in 1958 and is still *in situ.*

We find the same technique employed in some third- to fifth-century Egyptian funerary portraits. But there are no grounds for assuming that the earliest Christian icons were made in Egypt. That Egyptian portraits are more abundant than those from other Mediterranean lands (where they are known to have existed) is due to the climate of the Nile region, better suited to their preservation.

199. *Bawit. Icon of Bishop Abraham. Staatliche Museen, Berlin.*                                185

201. *Sinai, Monastery of St Catherine. St Sergius and St Bacchus. Kiev Museum.*

In the double icon of Sts Sergius and Bacchus we have a typical example of the commemorative art associated with the tombs of martyrs. The maker of this icon may well have modelled it on earlier sepulchral portraits. Those representing sainted bishops were presumably inspired by existing portraits of these prelates, and by the same token the icons of sainted monks derived from portraits of ascetics and founders of monasteries that had been made at the places where they lived.

The Mount Sinai icons and Bawit wall paintings exemplify this genre of local iconography. The icons of Christ and the Mother of God in Majesty—especially those showing them enthroned with saints around them—stem from the official portraits of emperors and dignitaries. The very fine icon of St Peter (Mount Sinai) reproduces the long, narrow shape of consular diptychs, and above the effigy of the saint are three medallions like those figuring in the diptychs above the consul's head. But here Christ replaces the emperor, the Virgin the empress, and an apostle the other consul of the year. Thus in both diptychs and icons we see above the leading personage those who conferred on him in the one case consular rank, in the other sainthood.

The fact that Christian artists practised transpositions of this order does not rule out the possibility that in some cases pagan icons were adapted to Christian themes. The iconic frescoes of Karanis, near the Fayum (now in the Kelsey Museum at Ann Arbor, Michigan), and some pagan icons in the Berlin museum, give us an idea of the nature of these prototypes.

186

202. *Sinai, Monastery of St Catherine. St Peter, detail.* 187

188       203. *Sinai, Monastery of St Catherine.  Virgin and Child with Saints and Angels, detail.*

204. *Bawit. Christ with the Abbot St Menas. Louvre, Paris.*

The historical icons depicting the Crucifixion and various Gospel scenes seem to represent a more advanced stage in the development of portable Christian paintings. Still, we cannot be sure of this, since Biblical themes often appear side by side on Christian third-century sarcophagi, and moreover some pagan icons in stone or bronze are adorned with sequences of mythological scenes, such as the Labours of Hercules, juxtaposed in the same manner.

Icons were evidently much appreciated throughout the Empire, and in all classes of society. They served as evil-averting talismans and prayers were addressed to them. Icons were used by communities, by towns and armies, and by private individuals. The Byzantine emperor Heraclius had images of the Virgin fastened to the masts of his ships.

Though they had an essentially devotional function, workmanship and aesthetic qualities being minor considerations, some of these icons have a very real beauty. Among the most impressive are the icon of St Peter, that of the Virgin enthroned among saints and angels, the two Mount Sinai icons, those of Sts Sergius and Bacchus, and the Virgin and Child icon in Santa Maria Nuova in Rome. Their styles vary but, as with the Bawit frescoes and the Fayum portraits, their stylistic qualities give no clue to their dating. Icons in the antique 'plastic' style may well have been contemporary with those treated in a schematic, strictly linear style.

189

206. *Icon with the Virgin and Child, detail. Santa Maria Nuova, Rome.* 191

◀ 205. *Icon with Gospel Scenes. Museo Sacro, Vatican City.*

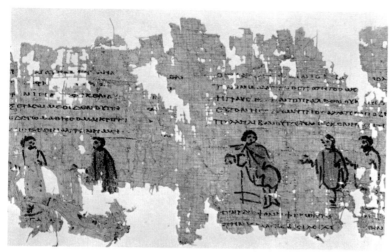

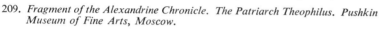

208. *Fragment of a Greek Manuscript. Bibliothèque Nationale, Paris.*

209. *Fragment of the Alexandrine Chronicle. The Patriarch Theophilus. Pushkin Museum of Fine Arts, Moscow.*

*Illuminated Manuscripts*

The original purpose of manuscript illustrations was to help to a better understanding of the text. This is why they make their first appearance in scientific works, treatises on mathematics, medicine, siegecraft, cosmography and history. We can get an idea of the nature of these early illustrated manuscripts from the papyrus rolls which the Egyptians buried with their dead and also from a fragment of a Greek papyrus now in the Bibliothèque Nationale, Paris.

From the second to the fourth century the papyrus roll *(volumen)* was gradually replaced by the book on parchment, stitched or bound *(codex)*. This new support provided the illuminator with an ideal ground for paintings large and small on every page. However, for a long while he failed to exploit this possibility and kept pictures and text distinct, on separate pages—differing thus from what was to be the practice of the illuminators of the Middle Ages.

The illustrations in books on scientific and similar subjects sometimes possess appreciable artistic qualities. For example, of the two illuminated copies of Aratus' *Astronomy* (one in the Leyden University Library, the other in the British Museum), the small pictures of personified constellations in the Leyden manuscript, which can be assigned to the mid-fourth century, have a beauty of their own.

A more or less contemporary calendar (for the year 354) which was made in Rome for a person of importance named Valentinus, is known to us now only by drawings made in the sixteenth and seventeenth centuries from a Carolingian copy of the original

207. *Ashburnham Pentateuch. The Story of Jacob and Esau. Bibliothèque Nationale, Paris.*

210. *Codex Vergilius Vaticanus. The Death of Dido. Vatican Library.*

manuscript. Most remarkable here are the series of decorative, richly ornamented archi-tectural compositions surrounding the figures (Constantius II and Gallus) and the images of personified months and towns. These frames prefigure the arcades in the Canon Tables of Gospel books.

The so-called 'Alexandrine' Greek Chronicle on papyrus (fifth century, Lenin Library, Moscow) and some pages of the Latin Chronicle of Ravenna (fifth and sixth centuries, Chapter of Merseburg Cathedral) contain small illustrations of the text, of no great artistic merit, in the margins. Far more interesting are the two Virgil manuscripts in the Vatican Library, the Vergilius Vaticanus and the Vergilius Romanus.

The Vatican Virgil (late fourth century) contains scenes of dramatic action taking place in settings of rocks, subterranean grottos, townscapes, seascapes and interiors. They seem to be the work of a highly skilful copyist. We find far more life and feeling in the full-page pictures of the second Virgil MS in the Vatican, the Codex Romanus. Agreeing with Carl Nordenfalk, I do not regard this manuscript as later than the Vergilius Vaticanus. It is less influenced by the decadent classical tradition and, while rather rustic, has an engaging spontaneity. Here the painter has deliberately avoided the technicalities that perplexed the illustrator of the Vatican Virgil : foreshortenings, renderings of space and three-dimensional form.

194

212. *Codex Vergilius Romanus. Shepherds tending their Flocks. Vatican Library.*

211. *Codex Vergilius Vaticanus. The Construction of a City. Vatican Library.*

213. *The Iliad. Battle Scenes. Biblioteca Ambrosiana, Milan.*

The *Iliad* in the Ambrosian Library of Milan, dating to about the year 500, enables us to compare a Greek work with the two Latin manuscripts of the *Aeneid* mentioned above. The *Iliad* miniatures are framed pictures deriving from a somewhat similar, but more dynamic tradition. Personally I would hesitate to ascribe them to a Constantinopolitan workshop, as Signor Bianchi-Bandinelli has recently done. These pictures are by the hands of several painters. The battle scenes teeming with figures in rapid movement come as a surprise, when we remember that, from its beginnings in the latter part of the fourth century, Byzantine art always aimed at dignity and repose, avoiding effects of hasty movement or dramatic action. Such is the style we find in the reliefs on the columns of Theodosius and Arcadius.

196

214. *Dioscorides, De Materia Medica. Portrait of Juliana Anicia. Nationalbibliothek, Vienna.*

215. *Dioscorides, De Materia Medica. Dioscorides receiving the Mandrake Root from Euresis. Nationalbibliothek, Vienna.*

On the other hand the portrait of Juliana Anicia, the lady who commissioned the illuminated copy of Dioscorides' *Materia Medica* now in Vienna was undoubtedly made at Byzantium. Placed in the centre of a circle divided by two intersecting squares defined by simulated braids, the likeness of the princess is strictly frontal and her expression serene. She is escorted by allegories and winged genii in the Alexandrine manner. Next come a series of portraits of the famous physicians cited in the text. All are in the antique style and copies no doubt of the portraits in an earlier version. The originals of some of the depictions of medicinal herbs may date back to the first issue of Dioscorides' book, in the reign of Nero.

197

216-217. *Vienna Genesis.* *Personification of the Well and Rebecca giving Eliezer Water to Drink.* *Nationalbibliothek, Vienna.*

Surprising though it may seem, the illustrated religious manuscripts of this period are even more rare than secular manuscripts. With the exception of the small group of Christian effigies in the Alexandrine Chronicle (Lenin Library, Moscow), which we have already mentioned, no religious manuscript prior to the sixth century has come down to us intact. Given their absence or fragmentary state, it is impossible to study the origins and evolution of the Christian illustrated manuscripts produced in the various parts of Christendom during the period we are here concerned with; all we have to go on are scattered vestiges of large works no longer extant.

No complete illustrated text of the Old Testament has survived. It would seem that of the books of the Old Testament it was Genesis that was most favoured by the illuminators of the period, and the Greek Genesis in the Austrian National Library at Vienna gives us an idea of their work. This is a de-luxe edition and its paintings may have derived from Jewish models.

Most of the miniatures in the Vienna Genesis directly illustrate the text under which they figure, at the bottom of the page. Sometimes we have a single rectangular picture in a landscape setting with bright or cloudy skies; sometimes (and more frequently) there are continuous sequences of small scenes set forth on one or two registers on a uniform ground of purple vellum. Both methods are in fact conventional and equally antique. To go back no further in time, we find them in the curious second- and third-century

198

218. *Vienna Genesis. Eliezer and Rebecca's Parents. Nationalbibliothek, Vienna.*

219. *Vienna Genesis, detail. The City of Nahor. Nationalbibliothek, Vienna.*

220. *Vienna Genesis, detail.  The Death of Deborah.*

221. *Vienna Genesis, detail.  The Death and Burial of Jacob.*

frescoes with mythological subjects in tombs at Hermopolis in Egypt.  There, too, as in the Vienna Genesis, there are scenes in landscape settings and also sequences of scenes set out in rows.

Despite the use of two distinct methods of presentation, the miniatures in the Vienna Genesis have, all in all, a certain aesthetic unity.  They are of special interest for the art historian since they represent a transitional phase in the history of painting.  While, in the main, keeping to the classical tradition, they contain innovations pointing the way, if at a far remove, to certain trends of medieval art.  Yet the divergences from the conceptions of the painters of antiquity—chiefly evidenced in the difficulty the artist experiences in making figures seem to move freely in the space provided—are relatively few and seldom carried far.  By and large the illustrations of the Vienna Genesis still rank among the paintings of antiquity.

200

222. *Vienna Genesis. The Episode of Potiphar's Wife. Nationalbibliothek, Vienna.*

223. *Vienna Genesis. Eliezer and Rebecca at the Well. Nationalbibliothek, Vienna.*

224. *Cottonia Genesis. The Lord with Three Angels (copy by Peiresc). Bibliothèque Nationale, Paris.*

225. *Codex Sinopensis. The Multiplication of the Loaves and Fishes, detail. Bibliothèque Nationale, Paris.*

Another Greek sixth-century Genesis, which formed part of the collection of Sir Robert Cotton but was greatly damaged by fire in 1751, contained two hundred and fifty miniatures intercalated in the text. The style of the surviving fragments (in the British Museum) is elegant and forceful, the colours are brilliant and pleasing to the eye. The Cottonian Genesis was a work of high aesthetic merit and these fragments show that the painter did more than merely illustrate the text, and interpreted it iconographically as well as literally. Thus, as M. T. d'Alverny has pointed out, in his illustrations of the Creation he took guidance from a philosophic treatise, Platonic in inspiration, by St Clement of Alexandria.

Like the Vienna Genesis, the two manuscripts to which we now turn, the pages of the Sinope and the Rossano Gospels, are in purple vellum. Purple being the imperial colour, it has been suggested (on inadequate grounds) that they were made in a scriptorium of the Great Palace of Constantinople. Other authorities assign to them an origin in Asia Minor or even further east. None of these hypotheses has any solid foundation and in my opinion their provenance remains an open question.

202

226. *Codex Sinopensis. Christ healing the Two Blind Men of Jericho. Bibliothèque Nationale, Paris.*

The art of the Sinope fragment (a portion of the Gospel of St Matthew) and of the Rossano Gospels gives an impression of being in a more realistic vein than that of the Vienna Genesis, since it departs more widely from the elegance of the antique style. It is also more concerned with enforcing a religious lesson, as we see in the representations of the prophets holding scrolls setting forth the intimate connection between the events described in the New Testament and their prefigurations in the Old. But evident as is this tendency, it does not warrant our assigning a later date to the manuscripts or assuming that they were executed in Asia Minor or Syria; regarding this point no evidence one way or another exists.

Of the Codex Sinopensis forty-three pages have survived and there are five illustrations covering the full width of the bottom of the pages, which are coloured purple. As a result of the declining influence of the antique style the presentation of the scenes and figures has a new vigour and dramatic quality. Conscious of the deep significance and poignancy of the Gospel scenes he depicts, the artist individualizes the faces and expressions of those participating in them (e.g. Herod's feast and the two blind men of Jericho).

203

227. *Codex Sinopensis. Herod's Feast with Salome receiving John the Baptist's Head.* *Bibliothèque Nationale, Paris.*

This will to inculcate religious truths by means of imagery is even more apparent in the Rossano Gospels (Museo Diocesano, Rossano, Calabria). One is even tempted to surmise that the Sinope and Rossano codices were made in the same scriptorium or anyhow the same town. But this is purely conjectural, nor is there any certainty as to their dating. Both certainly go back to the sixth century but there may have been a considerable interval of time between them.

All the illustrations of the Rossano Gospels are grouped on special pages at the beginning of the volume and each Gospel is preceded by a table and a portrait of the Evangelist. The illustrations are full-page pictures, with figures of the same height lined up on a narrow strip of ground. The dramatic action tends to take the form of processions or gatherings of participants in liturgical rites in a church or palace, and the painter has evidently given special care to creating effects of rhythm and euphony appropriate to these ceremonial occasions. Small though they are, these paintings, possibly inspired by contemporary mosaics, have an almost monumental grandeur rarely found in manuscript illustrations. This is particularly evident in the Communion of the Apostles, and in the scene of the Entry into Jerusalem figuring forth a triumphal *Adventus* of Christ the King. In the Garden of Gethsemane the figure of the kneeling Saviour seems crushed between the huge rocks of the mountainside and the massive superstructure of the picture. In the illustration of the parable of the Wise and Foolish Virgins, prominence is given to the Garden of Paradise, a beatific vision of the lot of the Virgins who at the Last Judgment have entered into their reward. But in the scene of Pilate on the judgment seat there is nothing visionary—only a starkly realistic image of a Roman tribunal. Here the

204

228. *Rossano Gospels.  Entry of Christ into Jerusalem.  Museo Diocesano, Rossano.*

205

229. *Rossano Gospels.  The Communion of the Apostles, detail.  Museo Diocesano, Rossano.*

230. *Rossano Gospels. The Last Supper. Museo Diocesano, Rossano.*

231. *Rossano Gospels. Parable of the Wise and Foolish Virgins. Museo Diocesano, Rossano.*

232. *Rossano Gospels. Pilate bidding the Jews choose between Christ and Barabbas. Museo Diocesano, Rossano.* 207

233. *Rabula Gospels. The Pentecost. Biblioteca Laurenziana, Florence.*

vertical layout may very well derive from that of some law-book, perhaps an illuminated copy of the Code of Justinian.

The text of the Rabula Gospels (Biblioteca Laurenziana, Florence) was written in the Syriac tongue and the style of the famous paintings in this manuscript is slightly less Hellenic. Both the name of the artist who made these miniatures and their date are uncertain, for the date, 586, usually assigned to the manuscript and the name Rabula apply only to the text, not to the illustrations. However there are no indications that the paintings in this book, the handsomest illuminated manuscript of the period that has come down to us, should not be dated, as is customary, to the sixth century. Here, too, we have for the first time purely decorative settings combined with a cycle of pictures on religious subjects. As in the Rossano Codex there is a clear-cut division between text and pictures, but here the latter are numbered and by reference to the Table of Contents the relevant passages in the Gospels are easily identified.

Standing between three pillars under a tapered cone, Eusebius of Caesarea and Ammonius of Alexandria present to us their work, the Canons. These are inscribed in an architectural setting of columns upholding arcades sprinkled with flowers, above which

234. *Rabula Gospels. Canon Tables. Biblioteca Laurenziana, Florence.*

235. *Rabula Gospels. Canon Tables and Marginal Decorations, detail. Biblioteca Laurenziana, Florence.*

birds are hovering. Outside the arcades, in the margins, are Old Testament figures and Gospel scenes, pictures without frames painted directly on the vellum ground. Next comes a series of large framed miniatures ranking among the finest examples of the Christian iconography of the East. Beginning with the Crucifixion and Resurrection, placed one above the other as on Palestinian ampullae, this picture sequence continues with the Ascension, the Call of Matthew and the Pentecost, and concludes with figures of the Virgin, standing, with the Child in her arms, and Christ seated between two bishops and two monks.

Whereas the marginal figures seem to be the work of a mere artisan or, at best, of an inexperienced artist, the large miniatures are, by general consent, of high artistic quality, combining as they do effects of dramatic action with highly realistic renderings of faces and movements. Differing from many authorities, I can see no reason why this style should be a purely Syrian creation. Can it be denied that in Greek and Latin paintings of this period we often find a strain of realism along with other more conventional or more abstract trends? This imitation of factual reality is not the hallmark of any specific

210

236-237. *Rabula Gospels, details. An Evangelist (?) and Christ ascending into Heaven. Biblioteca Laurenziana, Florence.*

place of origin. On the other hand it is interesting to note in the illuminations of this Syrian Gospel an unfailing fidelity to the aesthetic and technical procedures of contemporary Greek painting. This applies not only to the figural paintings but also to the remarkably effective ornamentation, which foreshadows many of the decorative schemes of the Middle Ages.

Traces, however, of a characteristically Syrian style can be detected and some of these reappear in other sixth- and seventh-century illuminated manuscripts. Thus in a sixth-century Syrian manuscript (Bibliothèque Nationale, Paris, No. 33) whose place of origin was Mardin we find the same curious practice of including Gospel scenes in the margins of the Canon Tables and immediately below them plants, animals and streams that evoke the earthly paradise. It is significant that, while the motifs here are Hellenic, this method of handling them is typically Syrian. Quite possibly during this period, which in Syria witnessed a massive infiltration of Greek culture, there continued to exist a folk art of an indigenous type still conforming to the ancient, unsophisticated art tradition. That during the last half of the fifth century and in the sixth the patronage of the

211

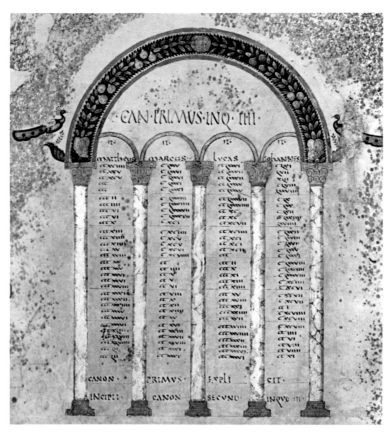

238. *Gospel Book. Eusebian Canon Tables. Vatican Library.*

Byzantine emperors reinforced the Hellenizing trend, is proved by the architecture and monumental decorations. Similarly the beautifully illuminated Syrian manuscripts, all dating to the sixth century, may well reflect the art of the Constantinopolitan de-luxe manuscripts which, sent there by the basileis (as attested in the texts), then were finding their way to Syria.

When at the end of the sixth century Syrian painting entered on a new phase in some localities, this Hellenizing trend underwent a setback. Thus in the Paris Bible 341 the head-piece of the Book of Wisdom is, iconographically, a new departure, and in it we see indigenous methods of rendering the human figure and drapery coming once again to the fore. This tendency to employ an idiom native to the region, already visible at Dura, was to recur in the illustrations of Syriac texts of the eleventh and twelfth centuries.

Illuminated Latin manuscripts of the period we are dealing with have fared even worse than the Greek and Syrian, for very few have survived. Among the religious works some Gospels copied and decorated in Italy call for mention, but their exact provenance has not been determined. Two leaves in the Vatican Library (Vat. lat. 3806) and a more complete manuscript in the British Museum (Harl. 175) provide fine examples of Gospel Canons of Concordances, but only one manuscript contains paintings of Christian themes. This is the Cambridge Gospels (Corpus Christi College MS 286) in which are two very fine miniatures simulating marble reliefs. The one depicting twelve scenes of the Passion according to St Luke has the look of a small icon. The other represents a sculptured tabernacle in which St Luke is seated, with his symbol above him, and twelve

212

PLASACRA DOTETLVCASTENET ORAIVVENCI

LEGIS
PERITUS
SURREXIT
TEDITANSILLU

EXETOLLIT
VOCEMQVAE
DAEMONLIER
DETVRBAS·

IHESVXIT
MULTOS·EOS
SALVADENT·

DEPICVL
NOA

YDROPI
CVM·SANABA
EUTVS

ZACHEUS
IN ARBORE

240-241. *Gospel Book of St Augustine, details. Scenes of the Life of Christ. Corpus Christi College Library, Cambridge.*

small scenes are inserted between the columns on each side of the evangelist. Curiously monolithic in effect, this painting seems to have been inspired by some antique votive relief of the same type as the carved tablet with a figure of Cybele in the former Saburoff Collection. There are grounds for thinking that this manuscript, which must have originally included over a hundred illustrations besides the four evangelist portraits, was brought to England soon after the close of the sixth century. That it served as a model during the Carolingian and Romanesque periods is proved by the insertion of the symbol of St Luke in the tympanum of the arch above his throne. Here, then, we have convincing proof of the fact that some illuminated manuscripts of the eighth and ninth centuries were imitations of sixth-century works.

While the pictorial methods of all the illuminated manuscripts we have been discussing vary to a greater or a less extent, there is one whose striking differences from the rest place it in a class apart. This is the Latin manuscript commonly called the Ashburnham Pentateuch, more properly the Tours Pentateuch (Paris, Bibliothèque Nationale, Nouv. acq. lat. 2334), datable to the early seventh century. As yet, there is no knowing in what scriptorium it was executed. Most authorities assign it to North Africa or Spain, but this is purely conjectural; personally I am inclined to think it may well have been made in Italy. The nineteen surviving full-page pictures illustrate the Old Testament narrative from the Creation to the departure of the Israelites from Egypt under the leadership

214

242. *Ashburnham Pentateuch. The Story of Adam. Bibliothèque Nationale, Paris.* 215

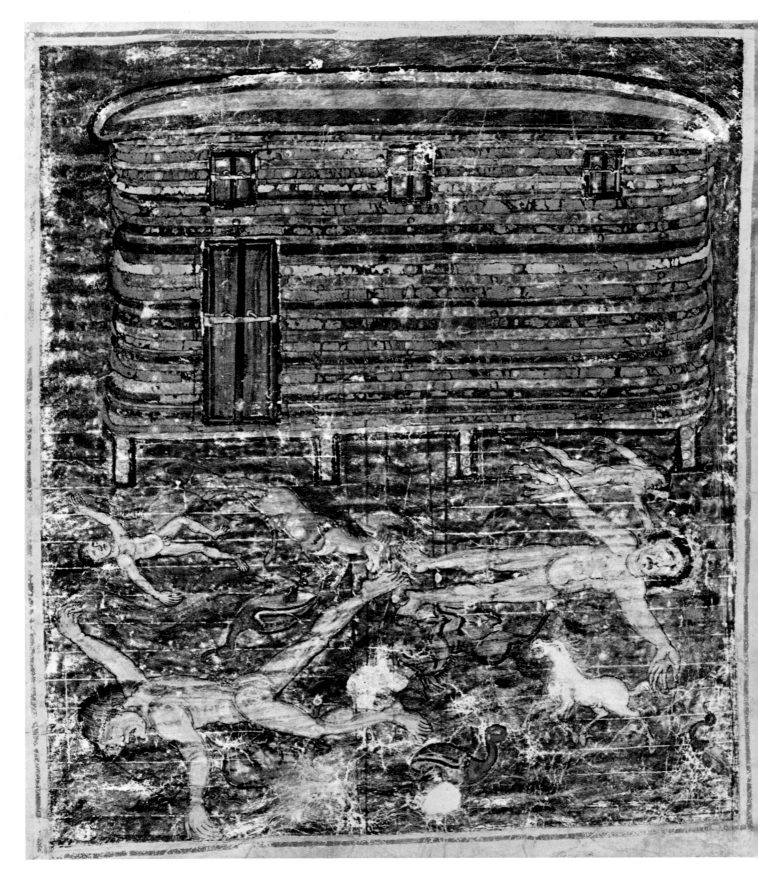

216      243. *Ashburnham Pentateuch. The Flood. Bibliothèque Nationale, Paris.*

of Moses. Most of these paintings are composite and contain a number of independent, juxtaposed scenes, often laid out in several registers on backgrounds of various colours, red, green, mauve or brown. The settings also vary; sometimes we have a landscape reaching to a considerable height, sometimes an architectural complex whose front walls are removed so as to disclose the figures within.

As regards their more archaic elements these paintings clearly derive from antique art and specifically recall the Roman mosaics and frescoes in which a sequence of more or less independent scenes is given a common panoramic background. Examples are the frescoes in one of the rooms of the Farnesina at Rome and the mosaic pavement of 'Lord Julius' in the Alaoui Museum at Carthage.

None the less the juxtaposition of the scenes and an almost total disregard of the space dimension foreshadow the aesthetic of the Middle Ages. With their gesticulating, beardless figures clad in billowing cloaks, their vividly coloured landscapes full of rugged cliffs and white buildings, these paintings, obviously inspired by Jewish versions of the Old Testament, point the way to certain Italian pictures of the ninth and following centuries, though retaining much of the climate of antique art. The large picture of the Deluge, for example, shows us corpses floating in the water which, quite in the medieval manner, occupy the greater portion of the scene. This singular anticipation of medieval art (recently pointed out by Bianchi-Bandinelli) invests the paintings in the Ashburnham Pentateuch with an exceptional historical interest. Yet these miniatures were essentially precursors, born out of their due time, and had no immediate effect on most contemporary works.

# 3. Sculpture

*Foreword*

Plastic art had been the chief loser in the aesthetic retrogression of the close of antiquity. However, in the widespread general revival of the arts that took place in the Theodosian period, sculpture played a considerable part and many great works of secular and religious sculpture were produced under the active patronage of Theodosius I, his son Arcadius (who reigned at Constantinople) and his grandson Theodosius II.

Completing the work of Constantine and, like him, desiring to create a Constantinople that would rank as a 'New Rome,' Theodosius and Arcadius gave orders for the erection of two gigantic columns, their shafts and bases covered with reliefs. The carvings on the Obelisk of Theodosius, brought from Egypt and set up on the Spina of the Hippodrome, were executed in the same technique, and when Theodosius II set up a triumphal arch and a 'Golden Gate' at the place where the victor made his state entry into the city, he had the front of the new gate decorated with mythological scenes in bas-relief.

We learn from records of the period that statues continued to be erected, as in the past, in government buildings and public squares. Some were effigies of the emperors and high officials, others of athletic champions and winners in the games in the Hippodrome. These representations of men on horseback or on foot and reliefs on commemorative stelae still entered into the repertory of votive sculpture, and the reliefs perpetuated the purest Roman tradition under its most official aspect. Thus, paradoxically enough, it was the imperial art that countenanced a pagan technique which, to the thinking of all pious Christians, was tainted with idolatry. This also explains why sculpture in the round was allowed so little place in religious art, relief rarely indulged in and, when permitted, was always on a modest scale.

We do not propose to study in detail the sculpture of the Theodosian period, marked by a steady decline in the realm of plastic art. Mention may, however, be made of the representation, on the base of the Obelisk of Theodosius, of the emperor and his son watching a chariot race from the imperial 'box.' Here the sculptor, bearing in mind the hierarchical status of the personages represented, made the emperor the largest figure, although he is furthest away from the beholder, while the people in the lowest tiers are

*244. Head of a Man. Kunsthistorisches Museum, Vienna.*

245. *Constantinople, Hippodrome. Base of the Obelisk, detail: Theodosius I with his Court.*

smaller, smallest of all being the racing-chariots. The effect of this 'inverted perspective' is that the spectator of the relief is not assumed to be located at any precise point in space and the scene is presented as if he were observing it through the eyes of the most important person figuring in it. This was the viewpoint recommended by Plotinus and his conception of space is illustrated in several other features of these same reliefs. In them space is not rendered plastically by the use of actual salience but merely suggested, as in a painting, by the steps of a staircase represented frontally and an arrangement of superimposed figures partially concealing each other.

The colossal bronze statue at Barletta, a work of the highest technical proficiency, may well have given a lead to the Latin and Byzantine figural sculptors. But perhaps the

220

246. *Constantinople, Hippodrome. Base of the Obelisk.*

248. *Figure in a Chlamys.  Corinth.* — 249. *Figure in a Toga.  Istanbul.* — 250. *Emperor in a Chlamys.  Berlin.*

relative paucity of fourth-century works that have survived does not warrant any definite conclusion as to the output of figures in the round during the fifth and sixth centuries.

Distinctive of some headless statues from Byzantine workshops are the way the toga is worn and the handling of folds.  The feeling for plastic form in space is dying out, there is a tendency to schematism in the treatment of draperies, and we find the sculptor harking back unconsciously to the fluted column-statues of ancient Greece.  Soon, too, the toga gives place to the chlamys falling in ample folds from shoulder to feet, with the horizontal pose of the forearm stressing the all-over rhythm of the composition.

One of the best surviving examples of Byzantine sculpture, the bearded head of a dignitary, is notable for the regularity of the features and the brooding melancholy of the

247. *Colossal Statue of the Emperor Valentinian I (?).  Barletta.*

253. *Head of the Empress Ariadne (?). Louvre, Paris.*

gaze. No less attractive, but more unusual, is the man's head in Vienna. It is unnaturally elongated, and the wide-open eyes under raised brows make a striking contrast with the tight-set lips with turned-down corners. The quiet resignation of the faces of these men, whose lot was cast in an iron age, gives them a look of spiritual grandeur of a quite exceptional order.

This other-worldly quality tended gradually to die out in the official portraits. Though some heads of empresses, like the one (greatly mutilated) in the Castello Sforzesco at Milan, retain an aristocratic elegance, the marble portrait of a princess in the Louvre is a mere soulless mask, heralding the medieval 'idol' of Sainte Foy at Conques.

The slightly arid Atticism of a group of marble reliefs dating to about 400 is all the more surprising since the sculptors employed by the Roman Senate during this period

254. *Aphrodisias. Dignitary in a Chlamys, detail. Archaeological Museum, Istanbul.* ▶

◀  251. *Emperor in a Chlamys. Museo Arcivescovile, Ravenna.*
252. *Aphrodisias. Dignitary in a Chlamys. Archaeological Museum, Istanbul.*

255. *Constantinople. Sarcophagus of a Child. Winged Angels holding the Monogram of Christ. Archaeological Museum, Istanbul.*

256. *Constantinople. Sarcophagus of a Child. Short Side, detail: Head of an Apostle. Archaeological Museum, Istanbul.*
257. *Constantinople. Sarcophagus of a Child. Short Side: Two Apostles. Archaeological Museum, Istanbul.*

258. *Constantinople. Fragment of a Sarcophagus. The so-called Psamatia Christ. Staatliche Museen, Berlin.*

seem to have broken with the ancient classical tradition. One of the best of these works (now in the Archaeological Museum, Istanbul) is the sarcophagus of a child found in a suburb of Constantinople not far from the Fatih mosque, on the former site of the Justinianian Church of the Holy Apostles near which a Christian cemetery once existed. On the long sides are two winged angels upholding the monogram of Christ and at each end are two apostles adoring the cross which stands between them. The heads are finely modelled and the carving is of a high order.

One of the masterworks of the period, the so-called Psamatia Christ (on a fragment of the side of a sarcophagus) has affinities with the sarcophagus carvings of Sidamara (Asia Minor) but the subjects here are Christian. Each figure is separated from the others by an arcade, but, though in high relief, it gives an effect of shallowness and the sculptor

229

260. *Constantinople. Medallion with the Bust of an Evangelist. Archaeological Museum, Istanbul.*

confines himself to hinting at the plastic values. Also, as compared with those on the child's sarcophagus at Istanbul, these figures seem to lack stability.

Some medallions in the Istanbul Museum, containing half-length figures of evangelists, prove that sculpture was not excluded from the decoration of fifth-century Byzantine churches. They also show that along with the 'suave' style then predominant in Constantinople there co-existed more robust and forceful figurations.

On the fragments (Istanbul Museum) of the base of a monumental column datable to the fifth century, which I believe to have been made in Constantinople, we see, framed in a vine-scroll pattern, some pastoral scenes, isolated figures, and—of particular interest—an eloquent representation of the Baptism of Christ. The Forerunner, a tall figure clad in a toga, towers above Jesus, whose naked, athletically moulded body is partly immersed in the waters of the Jordan. Their fluidity is indicated by parallel wavy lines scoring the course of the river. On the farther shore are two angels who have come

259. *Constantinople. Fragment of a Sarcophagus, detail: Five Apostles under a Mitre Arch. Istanbul.*

261. *Constantinople. Fragment of a Sarcophagus, detail: Christ enthroned with St Peter. Archaeological Museum, Istanbul.*

down from heaven to play the part of deacons. Their hands are cloaked in token of respect. Though this work is still in the classical spirit, its dramatic effect is largely lost owing to the sculptor's insistence on frontality, which tends to immobilize each figure and give it an unnatural rigidity.

The numerous rustic reliefs on sarcophagi exhumed at Constantinople make it clear that not only works of high artistic quality were produced in the capital. The schematism of some of these reliefs (often damaged) resulted in linear compositions of an interesting type and having much the same characteristics as the pagan tomb portraits made in the Balkans and Bithynia before the Peace of the Church.

Figure reliefs were used to adorn church furniture. Two excellent fifth-century ambos, now in the Archaeological Museum, Istanbul, were found, one in St George's,

232          262. *Constantinople. Column Drum, detail: The Baptism of Christ. Archaeological Museum, Istanbul.*

263-264. *Salonica. Ambo, details: One of the Magi and the Virgin and Child. Archaeological Museum, Istanbul.*

Salonica, the other in Tralles (western Asia Minor). Of the former justly famous ambo only two fragments of the outer hemicycle have survived. In arcades with conches, separating each figure from the others, we see the shepherds receiving tidings of the Nativity and the Kings of the East advancing towards the Virgin, who has the Child on her knees. These carvings are revealing; whereas all that lends itself to precise delineation—costumes, headdresses, jewellery—is treated with extreme precision, the sculptor no longer attempts to locate his figures in space, and falls back on the device of complementing the figures carved in relief with motifs engraved on the wall behind them (for example the trees behind the Magi). The same device had been employed a century earlier on another monument at Salonica, the arch of Galerius, and there is no question that it influenced the carvings on the St George ambo.

Many sculptors of the fifth and sixth centuries were at pains to reproduce the effects of painting. Though some plastic qualities still exist in the (extremely low) reliefs of the

234

267. *Antioch. Fragment of a Piece of Church Furniture: Joseph in Prison. Princeton University.*

◄ 266. *Antioch. Fragment of a Piece of Church Furniture: Daniel. Princeton University.*

Good Shepherd on the Tralles ambo and in the figures of Goliath and Daniel on a piece of furniture from the martyrium of Antioch-Seleucia, the technique which, at Antioch, frankly imitates marquetry-work and associates engraved designs with grounds of tinted cement, involves in practice the suppression of all truly sculptural qualities. There is no denying that these are admirable decorative works, but they remind us more of the floor mosaics in contemporary churches and do not properly belong to plastic art.

Some of the doors of Christian churches in Syria and eastern Asia Minor had carved frames, and these, from the fifth century on, were adorned with decorative motifs heralding certain themes that were to come to their full flowering in the sculptured church portals of western Europe during the Romanesque period. The most striking example

236

268. *Antioch. Fragment of a Piece of Church Furniture: Goliath.* *Princeton University.*

is in the church of Alahan Monastir, where we see, on one side of the door jambs, two archangels bestriding demons, and on the other, four busts of unidentifiable personages, possibly the four evangelists. The lintel contained a theophany (now in a mutilated state), resembling the painted Majesties in apses at, for example, Bawit. By the same token some of the iconographical themes employed on door-frames are the same as those of the apse mosaics and paintings of Cyprus, Bawit and Sinai. Instances are the angels, deriving from classical 'Victories,' placed above the doors of churches and upholding the Cross or the monogram of Christ, and a semicircle of medallions containing half-length figures of Christ and the apostles. Both these motifs reproduce themes employed in the decorations of Early Christian apses.

237

269. *Ahnas el-Medineh. Fragment of an Acanthus Frieze with a Bust of Hercules. Coptic Museum, Old Cairo.*

270. *Ahnas el-Medineh. Niche with a Pediment, detail: Nereid on a Sea Lion. Coptic Museum, Old Cairo.*

271. *Ahnas el-Medineh. Niche with a Pediment, detail: Pan pursuing a Bacchante. Coptic Museum, Old Cairo.*

In Egypt, where sculptors had a softer stone to work on, the Christian communities might have been expected to encourage a wider use of figure sculpture. However, judging by what remains, it seems to have been little if at all more frequent there than in the rest of the Levantine area.

The correspondence we noted between the iconographic themes in the apse and those on the façade later became a typical feature of Romanesque churches. Most of the relief carvings on Romanesque tympana, in France and elsewhere, repeat the themes of the apse paintings (e. g. Christ in Majesty). It is not yet known for certain whether the medieval artists reinvented this procedure or took it over from Early Christian churches.

Excavations at Ahnas el-Medineh have brought to light some typically pagan works in a style ranging from the rustic to the involuntarily grotesque. Placed in various parts of the building, usually without any regard to its architectural layout, are bacchanalian scenes, Nereids, Hercules, Leda and Venus. The general effect of these figures and their accessories—vine-shoots, acanthus leaves, shells—was richly decorative; and the well-balanced counterpoint of solids and shadows, of motifs and the gaps between them, was particularly effective.

273. *Ahnas el-Medineh. Nereid Dancing and Cupid on a Dolphin. Civico Museo di Storia ed Arte,*
*Trieste.*

272. *Ahnas el-Medineh. Fragment of a Pilaster, detail: Bearded Man with Two Figurines on his Shoulders. Coptic Museum, Old Cairo.*

274. *Sohag. Fragment of a Niche: Flying Angel with the Monogram of Christ. Coptic Museum, Old Cairo.*

242    275. *Sohag. Fragment of a Pediment, detail: Angel carrying a Cross. Coptic Museum, Old Cairo.*

276. *Ahnas el-Medineh. Niche, detail: Venus crouching in a Shell. Coptic Museum, Old Cairo.*

277. *Ahnas el-Medineh. Pilaster Capital: Two Flying Genii holding a Mask. Coptic Museum, Old Cairo.*

278. *Bawit. Lintel: Two Flying Angels holding an Image of Christ in Majesty. Coptic Museum, Old Cairo.*

279. *Egypt. Pediment, detail: Dionysos driving a Chariot. Dumbarton Oaks Collections, Washington.*

Similar works uncovered on various sites in Egypt prove that this type of art, which took its rise in the mid-fourth century and was to last until the Arab conquest (640), catered both for paganism in its decline and for the Christian religion superseding it. The emergence of Christian themes did not lead to the immediate extinction of the hybrid elements prevailing in the eastern marches of the Empire, and the two sources of inspiration constantly intermingled (e.g. the triangular pediment in the Mirrit Bouthos Ghali Collection, Cairo). Thus the winged angels upholding the mandorla with Christ in Majesty have a family likeness to their pagan counterparts, the two flying genii holding forth a mask on the pilaster capital from Ahnas el-Medineh.

Though most of the Coptic sculpture decorating churches was in wood, some fragments have survived thanks to the dryness of the climate. One of the most striking, now in the Coptic Museum of Old Cairo, is a lintel from the Church of Al-Muallaka in Cairo; it consists of a frieze of small agitated figures representing the Entry into Jerusalem and the Ascension. But the most interesting of the Coptic figure reliefs are undoubtedly the funerary stelae. In all we find much the same iconographic elements; all bear the figure

245

280. *Egypt. Funerary Stele: Orant. Coptic Museum, Old Cairo.*

of a praying woman with uplifted arms, usually flanked by two small crosses or two angels. Sometimes a touching expression is imparted to these posthumous portraits (assignable to the fifth and sixth centuries), though they are essentially symbolical rather than real likenesses.

The decline of figure sculpture in the fifth and sixth centuries was more pronounced in the Latin countries of the Mediterranean area than in the Greek and Levantine region. We have noted that the survival of secular statuary and relief in Constantinople was due to the imperial patronage of this branch of plastic art. This was not the case in the west. It is stated, however, in written records of the period that statues of emperors (some equestrian) existed and that an effigy of Theodoric figured on the façade of his palace at Ravenna.

The group of figure reliefs in stucco under the vault of the Orthodox Baptistery is unique of its kind and may well have been inspired by the imperial art of Constantinople. If so, the court of the emperors at Ravenna itself acted as intermediary. In this group we find imitations of 'tabernacles' with pediments within which are figures (prophets?)

281. *Egypt. Funerary Stele: Orant between Two Crosses. Coptic Museum, Old Cairo.*

282. *Ravenna, Orthodox Baptistery. Stucco: Prophet in a Simulated Tabernacle.*

and above them small religious scenes reproducing on a larger scale those on the corners of sarcophagi at Rome and Ravenna of the type of the Junius Bassus sarcophagus.

At Ravenna (as at Salonica, Constantinople and Tralles) the fronts of pulpits carried carved decorations which, though keeping to a distinctively indigenous idiom, have curious affinities with the imagery of the pavements in the Holy Land. Within juxtaposed or superimposed frames are praying figures of sainted patrons of the Church attended by a concourse of 'all that breathes' gathered together to listen to the message of salvation.

Of much more artistic interest are the handsome sarcophagi in Proconnesus marble which were produced in workshops at Ravenna at this time. They were inspired by Constantinopolitan models and this affiliation has all the more importance since it goes to show that in this period, otherwise marked by a general decline in sculpture, the Court deliberately encouraged the production of sculptural works of a superior order. The sides of the earliest of the Ravennate sarcophagi were hollowed out into niches containing the figure of the youthful Christ surrounded by apostles or delivering the Law to St Peter. In most works, however, the sculptor dispenses with architectural frames and presents

283. *Tralles. Ambo, detail: The Good Shepherd and his Dog. Archaeological Museum, Istanbul.*

284. *Ravenna. Ambo of Bishop Agnellus, detail.*
*Ravenna Cathedral.*

285. *Constantinople. Sarcophagus: Christ between the Four Evangelists (?), detail. Archaeological Museum, Istanbul.*

the figures on a smooth ground. Occasionally the iconographic themes are given a pastoral setting, showing the Lamb on a hill, with the four rivers of Paradise flowing below and two lambs acting as acolytes. Often palm-trees flank these scenes and the general effect (which includes clouds, sometimes in relief) reminds us of the apse decorations of Early Christian churches.

Other sarcophagi from Ravenna bear designs in low relief of birds and symbols of Christ set off by elaborately carved scrolls of stylized vine-shoots. This purely ornamental type of decoration lasted well into the seventh century, and was revived by the Aquitanian marble-workers; an example is the sarcophagus of St Drausius (died 680) in the Louvre.

250

286. *Ravenna. Sarcophagus: The Young Christ delivering the Law. San Francesco, Ravenna.* ▶

287. *Constantinople. Sarcophagus: Christ between the Four Evangelists (?). Archaeological Museum, Istanbul.*

288. *Ravenna. Sarcophagus of the Twelve Apostles: Christ delivering the Law. Sant'Apollinare in Classe, Ravenna.*

289. *Sarcophagus, detail: Figure of an Orant. Tarragona.*

290. *Ravenna. The Rinaldo Sarcophagus: Christ enthroned receiving Crowns. Ravenna Cathedral.*

291. *Ravenna. The Constantius Sarcophagus, detail: Lamb with Two Sheep. Mausoleum of Galla Placidia.*

292. *Sarcophagus of St Sidonius. Basilica of the Madeleine, Saint-Maximin-la-Sainte-Baume (Var).*

293. *Ravenna. Sarcophagus: Christ delivering the Law and giving Benediction. Museo Nazionale, Ravenna.*

294. *Sarcophagus of St Sidonius, detail: Tabitha raised from the Dead by St Peter. Basilica of the Madeleine, Saint-Maximin-la-Sainte-Baume (Var).*

295. *Sarcophagus: Christ with the Twelve Apostles. On the lid, Daniel. Church of Saint-Guilhem-le-Désert (Hérault).*

258

296. *Sarcophagus of Archbishop Theodore: Confronted Peacocks flanking the Monogram of Christ.  Sant'Apollinare in Classe, Ravenna.*
297. *Sarcophagus Lid, detail: Daniel in the Lions' Den.  Saint-Guilhem-le-Désert.*

It is rewarding to trace the gradual evolution of the funerary sculpture so abundantly produced in the workshops of south-western Gaul. To start with, there were more or less successful copies of Provençal sarcophagi; such are the sarcophagus of St Clair, bishop of Eauze (died 510), in the Musée des Augustins, Toulouse, and those in Spain deriving from Tarragona prototypes known as the 'San Pedro y San Pablo' sarcophagi. But very soon, both at Tarragona and in Aquitaine, sculptors began to lower the relief and to elongate figures so as to adapt them to the frame (sarcophagus of Saint-Guilhem-le-Désert, near Montpellier). Here we have an anticipation of the Romanesque sculptural practice of adjusting forms to the shape of the frames enclosing them.

Thanks to archæological research much new light has been thrown on the highly complex problem of the state of art at the close of Antiquity. Less weight now is given to the view that 'Oriental influence' accounted for the eclipse of plastic values, leading to an exclusive interest in linework and the suppression of the third dimension.

Of sculpture in wood some fragments have survived in Italy: the doors of Milan Cathedral and those of the basilica of Santa Sabina in Rome. Though, as a result of the ravages of time and restorations, we can get only an imperfect idea of the original aspect

298. *Sarcophagus of St Drausius, Bishop of Soissons, detail. Louvre, Paris.*

260

299. *Rome. Door of Santa Sabina, detail: The Crucifixion.*

of the Santa Sabina doors, they are of the utmost interest. Along with historical and symbolic subjects these panels represent Biblical scenes selected, it would seem, with an eye to their didactic value. The work of two or three hands can be detected in these reliefs, which have affinities both with the art of the catacombs and sarcophagi and with that of the ampullae of the Holy Land. Many Palestinian traits have been detected in the iconography of these wood carvings, which also contain marked reminiscences of classical art. The most striking panel of all contains a Crucifixion in which the naked, somewhat rigid body of Christ is treated in a thoroughly classical manner. This is also one of the earliest figurations of the Saviour in the 'crucifix' attitude (the woodwork of the Cross is not represented).

261

301. *Antioch. Frieze with Floral Reliefs.*

## Ornamental Sculpture

Our account of the statues and figure reliefs has by no means covered the entire field of plastic art in the fifth and sixth centuries. Indeed it may be said that the statues and anthropomorphic reliefs represent no more than a heritage of the last phase of classical art.

For, while figurative sculpture was gradually losing its appeal, the scope of ornamental sculpture was being steadily enlarged. In quest of new decorative effects craftsmen actively explored all the possibilities of stone- and wood-carving, of engraved or hammered metal, ringing the changes on different types of material and varieties of sheen, and exploiting contrasts of polished and unpolished surfaces and effects of light and shade. Both the quality and the quantity of works intended to beautify interiors of buildings and articles of furniture, whether secular or religious, made steady progress. And this widespread taste for lavish ornament, distinctive of the period under consideration, was one of its legacies to the Middle Ages.

The origins of the decorative sculpture of the fifth and sixth centuries can be traced back to the Parthian statues and reliefs whose influence made itself felt in all the lands of the Near East, in the Kingdom of the Nabataeans, at Palmyra and at Dura. This influence, which began in the first century of our era and lasted into the sixth and seventh centuries, directly or indirectly affected Coptic, Syrian, Armenian and Georgian sculpture. Confining ourselves to the lands which formed part of the Empire at the close of Antiquity, we shall now cite some examples of the early ornamental art prevailing in the provinces which were later to be the scene of a new type of Christian sculpture.

Ornamental work in the pre-Christian style figured around the gates and cornices of the temple of Bel at Palmyra. It consisted largely of vine and acanthus scrolls, garlands of laurel leaves, beaded strap-work, flower petals, heart-shaped festoons and egg-and-tongue mouldings. Entire scenes, single half-length figures or rows of figures are inserted in the scroll work and thanks to their flat, schematic handling and rhythmically disposed

300. *Rome. Door of Santa Sabina, detail: The Ascension of Elijah.*

302. *Antioch. Fragment of a Revetment from a Fountain. The Baltimore Museum of Art.*

accents, blend quite naturally into the overall decorative schemes. On the capitals we find a persistent use of classical motifs, but treated here in a more linear, more abstract style.

Excavations at Antioch have uncovered some remarkable fifth-century works in a similar vein: capitals with acanthus decorations and cornices with alternating geometric and floral motifs. The portals of Syrian churches, for example that of St Paul and Moses at Dar Kita (418), and the arches preceding the apse at Kalb Lauzeh (sixth century) give an idea of the ornamental sculpture figuring in fifth- and sixth-century Syrian churches. In them, along with a schematic style deriving from that of Palmyra (which in turn was a derivative of Parthian art), we find abstract geometric forms, probably stemming from the local Semitic tradition, to which were added in or about the sixth century some Byzantine motifs.

In Egypt, after the Peace of the Church, all decorative sculpture aligned itself to the 'new art.' But under the chisels of local craftsmen the formal ornaments of antiquity were treated as a mere decorative overlay, adaptable to all surfaces and covering them

303. *Bawit. Circular Relief between Two Columns. Staatliche Museen, Berlin*

like a tapestry. As a result, it lost much of its relief and proportions were no longer governed by any set scale. Originally inspired no doubt (as in Roman Syria) by the Greco-Iranian art of the Parthians, the new technique acquired in the Nile valley a Coptic accent. It was chiefly in the decorations of niches and friezes in low relief that Coptic art came to its full flowering. Here the progressive decline and geometrization of Alexandrian floral decoration had left the field open for new and striking developments. By the use of a deeply undercut ground the sculptor gave full play to light effects implemented by finely bevelled leafage.

Since the decorative motifs were apposed, exactly like pieces of embroidery, to stone or woodwork, it was natural enough that their motifs should resemble those of Coptic textiles: lion or bear hunts in settings of acanthus scrolls, and scenes of fishing from boats amid Nilotic water-plants.

One of the most elaborate specimens of this monumental decoration is that of a portal at Sohag in Egypt. Here the entablature, capitals and rhythmically disposed bands of decoration on the façade are adapted to the ornamental layout of the wall and combine to form an intricate, skilfully distributed complex of undulating or ribbed patterns.

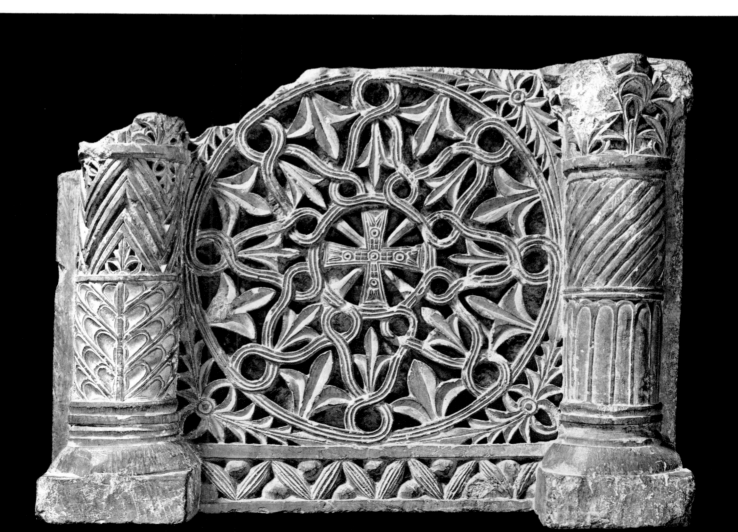

*304. Sakkara. Basket Capital with Vine Shoots and Bunches of Grapes. Coptic Museum, Old Cairo.*

Noteworthy are the new developments of the capitals, more varied here than in the other Mediterranean provinces. In them the influence of woodwork is often unmistakable, especially when they have the shape of multifoil baskets or lotus flowers. The surfaces are sometimes divided up into distinct compartments, each with motifs peculiar to itself. The carving on the columns is similarly fragmented, each segment forming an independent ornamental strip.

Less conventional than in the west, the closure slabs in chancels are similarly filled with decorations of various kinds, incised, engraved or fretted. Christian symbols and human figures rarely have a place in them and there is a taste for highly elaborate patterns anticipating the intricacies of Moslem decorative carving (with which they may easily be confused). If proof be needed we have but to compare the Bawit closure slabs with

305. *Sohag, Red Monastery (Deir el-Ahmar). Carved Frame of the South Door.*

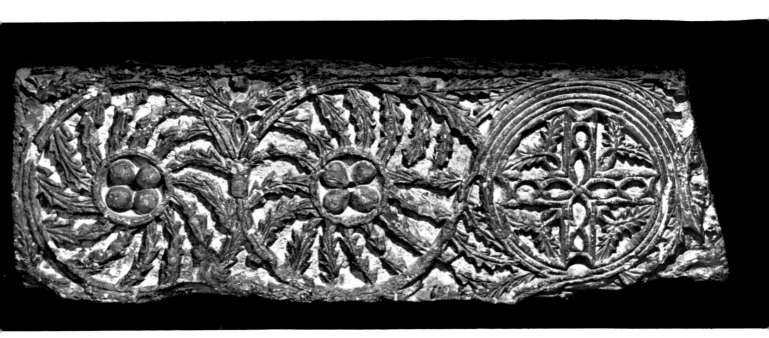

306. *Egypt. Frieze: Circles patterned with Crosses and Fruit forming Rinceaux. Coptic Museum, Old Cairo.*

307. *Alexandria. Capital shaped and patterned like a Wicker Basket. Coptic Museum, Old Cairo.*

308. *Salonica. Capital with 'Wind-blown' Acanthus Leaves.*

309. *Sakkara. Column Shaft. Coptic Museum, Old Cairo.*

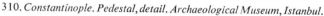

310. *Constantinople. Pedestal, detail. Archaeological Museum, Istanbul.*　　311. *Philippi, Church A. Corinthian Capital.*

the carved column-bases in the Omayyad castle of Khirbet el-Mafjar in Transjordania, wich date to the first half of the eighth century.

From the fourth to the early sixth century the characteristic motifs of classical decorative reliefs were still employed in friezes, cornices and capitals in the Greek cities of the Mediterranean coast and the Aegean basin. Such was the predilection for the Corinthian capital that it alone was in current use at the end of the fourth century. Then a new type, known as the Theodosian capital, was created. After originating in the Constantinopolitan workshops and being adopted throughout the eastern Mediterranean, it found its way to Jerusalem and even to Egypt (Monastery of St Menas). The decoration of the Theodosian capital consists of spiked acanthus leaves with serrated edges projecting from a pool of shadow, usually drilled, not chiselled out. This method of decoration stands midway between the classical Corinthian capital with its realistic sculptural orna-mentation and the wholly abstract motifs that come later.

Another type of capital, presumably of Iranian origin, also had a considerable vogue. This was the capital in two parts, the lower one basket-shaped or crowned with acanthus leaves, and the top consisting of animal protomes, sometimes accompanied by peacocks. These picturesque zoomorphic motifs had an immediate popular appeal, but they were abandoned in the Justinianian period when attempts were made to integrate the decorative sculpture more fully into the aesthetic of the building as a whole. Mention may be made in this context of the capitals with rams' heads and the corbels adorned with birds and animal forms produced at Korykos in Isauria towards the end of the fifth century. Here the influence of Constantinople is manifest, as also in the variant of the classical acanthus, known as the 'wind-blown acanthus,' which we find on capitals at Kalat Seman in Syria and other Mediterranean lands at the end of the fifth century.

269

313. *Philippi, Church B. Capital.*

The creative activity of the Byzantine craftsmen of the period can best be assessed by an examination of some characteristic examples of this decorative Constantinopolitan sculpture. On the Corinthian capitals of the first church at Philippi and on those of some pilasters now in the Archaeological Museum, Istanbul, the acanthus leaves, pointed or rounded, first cling to the stem, then project boldly forward before falling into a drooping position. Moreover, though the pronounced curves of some abaci still ensure the effect of massive solidity produced by the capital, there is also a tendency to exploit effects of light and shade to the detriment of outline and volume, the result being a sort of 'impressionist' technique with a liberal use of openwork ornament. It is in St Sophia

314. *Constantinople, St Sophia. Openwork Capital.*

at Constantinople that this type of capital can be seen at its splendid best. Particularly striking is the harmony between the decorative sculpture and the interior of the cathedral. Since they do not project beyond the surfaces of the capitals, cornices and spandrels on which they figure, the decorations do not mask the functional purpose of these elements but are subordinated to the overall architectural design. Otherwise the sculptor's fancy was given free play in these new creations, which scored a prompt success.

272

The impost capital was the most long-lasting innovation. After making its first appearance, undecorated, in 528 in the Bin Bir Derek cistern, in Constantinople, it was brought to perfection in the following decade in St Sophia. Impost capitals were used at Salonica, Parenzo, Venice and Ravenna, and as far afield as Egypt and Palestine.

It was at Constantinople, in the fifth and sixth centuries, that the various types of Byzantine capital came to their full flowering. The main centre of their production was located in the marble quarries of the Proconnesus (Marmara Island); from there, marked with inscriptions in Greek characters, they were shipped to all the Mediterranean lands. They made their way to North Africa, Spain and French Provence, but in the West the edifices in which they figured have perished; only the capitals themselves have survived.

A great number of openwork marble partitions serving as closures or supports of galleries were produced at Ravenna. Unlike those of Constantinople, where flat surfaces with plain geometric motifs (squares, lozenges, circles) carved in low relief were preferred, the Ravenna closure slabs display a remarkable medley of patterns: interlaces, rinceaux, crosses, wheels, acanthus leaves. They are akin to the closures of Bawit in Egypt and like them were inspired by floor mosaics with designs resembling those of carpets.

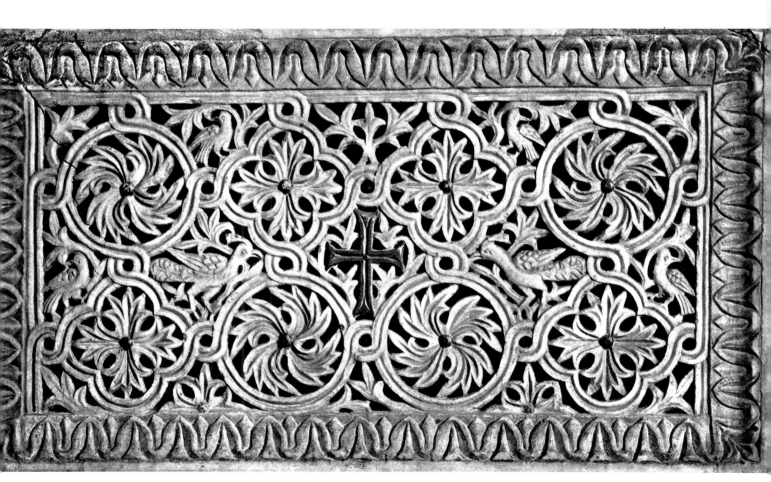

*315. Ravenna. Closure Slab. San Vitale, Ravenna.*

273

316. *Ravenna. Closure Slab. Sant'Apollinare Nuovo, Ravenna.*

317. *Ravenna. Closure Slab. Sant'Apollinare Nuovo, Ravenna.*

Stucco reliefs were in high favour at Ravenna, where in the fifth and sixth centuries they figured on the upper parts of walls, on soffits of arches and on vaults. This technique was well known in antiquity, but we have no means of determining its prevalence and distribution in the regions and in the period with which we are here concerned. It is less the surviving Byzantine works than the many ornamental stucco reliefs figuring in subsequent Islamic edifices that demonstrate the large part played by stucco on the eve of the Arab conquest and herald its widespread use both by the Omayyads of Syria and by the Lombards and Carolingians in Western Europe.

In Italy the carved decorations on Lombard openwork closures, baldachins and sarcophagi synchronize with the last phase of Ravennate art. Though of no great artistic merit, they prove that the taste for this type of decorative art did not die out in the Dark Ages. That the same is true of Gaul is proved by the Aquitanian sarcophagi. Nor should we fail to mention the kindred works produced in Northumberland in the seventh century and in Spain in the age of the Visigoth kingdoms.

It would have been rewarding to study in detail the outstanding monuments in each of these countries, emphasizing the remarkable persistence of relief work in various types of ornamental sculpture, geometric, vegetal, anthropomorphic and so forth. But such a study would take us too far afield and exceed the chronological limits of the present work.

# 4. Sumptuary Arts and Art Industries

Alongside the art industries catering for daily needs or the desire to own a replica of an original work, there existed another form of art gratifying the taste of wealthy patrons for costly artefacts. For, though a general decline of the cultural level and wide-spread impoverishment discouraged any mass production of works of art, this did not affect the de-luxe industries to the same extent. Even if relatively few in number, there still were princes and prelates capable of employing specialist craftsmen and thus ensuring the transmission of the more difficult techniques.

*Ivories*

The use of ivory as a material for de-luxe artefacts went back to a very early date; it was always much appreciated in antiquity, not only by reason of its rarity and costliness but also for the facilities it provided for delicate, minutely detailed carving, for the warmth of its natural hue and for the rich play of surface effects distinctive of highly polished ivory. Ivory was widely employed in the great age of the Roman Empire, but even more widely, so far as can be judged, in the period we are here concerned with.

This is borne out by the fact that it was only in the fifth and sixth centuries that ivory was used for certain official objects, notably the diptychs or small plaques used as covers for important documents. We have no reliable information as to the contents of the diptychs issued by the emperors. The consular diptychs contained the official notification of the Consuls' taking up their posts on January 1 of the year of issue. There is evidence of this practice for the period from 406 to 540, but it must have begun slightly earlier, for an Edict of 384 (Cod. Theodos. XV, 9, 1) enacts that the right of issuing ivory diptychs is henceforth reserved to the Consuls exclusively.

The popularity of the official, secular diptychs led to the making of similar objects having a Christian religious function on which were inscribed the names of those whose memory was hallowed in church services; indeed most of the ivories of this period served a memorial purpose. They fall into a small number of traditional categories, each com-

318. *Constantinople. Leaf of a Diptych: The Empress Ariadne, detail. Bargello, Florence.*

prising a group of secular objects and another group of similar, but Christian, objects.

Of no less interest are the ivory caskets, large and small, round or rectangular. Some are decorated with themes from classical mythology, while others, of the same shapes, bear Christian themes. The former contained jewellery, perfumes or medicines; the latter, Christian 'treasures': fragments of relics or the eucharistic Host. Lastly, we have the large episcopal chairs (or thrones), a heritage from classical antiquity. Adorned with carved ivory panels representing Christian themes, these were made for ecclesiastical use exclusively.

From the fact that the tusks of elephants which provided the ivory-workers with their raw material came from India and Africa it has often been inferred that most of the ivories must have been made in workshops at Alexandria and other Levantine cities. But, since the transport of elephant tusks presented no difficulty, there was nothing to prevent ivory-carvers from setting up their workshops in any Mediterranean city. What determined their choice was not the nearness of their headquarters to the source of their material but the size of the city in question, and in this respect the political centres of the Empire and other great cities of the Greek and Latin worlds served their purpose quite as well as Alexandria or Antioch. Moreover, whenever information as to the provenance of objects in ivory is forthcoming, it always leads us to Rome, Milan or Constantinople. This holds good especially for the imperial and consular diptychs, known to have been made in the cities where the high officials concerned resided.

Among the imperial diptychs we would draw attention to two detached leaves on each of which an empress figures. On one (Archaeological Museum, Vienna) we see her seated, on the other (Bargello Museum, Florence), standing. No names are given, but these are clearly sixth-century empresses. The same applies to the figure of a mounted emperor on a large diptych with five compartments (in the Louvre); he is usually identified either as Anastasius (491-518) or Justinian (527-565). Known as the Barberini ivory, this is one of the finest examples of this form of art. The theme of the reliefs is the triumph of an emperor over barbarians; a Scythian holds his lance, Scythians and Indians bring tribute, and a Roman general presents to him a statuette of Victory. A personification of Gaea upholds the hero's foot, thus showing that his power extends over the whole earth, and from the heights of heaven Christ is blessing his faithful vicegerent.

The consular diptychs are treated on much the same lines, but on them the consul, standing or seated in his chair of office, is often attended by personifications of the capitals, Rome and Constantinople. Sometimes we see him in the royal box at the circus, where he presided over the games held at his expense on the day of his taking office. In some cases the arena and the games themselves are also represented.

Another group of ivories may be safely assigned to Italian workshops, Milan in particular. Here, too, the themes are mostly of a non-religious order and, as with the consular diptychs, the figures represented often give a clue to their place of origin. The diptych of Stilicho, showing that soldier and great statesman with his wife and son, was almost certainly made in a Milanese workshop (c. 400). The leaves of a very fine diptych shared between the Victoria and Albert Museum and the Musée de Cluny may be safely assigned to Rome, not because of the subject (two pagan priestesses sacrificing) but because the names of two great Roman senatorial families, the Symmachi and the

319. *Constantinople (?).* *Leaf of the Diptych known as the Barberini Ivory. Louvre, Paris.*

320. *Constantinople. Leaf of the Areobindus Diptych.*
*Schweizerisches Landesmuseum, Zurich.*

321. *Constantinople. Leaf of a Diptych : The*
*Archangel Michael. British Museum, London.*

322. *Constantinople. The Barberini Ivory, detail: Triumph of an Emperor. Louvre, Paris.*

323. *Gaul (?). Leaf of a Diptych:*
*Muses and Poets. Louvre, Paris.*

324. *Apollo and Daphne. Museo Nazionale, Ravenna.*

Nicomachi, are inscribed above the figures. The inscription on a leaf of another diptych with a circus scene (Brescia Museum) contains references to another senatorial family, the Lampadii. The purely classical style and clear-cut execution of all the works of this group are accounted for by the fact that these great Roman families were resolutely anti-Christian and pro-pagan.

We also find this same cold and elegant neo-classicism in the carvings on two small plaques and a round box whose stylistic affinities suggest that they were made in the same town, probably one in northern Italy (Milan?). Here, however, the subjects are Christian: the Holy Women at the Tomb on the small plaques (Munich and Milan) and, on the box, the Sacrifice of Abraham and Christ Preaching. Each of these works, which date to about 400, is a small masterpiece in its own way, and all may be assigned to the same group, in virtue of their deliberate imitation of classical models and their feeling for plastic values.

282    325. *Constantinople. The Areobindus Diptych, detail: Games in the Circus. Schweizerisches Landesmuseum, Zurich.*

326. *Constantinople. Leaf of the Diptych of the Consul Magnus. Paris.*

327-328. *Rome. Apotheosis of an Emperor and the Emperor borne by the Winds. British Museum, London.*

329. *Rome. Diptych of the Consul Probus Anicius. Cathedral Treasure, Aosta.*

285

330. *Constantinople. Diptych of the Consul Anastasius, detail: Amazons and Tragic Actors. Bibliothèque Nationale, Paris.*

All these reliefs have points in common with the Christian sarcophagi of northern Italy. The same workshops also produced ivory caskets. None of them, so far as we know, was still pagan and wholly secular; nor do any belong to the intermediary type exemplified, as regards the Roman workshops of about the year 400, by the Pola casket. These ivory caskets were adorned, not with scenes culled from Christian iconography, but with representations of churches and of worshippers at their devotions, intermingled with apostle figures. Here we have a Christian adaptation of the themes much used on pagan caskets, such as the silver casket of Projecta (British Museum) on which this young married woman had herself portrayed with her husband and her servants in front of the thermae of her home.

Only one casket with purely Christian themes made in a north Italian workshop has come down to us (Brescia Museum) and it is of exceptionally high quality. Being made to contain relics, it is known as a 'leipsanotheca.' The sides and lid of this rectangular casket are covered with reliefs, whose layout resembles that of the sarcophagus reliefs. But here, as well as a main frieze and another, narrower one above it, there are two others.

286

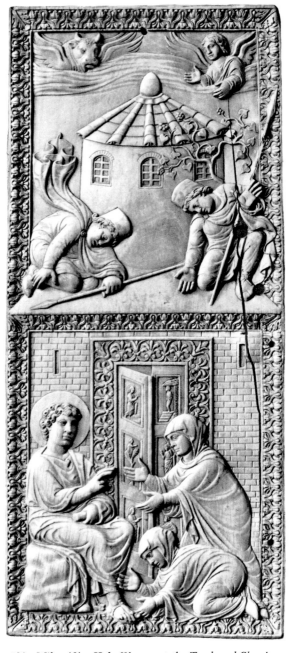

331. *Milan (?). Holy Women at the Tomb and Sleeping Soldiers. Castello Sforzesco, Milan.*

332. *Milan (?). Leaf of the Ascension Diptych. Bayerisches Nationalmuseum, Munich.*

Running along the bottom of the sides there is another narrow frieze and on top, along the edge of the flat lid, are rows of medallions containing busts of Christ and the apostles. Moreover, at each end of the sides there is a Christian symbol enclosed in a long narrow plaque of the same width as the feet of the casket.

Bold in his iconography, the Brescia craftsman is less so in his style; it is sedate, dignified, only moderately dramatic. He prefers arrested movement, languid gestures, to the effects of feverish haste favoured by so many ivory-workers of the period. The draperies are classical, elegantly designed, but unobtrusive, and there are few variations in the height of the relief. Though space is indicated, and the wooded landscape and articles of furni-

287

ture are clearly presented, nothing stands out particularly. In short we have here a perfect example of *classical* Christian art.

No less admirably executed, if less elegant, are two ivory book-covers in the Archaeological Museum, Milan. Each cover consists of several plaquettes grouped like those of the diptychs with five compartments. But, instead of the customary 'portrait' of Christ (or the Virgin), we here see the Lamb in glory, a cross beneath a square canopy, and the four rivers of Paradise gushing forth below. In the corners are figures of the evangelists with their symbols (showing that these covers originally contained a Gospel book), and all four sides have borders representing scenes of the Passion and the miracles. Both the iconography and, above all, the style of these small scenes have much in common with the works then being produced in the West and they are quite unlike the ivories we have the best grounds for assigning to the East. These fifth-century book-covers must have been in northern Italy when, a century later, the panel of the Lamb inset with polychrome gems was affixed to one cover and the cross, its pendant, to the other.

It is impossible to say whether Ravenna was a centre of ivory carving after its rise to political importance. True, in the massive ivory throne bearing the monogram of Maximian, Archbishop of Ravenna (545-553), we have the finest and largest example of Early Christian ivories, but it is commonly thought that this famous throne was not made at Ravenna. Is this view justified? This will probably remain an open question, given the lack of ivories demonstrably made at Ravenna and of any conclusive evidence as to the place of origin of other ivories of a similar type. There is no denying the affinities between the magnificent ornamental frames figuring on the throne and certain Coptic and Syrian works, such as the early eighth-century stuccoes at Khirbet el-Mafjar. But, on the other hand, the style and execution of the scenes and figures assimilates them to the Greco-Oriental ivories of the sixth century which can probably be assigned either to Syria or to Constantinople. A workshop at Ravenna may well have utilized Near Eastern models and employed Oriental craftsmen. Personally I incline to this last solution (endorsed by Stalfauth and G. de Jerphanion) in preference to the view that the commission for the throne was given to a Levantine workshop, and as for the ivories affiliated to it, I believe that most of them were made at Constantinople.

The Throne of Maximian has the form of a large high-backed chair with a semicircular seat and arm-rests. It is entirely covered, inside and out, with carved ivory plaques. Richly ornamented frames enclose rectangular panels, each representing a different scene. As on the Brescia leipsanotheca we find, side by side, scenes from both Testaments and effigies of God's annunciators, prophets and evangelists (corresponding to the apostles on the leipsanotheca). On both sides of the back are scenes of Our Lord's childhood and his miracles grouped round a medallion containing the figure of Christ the King, while, lower down, on the arm-rests are scenes from the tale of Joseph whose life foreshadowed that of Jesus. Still lower, on the front of the throne, are five niches containing standing figures of the four apostles and between them, carried by John the Baptist, the Paschal Lamb, symbol of the Redemption, who is also figured forth above, first by his Old Testament 'shadow,' then by the 'reality' of the Incarnation. Meyer Schapiro sees here a visual evocation of a passage in one of the Archbishop's sermons and this may well be so, though it is clear that details of the iconography of the evangelist figures

333. *Cover of a Binding: Scenes from the Life of Christ. Cathedral Treasure, Milan.*

334. *Ivory Throne of Bishop Maximian. Museo Arcivescovile, Ravenna.*

correspond to type forms created in the East, where apocryphal elements were freely introduced. On the other hand, the guardsmen with their curious headgear, their beards, their trousers and vaguely 'Scythian' aspect point to Constantinopolitan influences. Procopius tells us that during Justinian's reign there was a vogue for a type of garment worn by the 'Scythians,' meaning the nomad horsemen of the steppes who had settled temporarily on the north coast of the Black Sea. Actually 'Scythians' of this kind cannot have had any direct contacts with Ravenna, Egypt or Syria and the appearance

335. *Throne of Bishop Maximian, detail: Two Evangelists. Ravenna.*

336. *Throne of Bishop Maximian, detail: Joseph ordering his Brothers' Sacks to be filled with Corn. Ravenna.*

of such figures on the Throne of Maximian is all the more likely to have been due to Constantinopolitan influence, since very similar 'barbarians' are represented on the Barberini ivory panel, which was made at Constantinople.

To a very similar type of art belong the two diptychs in five compartments with religious themes which, made in the style of the imperial diptychs (here adapted to an ecclesiastical function), were most probably executed in the capital. We have an indirect confirmation of the Constantinopolitan origin of this group of ivories in the fact that one of these two diptychs with religious themes is preserved at Etchmiadzin, seat of the primate of the Armenian church, and the other, now in the Bibliothèque Nationale, Paris, was originally owned by the Abbey of Saint-Lupicin (Jura, France). Given its

337.  *Throne of Bishop Maximian, detail: The Meeting of Joseph and Jacob at Goshen.  Ravenna.*

position midway between these two extremes, Armenia and Gaul, Constantinople may very well have supplied churches in France and in Armenia with both of these very similar ivory carvings.

In most of these works, beginning with the throne of Maximian, we find (though not invariably) certain common features: low relief, smoothly polished surfaces, a tendency to cover all the space available, elongated figures with round heads and supple draperies fanning out around rapidly moving figures.  Outlines are firmly indicated by a fine, clear-cut line and we find the same precise linearism in renderings of wing-feathers, furniture, miscellaneous objects and the patterns on textiles.  This graphic technique (also used in the silverware) adds a pictorial touch to these plastic works.  But for the

339. *Constantinople. The Saint-Lupicin Diptych, detail: Christ enthroned between St Peter and St Paul.*

most part the makers of this group of ivories do not show so strong a penchant for classical elegance in their handling of draperies.

Many boxes of various shapes and sizes, notably the round pyxides of the sixth century, were produced in Constantinople and provincial workshops in contact with the capital. Their style varies greatly and when the scenes on them relate to local cults, like that of St Menas in Egypt, we may assume that they were made in Egyptian or Syrian workshops.

However, no systematic classification, by provinces, has yet been attempted, and few of the theories so far advanced as to the respective places of origin of the various pieces have, strictly speaking, any scientific basis.

The fact remains that family relationships are plainly seen between these ivory pyxides of the sixth century. But this need not mean that the pyxides in question were made in the same studio. The style and handling of some of them reappear in the ivory reliefs on medicine chests and in the designs on liturgical combs.

338. *Constantinople. The Saint-Lupicin Diptych. Cabinet des Médailles, Bibliothèque Nationale, Paris.*

340. *The Baptism of Christ. Musée des Beaux-Arts, Lyons.*

341. *Constantinople. The Saint-Lupicin Diptych, detail: Christ healing a Blind Man. Bibliothèque Nationale, Paris.*

342. *Pyxis, detail: Martyrdom of St Menas. British Museum, London.*

297

The life-size bronze statue was already going out of fashion at the close of Antiquity and need not concern us here. And though a fair number of bronze statuettes were still being produced at the beginning of our period, they too soon died out. This tendency was, however, counterbalanced by an extensive production of small works in precious metals, embellished with decorations in relief or engraved, many of them of remarkable elegance and beauty. We might almost say that, in the fourth, fifth and sixth centuries, what had hitherto been a craft practised by artisans was elevated to the status of a fine art.

Silverware of this period covers a curiously small range of objects, falling into well-defined categories. This narrowing down of the repertory—even more pronounced than with the ivories—suggests, yet again, a period of decadence. First, we have a group of ornamented plates and *missoria*, many of which stem from imperial art. Next there are the caskets, some of which bear secular decorations. The finest of these, a wedding present to a young woman named Projecta (now in the British Museum), was discovered in 1793 in Rome, on the Esquiline Hill. That Projecta and her husband, Secundus, were Christians is proved by the sacred monogram on the lid of the casket, followed by an inscription: *Secunde et Projecta vivatis in Chri(sto)*.

Like the ivory caskets, the non-Christian silver boxes had counterparts in the reliquary boxes of the period. Also, a few vessels—amphorae, chalices, cups and bowls—have come down to us, some made for religious, some for domestic use. Neither the forms of these objects nor the themes of their decorations underwent any substantial changes, and dating them would be almost impossible was it not that some of the finest pieces bear punched control stamps with the name of an emperor, or in some cases that of a city. From these we learn that a number of vessels, disks and dishes adorned with mythological scenes and executed in a very ancient technique were produced in Justinian's time and even under Heraclius (610-641)—which goes to show that there were no important developments in the decorative art of the gold- and silver-smiths between the fourth and the seventh century.

It would, however, be wrong to draw the conclusion that the art of metal work was completely stagnant in this period; on the contrary, we often find reflections of the changes in technique and taste that affected sumptuary arts at the close of Antiquity. For our present purpose these artefacts can conveniently be divided into two groups. First, then, we have the silverware adorned with finely rendered classical subjects: Nereids, Venus and Adonis, Silenus, Meleager's hunt, and Dionysiac scenes. Though by and large the handling is traditionalist, based on classical models, there are traces of a new sophistication, for example in the pointillist dappling of the body of Venus on the silver plate from Constantinople. Modelling was thus enhanced by pictorial effects, and plastic values were overridden by lightly incised, purely graphic motifs.

In the second group we find the same manner of treating bodies, but here applied more vigorously, and much sooner, than in the first. Of the two earliest examples, both in the imperial style, the oldest is the silver dish (datable to about 350) with a triumphal effigy of Constantius II on horseback. Again there is little emphasis on volumes, but

343. *Constantinople (?). Silver Plate with Silenus and a Maenad. Hermitage, Leningrad.*

344. *Rome.  Bridal Casket of Secundus and Projecta.  British Museum, London.*

300         345. *Rome.  Bridal Casket of Secundus and Projecta, detail: Bride and Bridegroom.*

346. *Silver Plate with Venus and Adonis.  Bibliothèque Nationale, Paris.*

348. *Constantinople (?). Missorium of Theodosius I, detail: The Emperor Theodosius. Academia de la Historia, Madrid.*

much attention is given to outlines, brought out by other incised lines which, filled in with niello, vary the hue of the silver ground. The niello technique, tentative here, was used more skilfully and lavishly in another, larger dish of the same kind, the famous *missorium* in the Academia de la Historia, Madrid, which represents the investiture of a high dignitary by Theodosius I, in the presence of his two sons. The silversmith has employed the repoussé technique only very sparingly for rendering the volumes of heads and arms; it is in his treatment of entire surfaces and his skilful use of engraved lines and black patches of niello that he excels. That without the least recourse to colour he can produce the illusion of a painted picture is due to the suggestive quality of his linework, which creates an effect of space around the three seated, frontally posed royal figures.

A hoard of lightly gilt silver dishes found in Cyprus is shared between the Nicosia Museum, the British Museum, the Pierpont Morgan Library and the Metropolitan Museum, New York. The reliefs on these dishes illustrate various episodes in the life of David, treated in much the same manner as the monarchical themes, with views of palaces and State ceremonies. But there are also landscapes and figures, these latter modelled quite in the classical manner; in other words this art is no less antiquizing

347. *Constantinople. Silver Plate with Equestrian Portrait of Constantius II. Hermitage, Leningrad.*

349. *Constantinople (?). Missorium of Theodosius I, detail.*

350. *Constantinople (?). Missorium of Theodosius I, detail: Abundance.*

351. *Constantinople (?). Missorium of Theodosius I. Academia de la Historia, Madrid.*

352. *Constantinople. Silver Plate with the Marriage of David, detail. Museum of Antiquities, Nicosia.*

than that of the vessels with mythological scenes, and as 'imperial' as the scenes on dishes bearing effigies of the emperors.

Only one of the distinctively Christian objects displays any marked technical proficiency: a reliquary box forming a cube, each of its sides adorned with scenes of the Last Judgment or of Veneration (Daniel, the Magi and the shepherds). The attitudes are convincing, gestures meaningful, forms vigorously modelled. This reliquary was probably made at Milan, where it still is.

Several other silver reliquaries of the period are extant; they are adorned, in the repoussé technique, with images from the cycle then in favour: Christ crowned and crowning, the Four Rivers of Paradise, the Cross (at whose foot the rivers take their rise), candlesticks, saints, sheep of the Early Christian type. Some are of African origin, others must have been made in Italy. The large silver cross presented by the emperor Justin II to the City of Rome was probably brought from Constantinople.

306          353. *Constantinople. Silver Plate: David receiving Samuel's Messenger. Museum of Antiquities, Nicosia.*

354. *Constantinople. Silver Plate: David killing a Bear. Museum of Antiquities, Nicosia.*

355. *Constantinople. Silver Plate with the Marriage of David. Museum of Antiquities, Nicosia.*

356. *Reliquary with Busts of Saints in Medallions. Museo Sacro, Vatican City.*

357. *North Africa. Lid of the Reliquary called Capsella Africana: Christ Crowned. Museo Sacro, Vatican City.*

310    358. *Lid of a Reliquary with the Virgin Enthroned. Cathedral Treasure, Grado.*

359. *Silver Cross of Justin II. Treasure of St Peter's, Vatican City.* ▶

361. *Milan. Reliquary with Old and New Testament Scenes. San Nazzaro, Milan.*

Many pieces of church plate in silver have been discovered in Syria. Best known is the famous chalice from the Kouchakji Collection now in the Metropolitan Museum, New York. When it came to the notice of archaeologists some thirty years ago, the suggestion was put forward that this chalice was the one used by Our Lord at the Last Supper, the Holy Graal. Others, however, declared that it was a modern counterfeit. Today there is no doubt of its authenticity, but it is generally agreed that the workmanship is of an inferior order. It is believed to have been discovered in North Syria.

In nearby Palestine, there was an active production of small silver flasks used to contain holy oil. The best known of them come from Jerusalem and are adorned with small reliefs in repoussé, representing the Holy Sepulchre and Gospel scenes. Several of these ampullae are now preserved at Monza and Bobbio.

360. *Syria (?). The Antioch Chalice. The Metropolitan Museum of Art, New York. The Cloisters.*

362. Syria (?). The Riha Paten : Communion of the Apostles. Dumbarton Oaks Collections.

314    363-364. Palestine. Pilgrims' Flasks (Ampullae): Ascension and Resurrection. Cathedral Treasure, Monza.

365. Syria. The Stuma Paten: Communion of the Apostles. Archaeological Museum, Istambul.

366-367. *Syria. The Homs Vase. Louvre, Paris.*

Among the other finds made in Syria are chalices, candlesticks, spoons, reliquaries and similar objects, some bearing figures in repoussé. Notable is the large and handsome ecclesiastical vessel (Louvre) known as the Homs Vase, around which are reliefs in an agitated, somewhat impressionistic style of Christ and the Apostles. Also found in Syria —at Stuma and Riha—were the two silver patens with scenes of a Communion of the Apostles, now in the Istanbul Museum and Dumbarton Oaks, Washington, respectively. These are provincial works and the figures have no pretensions to classical beauty; nevertheless the lifelikeness of gestures and expressions is remarkable. On the strength of works of this type some have spoken of 'descriptive realism' as a trait of Syrian art—but the reliefs on the Homs Vase hardly bear this out and were evidently conceived in a very different spirit.

Of the jewellery of the period little is known so far, and a systematic study of it has only just begun. Hence I will confine myself to some account of two classes of works of personal adornment: bracelets and neckpieces.

Many of the bracelets are broad and massive but there are also lighter ones made of a round band of filigree work bearing plant and floral motifs with large, delicately carved leaves. Small medallions with figures in repoussé (the Virgin or wedding groups) are sometimes attached to these bracelets and occasionally the medallions are replaced by gold coins.

We find more variety in the designs of necklets, which often consist of a row of medallions soldered on a concave strip of metal or linked together by clasps fixed to

368. *Gold Medallion of Licinia Eudoxia. Bibliothèque Nationale, Paris.*

369-370. *Constantinople. Gold Medallion: Virgin and Child, Nativity, Adoration of the Magi, and Baptism of Christ. Dumbarton Oaks Collections.*

371. *Gold Bracelet with Floral Designs. Staatliche Museen, Berlin.*

372. *Gold Bracelet with an Orant. British Museum, London.*

318

373. *Gold Bracelet with Plant Motifs. The Metropolitan Museum of Art, New York.*

374. *Gold Cross with Christ and Four Medallions.*
*Dumbarton Oaks Collections, Washington.*

375. *Necklet with the Annunciation on a Medallion. Staatliche Museen, Berlin.*

their frames. On others we find isolated medallions or crosses to which are appended wolf-tooth amulets, tiny amphorae or sirens, or coloured stones in metal settings hung on slender chains. Sometimes however (as with the bracelets we have just mentioned) the decoration consists of large leaves carved in high relief. Repoussé reliefs illustrating Christian subjects also appear on these pendants: on the crosses, the figure of the cruci-fied Christ surrounded by busts of Apostles; on the medallions, scenes of Christ's miracles, images of angels and personifications of virtues.

The general effect of this work is sumptuous, pleasing to the eye, and as a rule there is little use of the garish colours so often found in medieval and barbarian jewellery. But this impression may be due to the fact that so little has survived of the silverwork of the last centuries of Antiquity. In the case of most of the trinkets of the period we find gems and cloisonné enamel plaques affixed to gold, not silver, objects. The diadems and crowns of emperors and empresses were, naturally enough, in gold and, richly spangled with cabochons and rows of beads, gave the effect of a veritable blaze of colour.

We get an idea of this sumptuous polychromy from the cover of the Gospel of the Lombard Queen Theodelinda (in the Monza Treasure) with its wealth of multicoloured gems, beads and gold. The same applies to the ecclesiastical vessels represented in contem-

319

376. *Glass Pail with Dionysian Scenes. Treasure of St Mark's, Venice.*

porary imagery and also (but exceptionally) to the articles of furniture in palaces and the larger churches, which were made of gold and decorated on similar lines. The description given by Paulus Silentiarius, court poet of Justinian, of the church of St Sophia at Constantinople has much to say of goldsmiths' work of this kind, but there it was on an exceptionally large scale.

Very few glass vessels of Late Antiquity with figure decorations or other motifs have come down to us. In the treasury of St Mark's at Venice there are two interesting pieces of glassware: small pails in lightly tinted glass, adorned with darker figure motifs: hunting and Dionysian scenes. A bowl at Cologne bears moulded busts of two men, probably Constantine's sons. On some vessels we find monochrome images produced by cutting grooves in the glass walls, and here the themes are Christian. An example of this technique is the eucharistic chalice of Palestinian origin in the Dumbarton Oaks Collection in Washington, bearing an image of the Holy Sepulchre. Another chalice with figures of St Peter and St John, in the guise of fishermen, has been recently discovered in Tunisia.

377. *Glass Pail with Dionysian Scenes, detail: a Maenad. Treasure of St Mark's, Venice.*

378. *Glass Pail with Hunting Scenes. Treasure of St Mark's, Venice.*

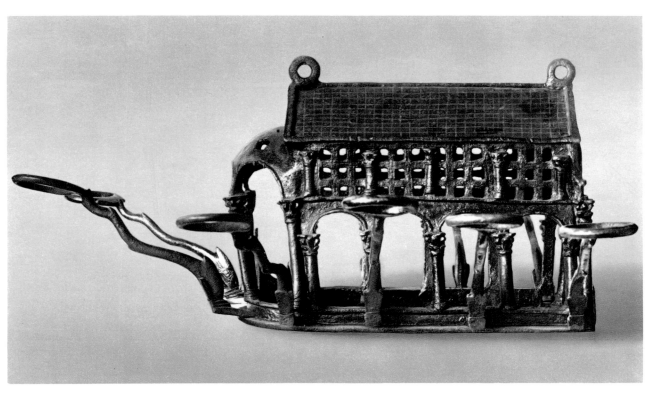

379. *Tunisia. Bronze Lamp in the form of a Church. Hermitage, Leningrad.*

## Figured Textiles

In the early centuries of the Christian era there was a widespread vogue for costly, brightly coloured materials throughout the Roman world. These were used both for garments and for interior decoration. Asterius, Bishop of Amasia (fifth century), tells us that after the Peace of the Church Christians did not deny themselves 'the curious pleasure' of wearing clothes adorned with Gospel images. Though discouraged by the clergy, a practice developed in all the Christian lands of embroidering or weaving religious scenes on ecclesiastical vestments, many examples of which have come down to us.

Except for some fragments dating to the first three centuries of the Christian era brought to light by excavations in the Near East—mainly at Palmyra and Dura Europos—all the surviving figured textiles come from Egypt and date to the third, fourth, fifth, sixth and seventh centuries. (There were, of course, later ones, but they lie outside the scope of the present volume.)

We have no means of determining the sources of the second- and third-century silks and woollens found at Dura and Palmyra, but it has been suggested, on good grounds, that they were made in Syria. This must, however, be regarded as a special case. Though attempts have been made to localize outside Egypt the places of origin of the textiles which have been preserved by the dry soil of the Nile Valley, their provenance remains conjectural. This being so, it is equally impossible to maintain either that none of the

*380. Egypt. Personification of the Earth. Hermitage, Leningrad.*

decorated stuffs in current use in the Roman Empire were imported from Egypt, or that all the de-luxe fabrics unearthed in Egyptian soil were necessarily of local manufacture.

A fragment of a textile bearing the name *Heraclea* on a medallion has recently been found and a woven inscription enables us to assign it to a gynaeceum situated on the shore of the Sea of Marmara, not far from Constantinople, where work of this kind was executed for the Great Palace of the Emperor in the new capital. This find raises our hopes that it may be followed up by others and that we may soon be able to trace the evolution of this branch of art during the last centuries of Antiquity and the first of the Byzantine era. As things stand, however, no reliable chronology of the extant fabrics can be established, and we must confine ourselves to a general survey of some of the figured stuffs that have come down to us, without specifying their places of manufacture, their dates and the scale on which they were produced in the various regions of the Empire.

The aesthetic qualities of the textiles depended on several factors, many of a technical order. The materials employed were silk, wool and linen. The weaving technique, which varied from place to place, falls into three categories: weaving proper *(Weberei)*, tapestry *(Wirkerei)* and embroidery *(Stickerei)*, each producing a distinctive surface effect. The ornaments sometimes formed dense, clearly outlined masses, round, oval, star-shaped or rectangular, telling out on a pale, uniform ground. Sometimes they consisted of free-flowing arabesques, with each element fanning out across the monochrome surface. And lastly, we find compositions framed in a single all-inclusive contour (the 'compact image'), but dividing up the field between several self-contained, independent motifs. The makers of these compositions (affiliated to the technique of appliqué work) aimed at covering the entire surface of the stuff with ornamentation up to the very edges. This last method, of ornamented *pièces rapportées*, in wool or silk, was frequently employed on stuffs of this period: they were made to be sewn on to linen garments.

The pigments used seem to have come from several different places. But the place where the stuff was woven and the one where the colouring was done were not necessarily identical with the one where the dye was manufactured. The colours varied according to the technique employed and also from one period to another, though sometimes remaining unchanged over a considerable time. Thus for several centuries we find a predilection for sober, usually dark colour-schemes, limited to one or more shades of the same hue, two shades of brown for example. These subdued, almost monochrome schemes were among the earliest employed. They were definitively supplanted by a range of stronger, livelier colours only in the period immediately preceding the rise of Islam and the Arab Conquest.

In both classes of textiles, those with decorations forming compact, coherent designs and those in which the field is divided up between independent, juxtaposed units, we find a frequent use of the 'inhabited' vine scroll and of scenes of hunting various kinds of game on foot or on horseback, directly deriving from the decorative art of the last centuries of paganism. Nothing survives of the religious significance of these motifs, or, when any trace exists, it assumes the form of some vague superstition. The scenes of putti and men fishing from boats, or standing in clumps of Nilotic plants, are more specifically Egyptian, but here, too, we question if the weaver had in mind anything more than the decorative value of these motifs. They may, indeed, have originated far from Egypt, more especially in Rome, where they had the exotic, adventitious glamour of a species of *chinoiserie*.

324

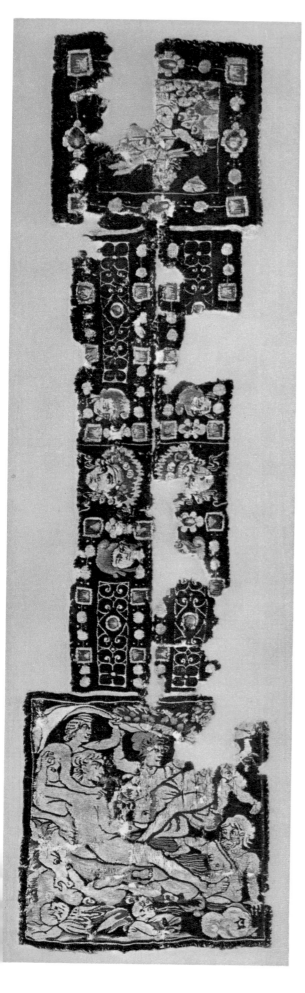

382. *Egypt. Chosroes I watching a Battle. Musée Historique des Tissus, Lyons.*

381. *Egypt. Fragment of a Tunic. The Museum of Fine Arts, Boston.*

325

383. *Egypt. Two Naiads. Dumbarton Oaks Collections, Washington.*

Equally popular are triumphal themes in black on white: winged genii carrying the portrait of an anonymous victor or holding forth a wreath, horsemen riding down the foe, offering-bearers. The Bacchic themes resemble those of the coloured textiles described above: 'inhabited' vine scrolls, hunting scenes, processions. Sometimes we have *disjecta membra* of what had been originally complete scenes: usually isolated figures of winged genii or personifications of the elements. Thus on the magnificent Dumbarton Oaks textile we see a young woman personifying 'Hestia' (the hearth) and a group of genii presenting her with inscribed votive disks. Also at Dumbarton Oaks is a superb woollen stuff adorned with two naiads, one gazing at her reflection in a shell. Here the modelling of the faces, woven in threads of many colours, is particularly effective.

The art of these textiles, which flourished, it seems, more at the beginning than at the end of the period we are dealing with, falls into the class of the 'arts of reproduction' so prevalent in Late Antiquity. They obviously conform to the Greco-Hellenistic tradition and contain no reminiscences of Pharaonic art.

The designs on some sixth-century stuffs from Antinoe form a class apart, being clearly of Iranian inspiration. They contain such familiar Sassanian motifs as masks, kings enthroned and battle scenes. We cannot as yet be sure whether they were imported from Persia or made, after Iranian models, in some factory located within the Empire.

Pertaining to another type of art and quite different in appearance are two handsome fragments of tunics in the Boston Museum of Fine Arts. They have representations in

326

384. *Egypt. Naiad looking at her Reflection in a Shell, detail. Dumbarton Oaks Collections, Washington.*

327

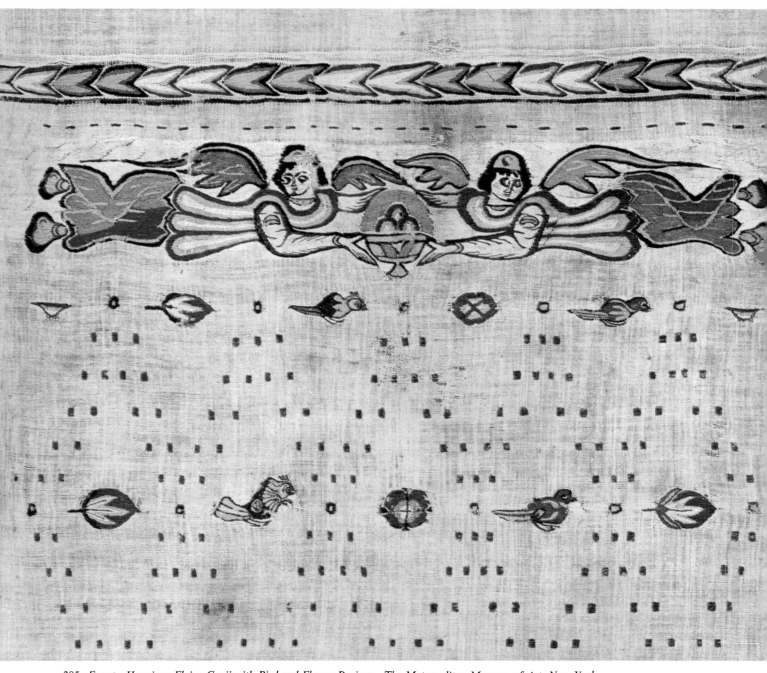

385. *Egypt. Hanging: Flying Genii with Bird and Flower Designs. The Metropolitan Museum of Art, New York.*

328

386. *Egypt. Hanging with an Orant. The Detroit Institute of Arts.*

monochrome of mythological scenes and, in *trompe-l'œil*, necklets set with coloured gems. They are datable to the fifth century. Their place of origin is unknown, but they seem to come from the Eastern Mediterranean area.

The upper parts of the most elegant of the figured curtains bear a frieze-like design having the same motifs and layout as the decorations on door-panels and book-covers. These include an *imago clipeata* above a pillar, angels or genii carrying victors' wreaths, mounted men lined up under an arcade—seemingly wardens of city gates, like those of the Middle Ages.

Not all the figured curtains were so ornate; there were also decorations of a quite simple type, limited to the repetition of a few motifs: rows of trees, faces, leaf or flower patterns. Presumably these curtains were hung on the inner walls of rooms and went down to the plinths. This, anyhow, is how they are represented in a number of mural paintings, and it was obviously the most effective way of displaying silks with printed designs arranged in rows. The images, all of small size, could thus be easily 'read' once the fabric was fixed to the wall.

388. *Egypt. Fragment of a Garment: Hare nibbling a Bunch of Grapes. Private Collection.*

387. *Egypt. Hanging with Busts in Medallions and Horsemen.* **The** *Metropolitan Museum of Art, New York.*    331

389. *Egypt. Hanging known as the Antinoe Shawl, detail: Bacchic Thiasos. Louvre, Paris.*

The largest and finest of the stuffs of pagan origin, the Antinoe shawl, is in the Louvre. It is a fourth-century work, representing a long line of satyrs and maenads, caught up in the frenzies of a Bacchic *thiasos*. The designs are admirable, and the decorative effect of this hanging must have been magnificent in its pristine state. It has two wide borders in which soberly rendered scenes of the life of Dionysus struck a contrast with the dynamic movement of the revellers. Accompanied by explanatory inscriptions, the Dionysian episodes form an unbroken sequence, without any vertical divisions.

Similar textiles were produced by the Christians, but in them pagan were replaced by Christian themes. The famous Christian 'veil' in the Berlin Museum conforms to the threefold layout of the Antinoe shawl, the large central frieze being composed of prophets and apostles, while the borders contain representations of churches with the names inscribed. These 'iconographic catalogues' of churches resemble those of the floor mosaics in some sacred edifices of the Holy Land. However, this veil was not copied from the pavements, for the pictures of churches usually figured on a wall or an iconostasis—though occasionally their themes were reproduced in floor mosaics.

332

390. *Egypt. Fragment of a Hanging with Fish Designs. Louvre, Paris.*

391. *Egypt.  Hanging with the Nativity in an Ornamental Medallion.  Vatican City.*

From a description of the interior of St Sophia compiled when it was being built we learn that the churches founded by Justinian and Theodora were represented on the veil of the iconostasis.  It would seem that this was also the place assigned to the curtain in the Berlin Museum and to many other figured silks carrying portraits and Biblical scenes. Textiles similarly ornamented are preserved in the Berlin Museum, the Victoria and Albert Museum, and many other collections, and they merit more attention than is usually given them in iconographic studies.

Hung across the closure of the choir or between its colonnettes (at the place where, in later times, the icons were displayed), they formed as it were a silken screen of pictures which could be drawn aside at certain moments in the course of the service.  The themes on stuffs of this kind were appropriate to these choir screens, which subsequently were converted into iconostases. Among the themes were those of the Wise and Foolish Virgins (Edinburgh Museum), Christ and the Apostles, Old Testament paradigms of Salvation (such as Daniel in the lions' den)—all of them themes which were to figure in the choirs of medieval churches.

392. *Egypt.  Hanging with the Annunciation in a Medallion.  Museo Sacro, Vatican City.*

Another group of stuffs with Old or New Testament motifs enclosed in medallions may have served to adorn the lower walls of churches. The finest example is the purple silk bearing an Annunciation now in the treasury of the Sancta Sanctorum (Museo Sacro, Vatican). Another silk in the same treasury represents the Nativity. These two pieces strikingly resemble two well-known cycles of sixth- or seventh-century wall paintings: those in the central apse of Santa Maria Antiqua in Rome, and the scenes from the life of David in a chapel at Bawit in Egypt.

In the apse of Santa Maria Antiqua the paintings on the plinth took the form of a simulated textile draped over the wall and patterned with various motifs, including a medallion with a Gospel scene. In the Bawit chapel, too, the painted plinth simulated a textile, but here the design consisted of a series of *emblemata*, appliqués in embroidery representing various episodes of David's combat with Goliath.

# Conclusion

## The Byzantine Legacy to Medieval Art

To what extent was medieval art conditioned by the art that preceded it, the subject of this volume?

In the centuries following the age of Justinian and his immediate successors circumstances were by and large unfavourable to cultural and creative activities in the Mediterranean lands. Indeed, during the seventh and eighth centuries (the so-called Dark Ages) art came almost to a standstill. True, there were exceptions, notably in outlying regions such as the British Isles and Transcaucasia, and, a little later, under the Omayyads, in the Caliphate of Damascus. But the great art centres, those which were later to resume and transmit the art tradition of the Mediterranean world, remained to all intents and purposes inactive until the art revival that took place at the end of the eighth and in the ninth century, both in the newly founded Carolingian Empire and in the Byzantine Empire, after the passing of iconoclasm and the rise to power of the Macedonian dynasty. A contemporaneous and similar revival took place under the Abbasid caliphs at Baghdad and in all the lands conquered by the Moslems. Moreover other art centres in Armenia, Georgia, Spain and Egypt, some very active though of minor importance, developed as the first millennium drew to its close, simultaneously with, or a little after, the major centres.

In our survey of the legacy of the arts studied in the preceding pages, we shall take into account not only their immediate aftermath in the Dark Ages but also the part they played in subsequent 'renaissances.' This heritage was fundamental to the art activities of both these periods, since in each of the 'renaissances' we find a deliberate harking-back to the creative achievements of Late Antiquity. In other words, the heritage of Antiquity was transmitted both to the arts which were a direct (if rather meagre) continuation of the art we have studied in this volume, and also to certain more vigorous forms of art which were to have a long and fruitful career, but which, chronologically, were not its direct successors. This distinction is essential for a proper understanding of the origins and background of medieval art, but it must not be pressed too far. For the Dark Ages did not involve a total cessation of art activities or the closure of all the craftsmen's workshops,

337

and the pioneers of later 'renaissances' were not always obliged to look back, beyond the Dark Ages, for their models.

Byzantium was exceptional in its unwavering fidelity to tradition, and if elsewhere the medieval art that came to its full flowering between the ninth and eleventh centuries differed so widely from the art of the age of Justinian, this was not so much because the medieval artist failed to appreciate that art as because he came under the influence of arts foreign to the Mediterranean tradition during and after the intermediary period. I have in mind the arts of Iran, China and India which still held their ground in the regions dominated by the Moslems. We must also allow for differences between techniques, between categories of monuments and artefacts, and between countries, when we seek to estimate the imprint made by the Mediterranean arts of the period dealt with in this volume on works of a later age.

Thus, in the field of religious architecture, the achievements of the last phase of the Roman Empire had far-reaching consequences. It was then, as we have seen, that the basilical plan came into favour as being most suitable for Christian places of worship, and this layout is still favoured by present-day builders of churches. The prototypes of the churches with three aisles, an apse and bell towers which have persisted through the ages, were the Christian edifices built between the reign of Constantine and the Arab invasions. True, there are differences between the belated versions of ancient architectural plans and those of the fourth, fifth and sixth centuries. But the basic characteristics remain the same, a fact that testifies to the lasting importance of those earliest creations of a specifically religious art. The architectural history of the baptistery is limited in time and scope, but special edifices for the celebration of the rites of baptism continued to be built in the Middle Ages, in western Europe and above all in Italy. Here the baptisteries kept to the polygonal plan with a central dome characteristic of those of the Constantinian era.

The third type of Christian edifice current in Antiquity, from the fourth century on, was the martyrium, a chapel or oratory erected in memory of a martyr and often enshrining a relic. Its architectural plan stemmed from that of the Roman mausoleum, whose traditional vaults and specific features it imitated. In the Middle Ages and still more in the Renaissance (including its Baroque sequel) mausolea inspired by those of the Romans and Early Christians were still erected. But their derivative, the martyrium serving for religious worship, became rare in the West during the Middle Ages and was frequently replaced by a crypt beneath a church, in which the holy relics were preserved. In the Byzantine and Transcaucasian regions, however, from the sixth century on, some martyria served as ordinary places of worship, for which purpose, with their centralized structure and domes, they were well suited. In other words, far from dying out, the tradition of this type of edifice gained strength in the Middle Ages, and it has persisted in those parts of the Christian world until our time.

In this context it is interesting to note that though the Latin races on the one hand, and the Greeks, Caucasians and Slavs on the other, kept to different types of sacred buildings—symbolic in their way of the separation of the Western and Eastern Churches—both these types (basilicas and centralized buildings with domes) stem from architectural plans dating to the close of Antiquity.

It was in the first centuries of the Christian era that, adapting the new religion to an already current usage, the practice arose of partaking in a commemorative meal on the grave of a dead friend or kinsman. When the deceased had won the rank of sainthood, the tombstone on which the ceremonial repast took place became a eucharistic altar and the body beneath a sacred relic. The link between them was consolidated, so to say, by services regularly held on the tomb, paralleled by the cult of relics in the apsidal prolongations of churches. The earliest examples date back to the age of Constantine (Bethlehem, St Peter's) and to this practice, elaborated in the following centuries, was due the remarkable architectural development of the choir in the Christian basilicas of the Latin countries, and the subsequent proliferation (in the twelfth and thirteenth centuries) of radiating chapels in the chevets and spacious crypts below.

Jewish and Arab places of worship—synagogues and mosques—also owed much to the architecture of Late Antiquity. Over a long period the Moslems kept to the basilical plan in their mosques as the Christians did in their churches. This view holds good even if, following Sauvaget, we assume that the Omayyad mosques on the basilical plan derived from the royal palaces. As for the synagogues, they retained this plan long after the Arab invasion—as is proved, for example, by the synagogue of Toledo, built in the eleventh century, which later became the church of Santa Maria la Blanca.

The systematic orientation of religious edifices in a specific direction (the altar facing east in Christian churches, the chevet pointing to Jerusalem and Mecca in synagogues and mosques) originated among the Jews at the beginning of our era, and they transmitted it to the Christians and Mahometans. This tradition, which has persisted to the present day, determined the orientation of churches, synagogues and mosques alike (though, on occasion, the builders of Christian churches took certain liberties in this respect). The continuity of ancient traditions is particularly evident in Byzantium. Here we can study a type form of religious architecture all the more easily identifiable since, from the sixth century on, it markedly diverged from that of the other Christian lands. It had a remarkable compactness, contrasting with the basilical plan which was preserved in all other parts of the Christian world, and its far-flung vaults crowned with a dome differentiated it sharply from the traditional wooden roofs of basilicas in the other provinces. Thus, from an early date, Byzantine church architecture acquired the specific aspect which it was to retain for over a thousand years. And since it evolved less in the Middle Ages than did church architecture of the West, that of the Byzantines remained, in all essentials, a sort of fossilized form of a certain architecture of Late Antiquity.

In the vast domain of the figural arts the legacy of Late Antiquity was no less considerable, though varying according to the countries and techniques involved. Indeed the basic principles of figurative art, as established in the third century and a little later, were never called in question during the long period which, in western Europe, witnessed the rise of Carolingian, Ottonian and even Romanesque art, and, in the Byzantine area, covers all the works produced up to the end of medievaldom and the beginning of the modern age. Everywhere we find a tacit acceptance of these principles, a compromise between the representation of figures and objects located in space and the contrary trend towards the projection of every image on to the flat surface of wall or manuscript. Lending itself to a great variety of interpretations, this compromise could be adapted to the artist's personal taste or to that of his environment. But, all in all, none of the variations to which the art of the Early Middle Ages owes its wonderful vivacity, diverged to any great extent from the aesthetic current at the close of Antiquity. The earliest schools of Moslem artists (at Baghdad, Samarra and in Fatimid Egypt) took guidance from the same aesthetic. However, this influence gradually waned and in the twelfth and thirteenth centuries Moslem painting tended towards a new type of art in which Asiatic contributions played an outstanding part.

In Europe, and even more at Byzantium, the art of the Early Middle Ages conformed to the aesthetic of Late Antiquity; this applies both to many of its motifs and to specific forms and techniques, to the drawing and modelling of bodies and draperies, to renderings of gestures and attitudes, landscape and architecture, methods of foreshortening and the disposition of figures and objects in normal or 'inverted' perspective. In whatever way the artist interpreted his subject, he never overstepped the limits implicitly imposed by the tradition of his formative years, a tradition directly linking up with Late Antiquity. Even the atavistic notion of a Golden Age of the arts that had long since passed away, but which it was the artist's duty to struggle to regain, formed part of the heritage transmitted from Antiquity to the Middle Ages. But it should be added—and this is a fact that has been clearly proved by recent research-work—that the ideal of 'antique art' which haunted the imagination of the Early Middle Ages was not the classical Greek or Roman art of the early periods, but the art of the last centuries of Antiquity, and, more particularly, that of the works, already Christian but still 'antique' in taste and composition, which were more accessible, both factually and spiritually, to medieval man.

Thus in the art-forms of this period we find intermittent or parallel continuations of an earlier tradition; for example in the apse mosaics of the Roman basilicas from the sixth to the ninth century (and even later), and in the illustrations copied from one manuscript to another. Sometimes the conservatism of works of this kind makes it difficult to date them—as is the case with the recently discovered frescoes in the Cividale Tempietto and those of Mustair in the Grisons (Switzerland); also with the miniatures in a Greek Gospel (Leningrad, 21) and a Greek Psalter (Grec 139) in Paris.

But we have sometimes equal difficulties in dating works in which, instead of keeping docilely to the normal classical tradition, the artist deliberately harks back to very early models and meticulously copies them. For these reversions to ancient prototypes always led to a revival of classical forms and procedures—the same with each 'renaissance.' A recent example of the problems confronting us in such cases is the difficulty in dating the Castelseprio frescoes, discovered in 1944, whose fidelity to classical art is particularly marked. Here the antique elements tell us more about the age of the model than about the time when it was imitated at Castelseprio.

This imitation of models of Late Antiquity reached its climax in the art of the Carolingian painters and sculptors and their Constantinopolitan contemporaries, and the fact that after an interval of three centuries and more artists reverted to the same forms and the same techniques throws a revealing light on the spirit of the age. It proves, *inter alia*, that during the interval there had been no change of orientation in the aesthetic training of painters and sculptors, and that classical models were still regarded as the acme of perfection. There is, however, a shade of difference between the almost simultaneous productions of Byzantium and the West; in the capital of the Greek Empire the imitation of classical models sometimes had an exactitude never practised in the western art centres. Presumably this was because an intellectual and technical tradition held its ground immutably at Constantinople, whereas the westerners worked under different social and ethnic conditions. Thus, though we sometimes hesitate between the fifth and tenth centuries when it comes to dating certain genres of Byzantine painting (such as the famous Joshua Roll), none of the illustrations in Carolingian manuscripts has ever been ascribed to an earlier period.

These differences notwithstanding, the Carolingian painters and ivory-carvers, like their Greek contemporaries, made a practice of reproducing, down to the least detail, the iconography of works created in Late Antiquity. And for this reason the art studied in the foregoing pages is fundamental to the history of Christian art. For throughout the ages Christian artists referred back to the various iconographical versions of the symbolic and, above all, the narrative themes which had taken form between the third and sixth centuries, and copied again and again their general disposition and even incidental details. It is to the catacomb paintings that we must look for the prototypes of the traditional depictions of the Adoration of the Magi; to sarcophagus reliefs, for those of the Baptism of Christ and the Trial before Pilate; to the Palestinian ampullae, for those of the Nativity, the Visitation, the Holy Women at the Tomb and the Ascension.

By the same token it is to the imagery brought to fruition under the auspices of the imperial court in the last centuries of antiquity that we owe, *mutatis mutandis*, several of the figurations which have left the deepest imprint on the minds and memories of Christians throughout the ages, and continue to answer, by and large, to our visualizations of God, of the divine majesty, the celestial kingdom and the Last Judgment. It is almost always in terms of the iconographic language of Late Antiquity that we picture the Christian 'world beyond the world.' For more works of art bearing on the basic themes of the Christian faith were produced during the centuries covered by this volume than in later times. And though there can be no question of equating the iconography of the Byzantine age to the dogmas promulgated by the various Councils held in the same period—the images created at the close of antiquity never set up to be an iconographic 'article of faith' on an equal footing with the Creed prescribed by the ecclesiastical authority— this imagery is none the less fundamental to the entire history of Christian art.

# Plans

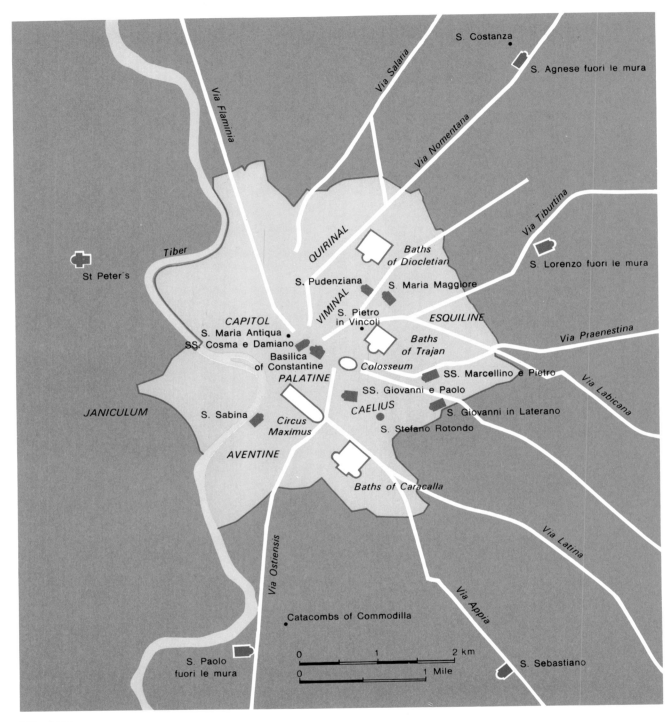

S. Costanza
S. Agnese fuori le mura
Via Salaria
Via Flaminia
Via Nomentana
Via Tiburtina
QUIRINAL
Tiber
Baths
of Diocletian
S. Lorenzo fuori le mura
St Peter's
S. Pudenziana
S. Maria Maggiore
VIMINAL
S. Pietro
in Vincoli
ESQUILINE
CAPITOL
Via Praenestina
S. Maria Antiqua
Baths
of Trajan
SS. Cosma e Damiano
Via Labicana
Basilica
of Constantine
Colosseum
SS. Marcellino e Pietro
PALATINE
SS. Giovanni e Paolo
JANICULUM
S. Sabina
CAELIUS
S. Giovanni in Laterano
Circus
Maximus
S. Stefano Rotondo
AVENTINE
Baths of Caracalla
Via Latina
Via Ostriensis
Catacombs of Commodilla
Via Appia
0        1        2 km
S. Paolo
fuori le mura
0              1 Mile
S. Sebastiano

393. *Rome*.

344

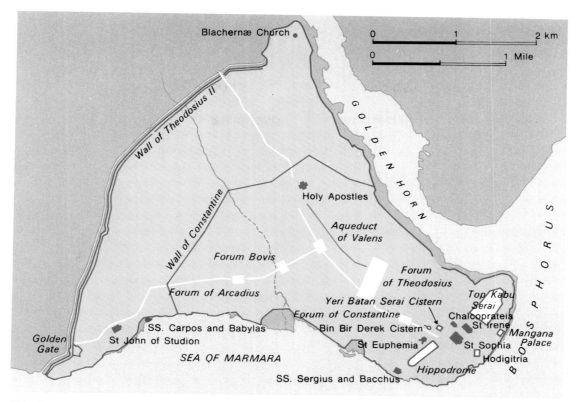

394. *Constantinople*.

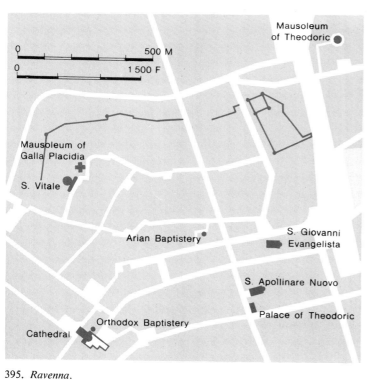

395. *Ravenna*.

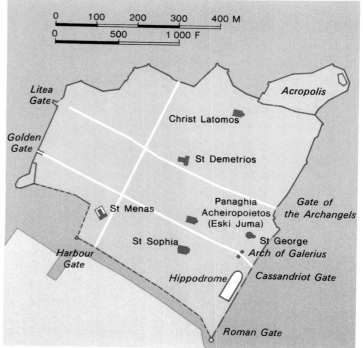

396. *Salonica*.

345

# ITALY-GAUL

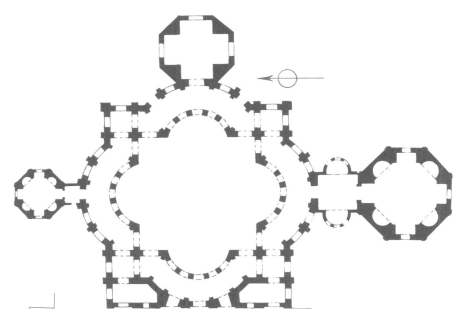

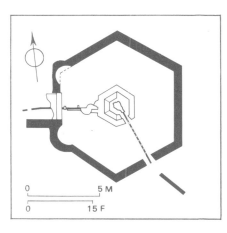

398. *Portbail (Manche). Baptistery.*

399. *Parenzo. Basilica and Baptistery.*

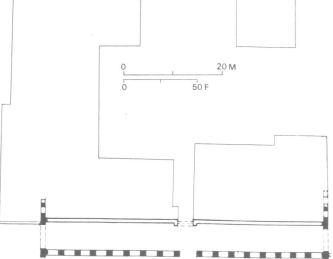

397. *Milan. Church of San Lorenzo.*

In some cases it has not been possible to indicate the exact orientation.

346

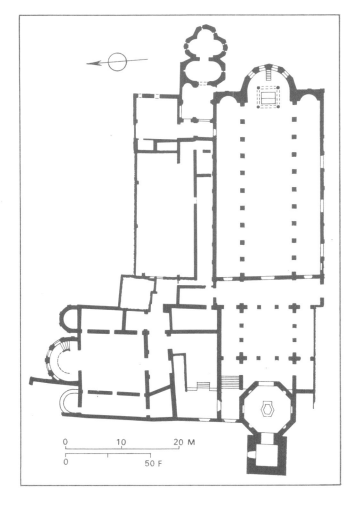

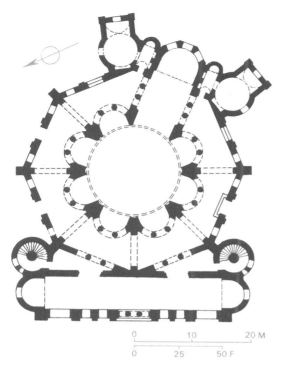

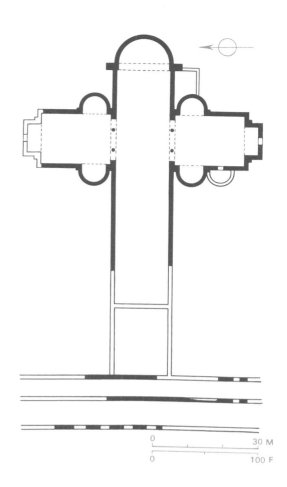

400. *Ravenna. Church of San Vitale.*     401. *Milan. Santi Apostoli.*

# MEDITERRANEAN AFRICA

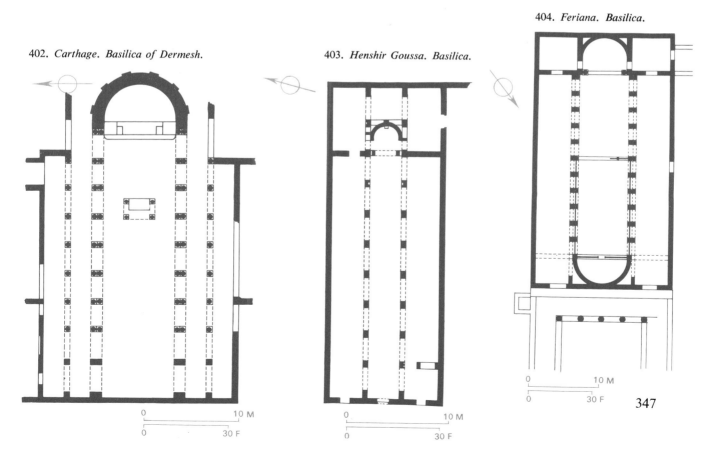

402. *Carthage. Basilica of Dermesh.*        403. *Henshir Goussa. Basilica.*

404. *Feriana. Basilica.*

347

# EGYPT

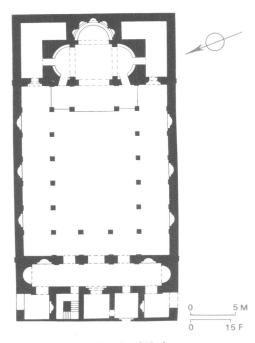

412. *Dendera. Room in the Temple of Hathor converted into a Church.*

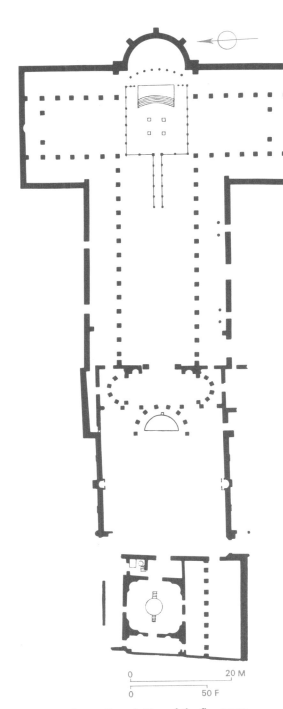

411. *St Menas. Overall Plan of the Sanctuary.*

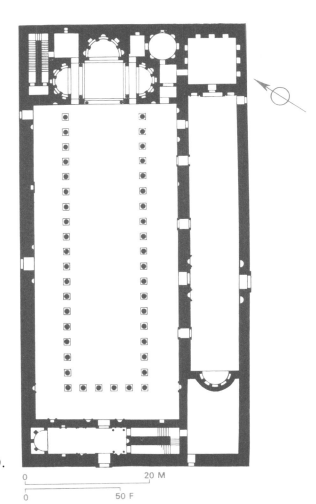

413. *Sohag. White Monastery (Deir el-Abiad).*

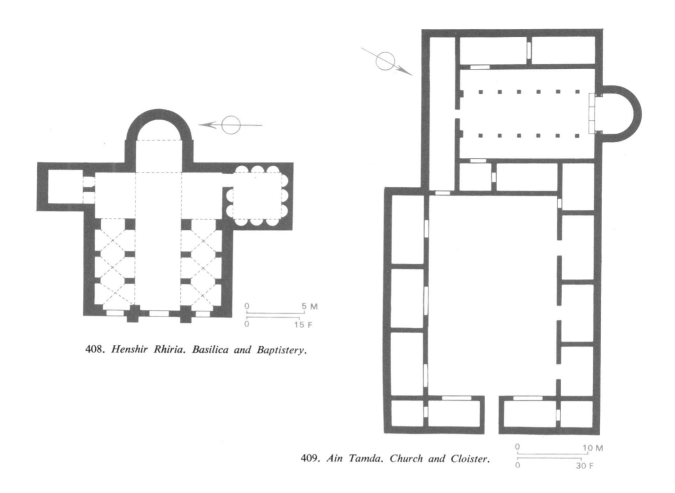

408. *Henshir Rhiria. Basilica and Baptistery.*

409. *Ain Tamda. Church and Cloister.*

0      5 M
0      15 F

0      10 M
0      30 F

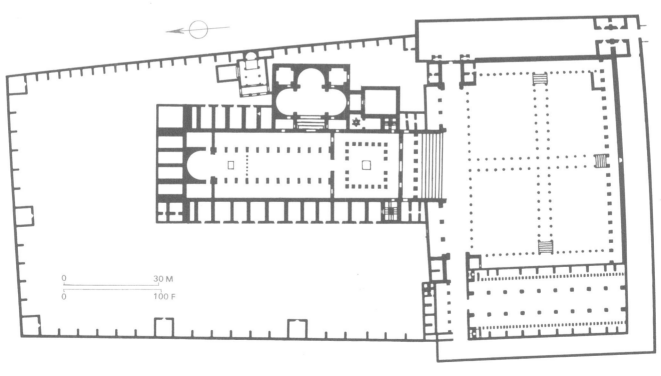

0      30 M
0      100 F

410. *Tebessa. Overall Plan of the Early Christian Buildings.*

349

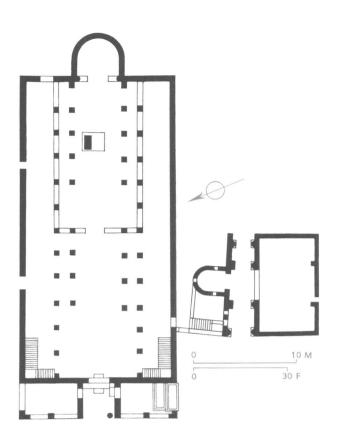

405. *Tipasa. Basilica of St Salsa and Martyrium.*

406. *Tabarka. Basilica and Detail of the Baptistery.*

407. *Mididi. Basilica. Plan and Longitudinal Section.*

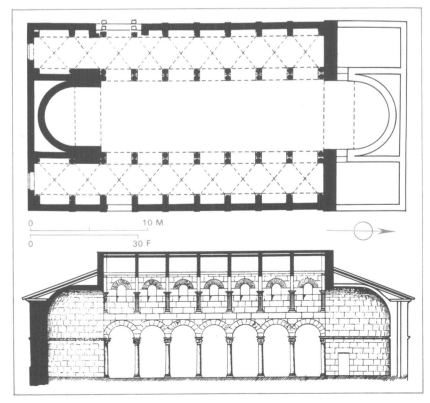

348

414. *Sakkara. Overall Plan of the Monastery of St Jeremiah (excavations).*

# SYRIA

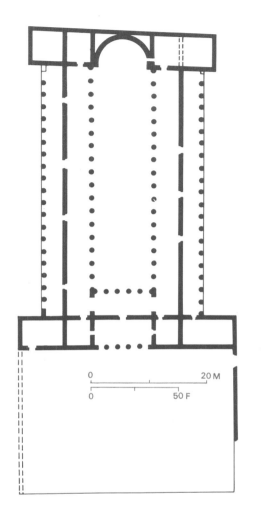

◄ 415. *El Hosn. Church I.*

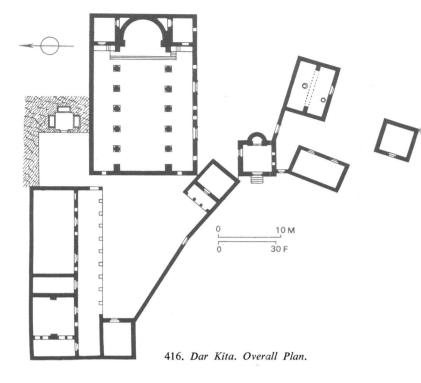

416. *Dar Kita. Overall Plan.*

417. *Ir-Ruhaiyeh. Overall Plan of the Three Churches.*

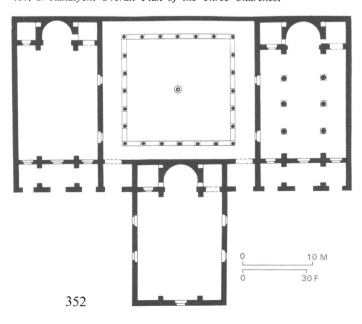

418. *Deir Seman. West Monastery.*

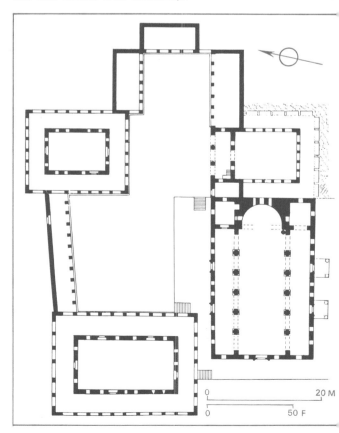

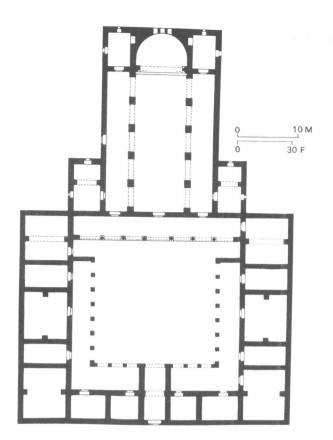

419. *Ed Deir. Church and Atrium.*

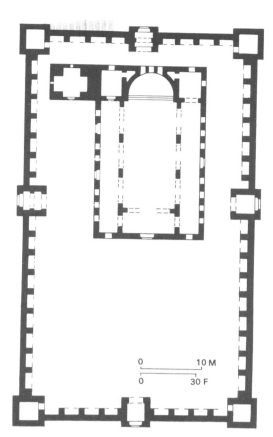

420. *El Anderin. South Church and Peribole.*

421. *Ruweiha II. Church of Bizzos and Mausolea.*

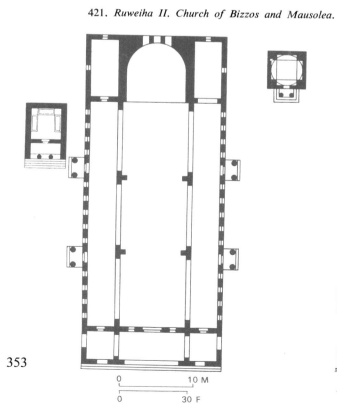

422. *Kasr Ibn Wardan. Longitudinal Section.*

# PALESTINE

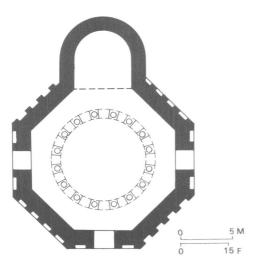

430. *Jerusalem. Church of the Tomb of the Virgin.*

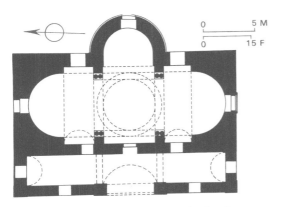

432. *Jerusalem. Church of St John the Baptist.*

433. *Beit Alpha. Synagogue.*

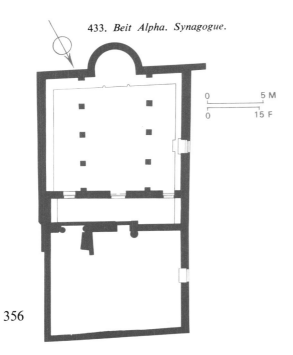

356

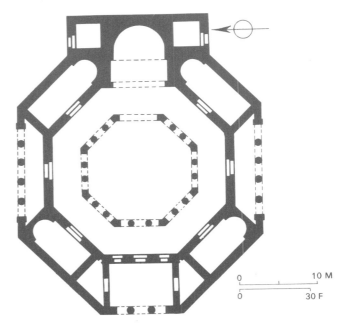

431. *Mount Garizim. Church of the Virgin.*

434. *El Tabgha. Basilica of the Multiplication of Loaves and Fishes.*

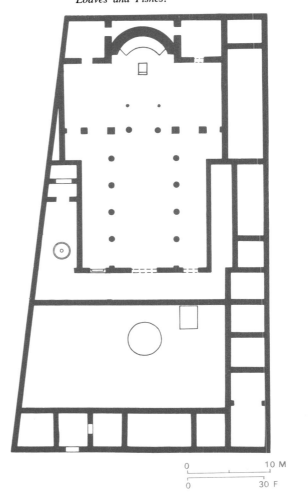

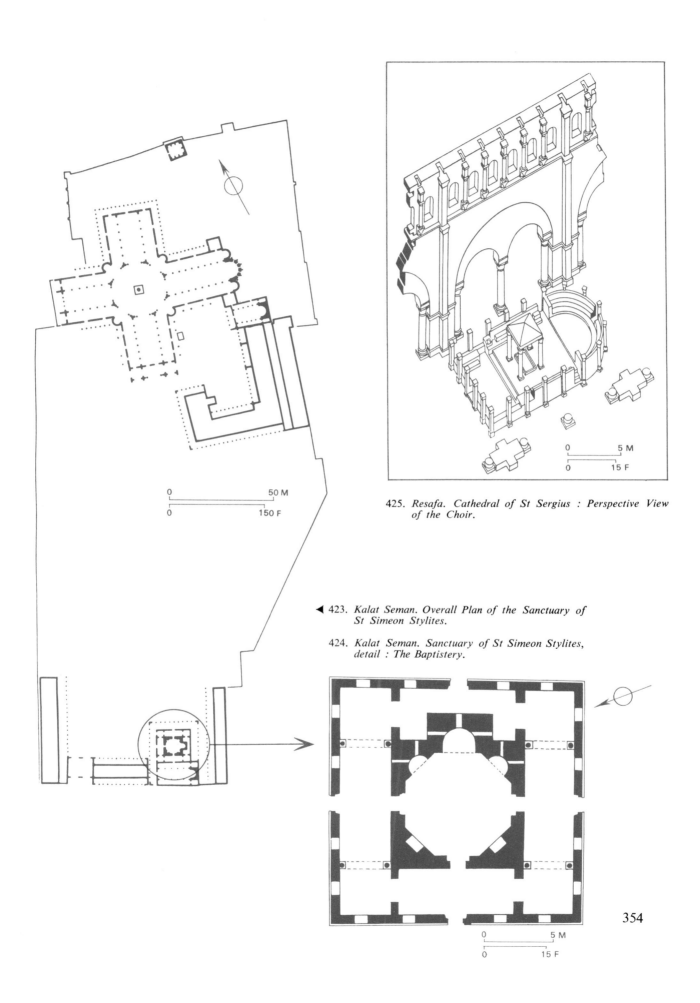

425. *Resafa. Cathedral of St Sergius : Perspective View of the Choir.*

◀ 423. *Kalat Seman. Overall Plan of the Sanctuary of St Simeon Stylites.*

424. *Kalat Seman. Sanctuary of St Simeon Stylites, detail : The Baptistery.*

354

426. *Bosra. Plan of the Cathedral.*

427. *Bosra. Section of the Cathedral.*

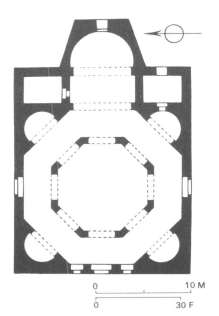

428. *Ezra. Church of St George.*

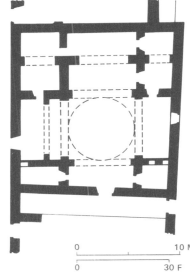

429. *Shagra. Martyrium.*

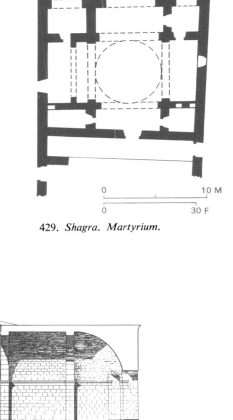

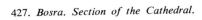

355

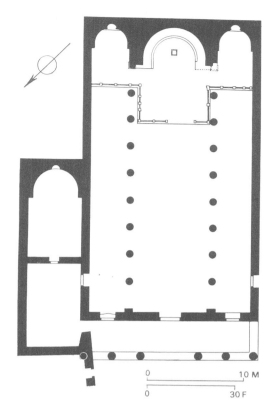

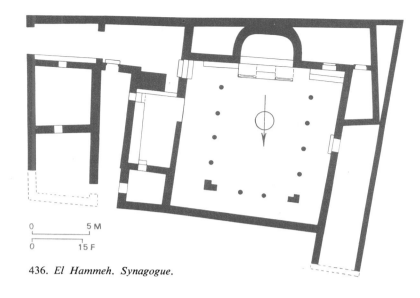

436. *El Hammeh. Synagogue.*

◀ 435. *Gerasa. Church of Sts Peter and Paul.*

# MESOPOTAMIA

438. *Al Hirah. Church XI.* ▶

437. *Damgan. Sassanian House.*

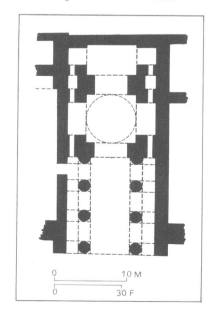

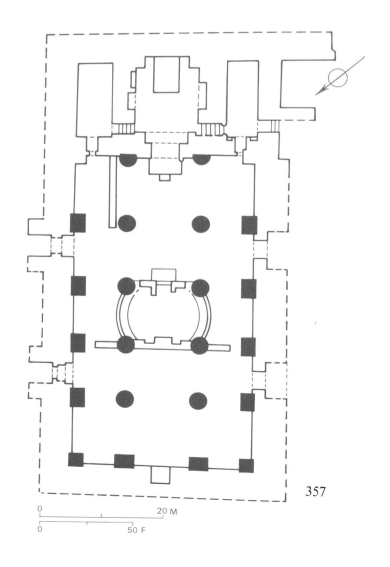

357

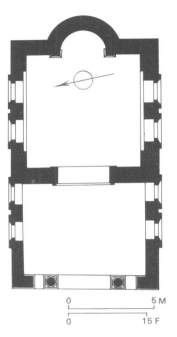

439. *Nisibis. Martyrium of St James of Nisibis.*

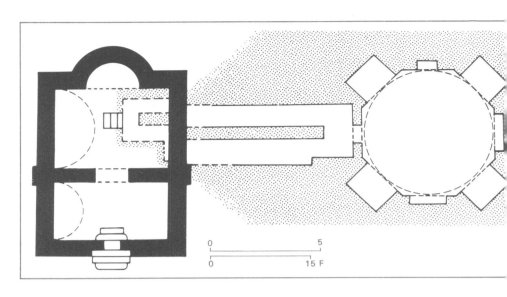

440. *Behnam. Church and Underground Room.*

442. *Kartamin. Detail of the Monastery Church.* ▶

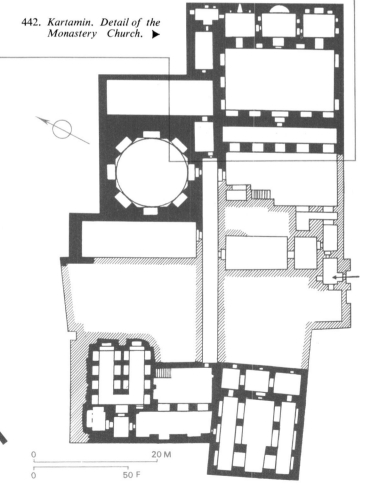

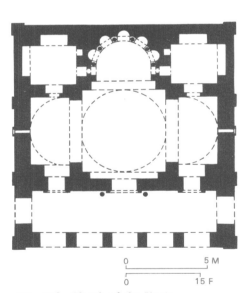

441. *Hah. Church of the Virgin.*

443. *Kartamin. Overall Plan of the Monastery.*

# AEGEAN REGION AND CONSTANTINOPLE

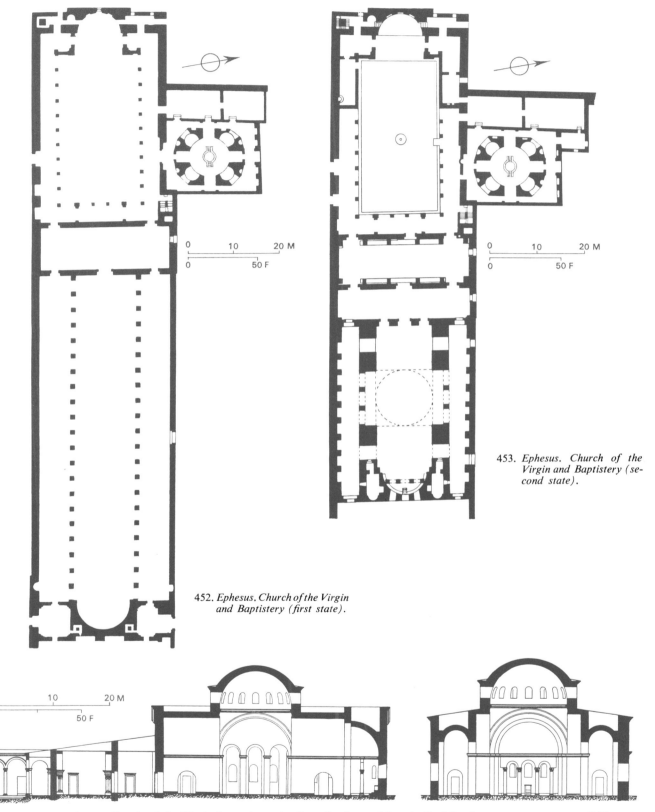

452. *Ephesus. Church of the Virgin and Baptistery (first state).*

453. *Ephesus. Church of the Virgin and Baptistery (second state).*

454. *Ephesus. Church of the Virgin (second state): Cross-Section and Longitudinal Section.*

361

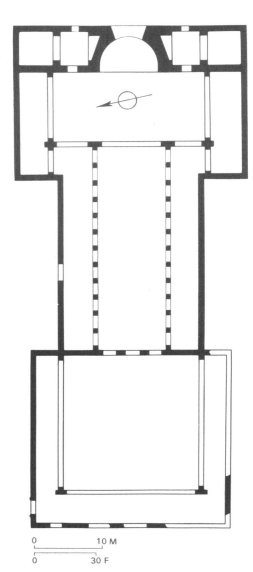

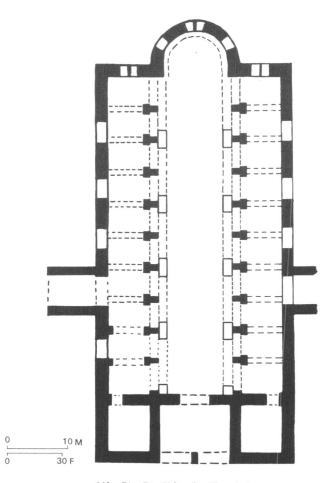

449. *Bin Bir Kilisseh. Church I.*

0    10 M
0    30 F

448. *Perga. Church.*

450. *Bin Bir Kilisseh. Church III.*

451. *Aspendos. Basilica.*

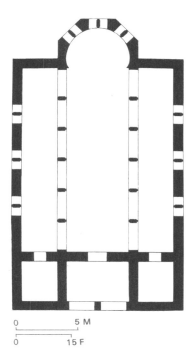

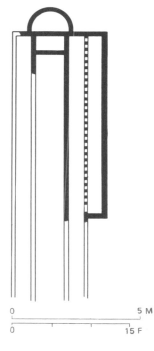

0    5 M
0    15 F

0    5 M
0    15 F

# ASIA MINOR

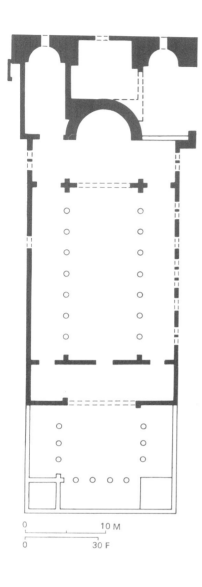

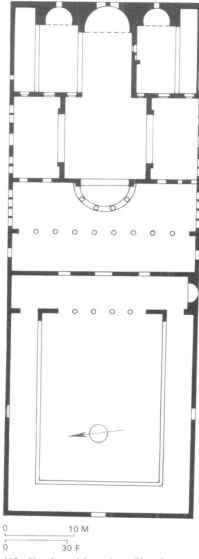

447. *Meriamlik. Basilica (reconstruction).*

444. *Korykos. Church 'extra muros'.*    445. *Korykos. Martyrium Church.*

446. *Side. Baptistery.*

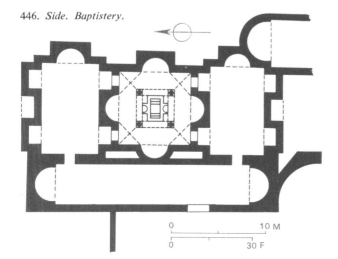

359

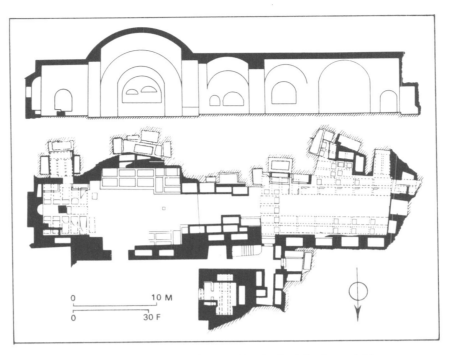

455. *Ephesus. Church of the Seven Sleepers: Longitudinal Section and Plan.*

456. *Salonica. Basilica of St Demetrios.*

457. *Athens. Ilissos Basilica.*

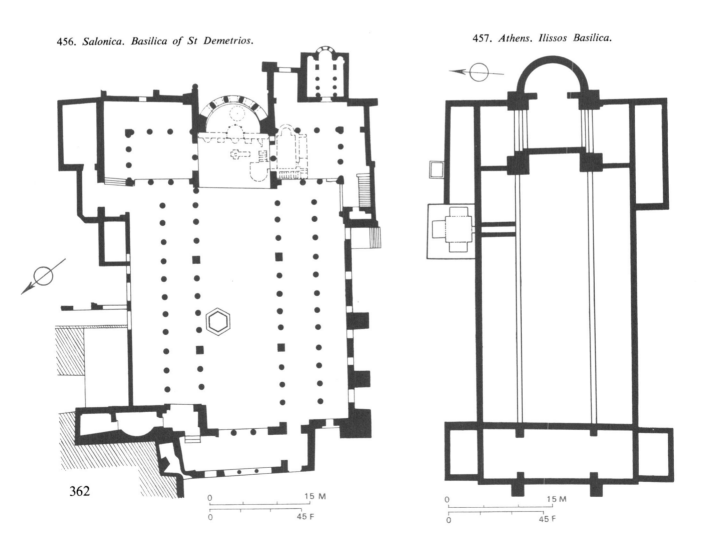

362

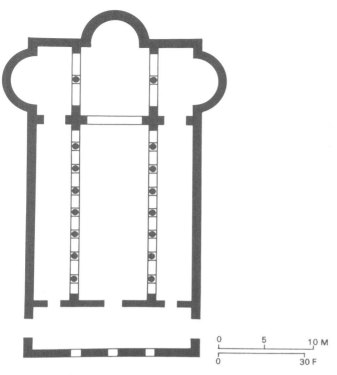

458. *Dodona. Basilica.*

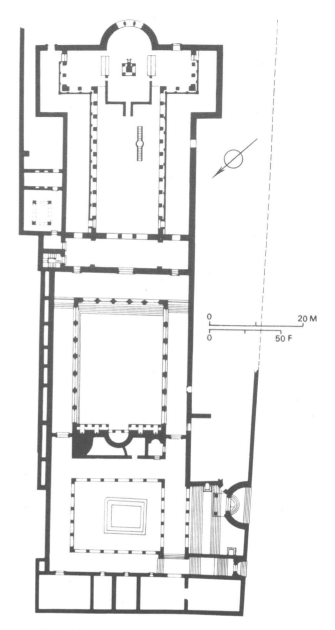

459. *Philippi. Church A.*

460. *Salonica. Oratory of Christ Latomos: Elevation, Section and Plan.*

363

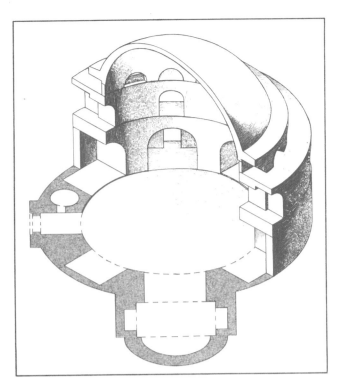

461. *Salonica. Church of St George.*

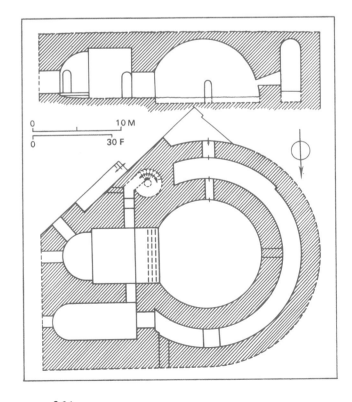

0          10 M

0          30 F

462. *Ephesus. Church of St John (second state).*

0          20 M

0          50 F

463. *Constantinople. Martyrium of Sts Carpos and Babylas: Section and Plan.*

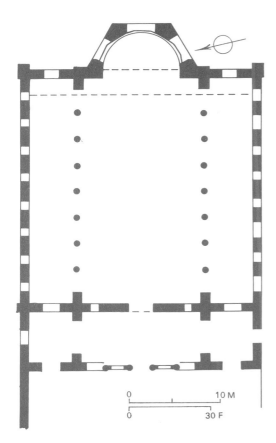

464. *Constantinople. Basilica of the Monastery of St John of Studion.*

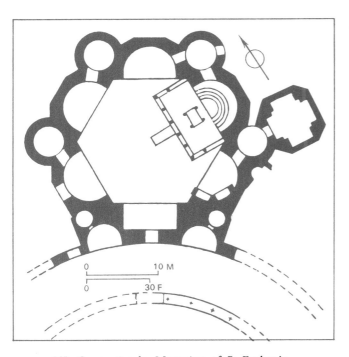

465. *Constantinople. Martyrium of St Euphemia.*

466. *Constantinople. Yeri Batan Serai Cistern: Section and Plan.*

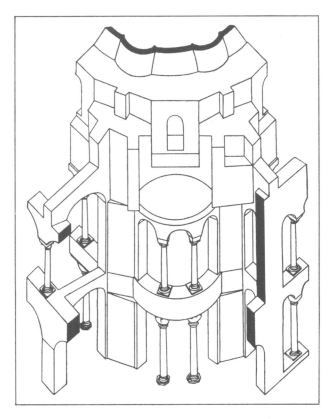

467. *Constantinople. Church of Sts Sergius and Bacchus: Dome-Canopy.*

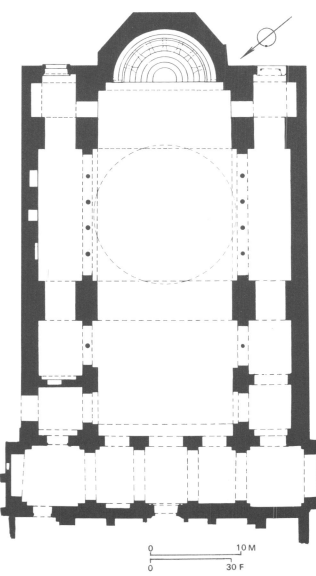

468. *Constantinople. Church of St Irene.*

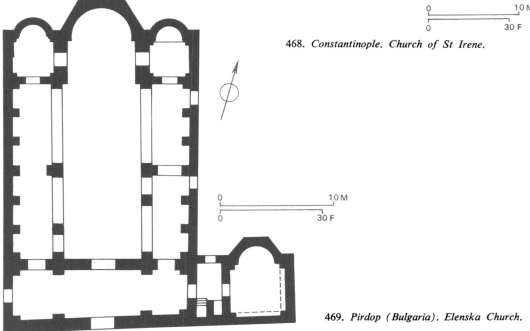

0            10 M
0            30 F

469. *Pirdop (Bulgaria). Elenska Church.*

# Chronological Table

| | MEN | EVENTS |
|---|---|---|
| 380 | Siricius, Pope (384-399) | 380 — Imperial edict establishing Christianity as the official religion of the state. |
| | Arcadius I, Emperor of the East (395-408) | 391 — Imperial edict prohibiting pagan worship. |
| | Honorius I, Emperor of the West (395-423) | 394 — Olympic Games abolished. |
| 400 | Theodosius II, Emperor of the East (408-450) | 404 — Ravenna becomes the capital of the Western Empire (until 476). |
| | | 405 — Gladiatorial combats forbidden. |
| 420 | | 410 — Capture of Rome by Alaric. |
| | Sixtus III, Pope (432-440) | 431 — Council of Ephesus: Mary proclaimed 'the Mother of God.' |
| 440 | Leo the Great, Pope (440-461) | |
| 450 | Marcian, Emperor of the East (450-457) | |
| | Leo I, Emperor of the East (457-474) | |
| 460 | Simplicius, Pope (468-483) | |
| | Zeno, Emperor of the East (474-491) | |
| 480 | | 476 — Odoacer deposes Romulus Augustulus, the last Emperor of the West. |
| | Anastasius I, Emperor of the East (491-518) | 488 — Zeno abandons Italy to Theodoric. |
| 500 | | |
| | Justin I, Emperor of the East (518-527) | |
| 520 | Justinian I, Emperor of the East (527-565) | |
| | | 533 to 555 — Under Justinian, reconquest of Italy and Africa by the Byzantines. |
| 540 | | 540 — Ravenna taken by the Byzantines. |
| 560 | Justin II, Emperor of the East (565-578) | |
| 580 | Tiberius II, Emperor of the East (578-582) | c. 580 — Exarchate of Ravenna established. |
| | Maurice, Emperor of the East (582-602) | |
| 600 | Phocas, Emperor of the East (602-610) | |
| | Heraclius I (610-641) | |
| 620 | | |
| | | 626 — Siege of Constantinople by the Persians and Avars. |
| 640 | | c. 640 — Conquest of Syria, Palestine and Egypt by the Moslem Arabs. |

| | |
|---|---|
| 382 | Church of San Nazzaro (Santi Apostoli), Milan. |
| 384-399 | Church of Santa Pudenziana, Rome, founded by Pope Siricius. |
| 385-386 | Basilica of the Martyrs (Sant'Ambrogio), Milan. |
| 386 | Church of San Paolo fuori le Mura, Rome, founded by Valentinian II. |
| c. 400 | Salonica, mosaics in St George and Christ Latomos.<br>Second basilica of St Menas, near Alexandria, founded by Arcadius.<br>Two basilicas of Sohag, Egypt. |
| between 400 and 640 | Monasteries of Bawit and Sakkara, Egypt, and their wall paintings. |
| c. 413-440 | Building of the walls of Constantinople. |
| 418 | Church of Dar Kita, Syria. |
| c. 430 | Church of Hermopolis, Egypt. |
| 432-440 | Church of Santa Maria Maggiore, Rome, and its mosaics. |
| between 439 and 564 | Baptistery of Cimiez, Nice. |
| c. 450 | Church of Alahan Monastir, Cilicia.<br>Synagogue of Gerasa, Palestine. |
| 470 | Mosaics in the San Vittore chapel of Sant'Ambrogio, Milan. |
| c. 475-490 | Church of Mount Garizim in Samaria, Palestine. |
| c. 480 | Church and monastery of Kalat Seman (St Simeon Stylites), near Antioch. |
| c. 500 | Illustration of the Dioscorides Codex (Nationalbibliothek, Vienna). |
| 519 & 558 | Sant'Apollinare Nuovo, Ravenna. |
| 528 | Painting of the Donatrix Turtura in the Catacomb of Commodilla, Rome. |
| c. 530 | Synagogues of Gerasa and Apamea converted into churches. |
| 532-537 & 558-562 | Construction of St Sophia, Constantinople. |
| 532-547 | San Vitale, Ravenna. |
| 536-546 | Construction of the Church of the Holy Apostles, Constantinople. |
| c. 540 | Church of SS. Peter and Paul, Gerasa (Palestine). |
| 549 | Consecration of Sant'Apollinare in Classe, Ravenna. |
| 564 | Church of Kasr Ibn Wardan, Syria. |
| 586 | Rabula Gospels written in Syriac (Biblioteca Laurenziana, Florence). |
| c. 600 | Apse mosaics in the Church of St Catherine, Mount Sinai.<br>Figured ampullae from Jerusalem, at Monza and Bobbio.<br>Silver dishes with figural reliefs from the Kerinia Treasure, Cyprus (Cyprus and New York). |
| c. 640-650 | Silver dishes with figural reliefs in the Hermitage, Leningrad. |

# Glossary-Index

ABBACYR (St). Alexandrian physician martyred at Canope in the 4th century, *p.* 168; *fig.* 179.

ABBASIDS. Third dynasty of Arab caliphs, from Abu-l-Abbas (750) to the death of Mustasim (1258), *p.* 337.

ABEL. Son of Adam and Eve, *p.* 156; *fig.* 168.

ABGAR. Name of eight kings of Edessa in Mesopotamia (132 B.C. to 216 A.D.), *p.* 60.

ABRAHAM. Biblical patriarch, forefather of the Hebrews, *p.* 145, 156, 185, 282; *fig.* 156, 157, 169, 200.

ABRAHAM. Abbot of Bawit, *fig.* 199.

ADAM. The first man created by God (Genesis, chapters 1-5), *fig.* 242.

ADAUCTUS (St). Roman martyr (died 304), companion of St Felix, *p.* 167; *fig.* 176.

ADONIS. In Greek mythology, a beautiful youth loved by Aphrodite (Venus), *p.* 298; *fig.* 346.

AEGEAN SEA. Between Greece and Asia Minor, *p.* 71.

AENEID. Latin epic by Virgil, *p.* 196; *fig.* 210, 211.

AGNELLUS. Archbishop of Ravenna (556-569), *fig.* 284.

AHNAS EL-MEDINEH. Village in Egypt, *p.* 239; *fig.* 269-273, 276, 277.

AIN TAMDA. Ancient town of Algeria, south of Aumale, *p.* 30.

AIX-EN-PROVENCE. City in the South of France, *p.* 27.

AK KALA, in Greek KANYTELIDEIS. Ruins in Cilicia, south-east of Seleucia, on the Mediterranean coast near Korykos, *p.* 62.

ALAHAN or ALAHAN MONASTIR or KHODJA KALESSI. Ancient town in Cilicia, between Karaman and Mut, *p.* 64, 66, 237; *fig.* 62, 63.

ALARIC I. Visigothic king (396-410) who invaded Italy (408) and sacked Rome (410), *p.* 11, 25, 84.

ALCANTARA. Town in western Spain (province of Caceres), on the Tagus, *p.* 30.

ALCARACEJOS. Town in southern Spain (province of Cordoba), *p.* 30.

ALEXANDRIA. Egyptian city and seaport on the Mediterranean, at the mouth of the Nile, founded in 332 B.C. by Alexander the Great. Greco-Roman, then Byzantine metropolis before being taken by the Arabs in 642 A.D., *p.* 2, 35, 57, 170, 278; *fig.* 307.

ALVERNY (Marie-Thérèse d'). French scholar, honorary Curator of the Department of Manuscripts at the Bibliothèque Nationale, Paris, *p.* 202.

AMBROSE (St). Father and Doctor of the Church (c. 340-397), bishop of Milan (370-397), *p.* 15, 165; *fig.* 175.

AMIDA. Town in northern Mesopotamia, on the Tigris, *p.* 59, 61.

AMMONIUS OF ALEXANDRIA. Monk in one of the monasteries of Nitria, *p.* 208.

ANASTASIUS I. Emperor of the East (491-518), *p.* 60, 278.

ANASTASIUS (Flavius Sabinianus Pompeius). Consul in 517, *fig.* 330.

ANATOLIA. Asia Minor, *p.* 71.

ANAZARAB. Ancient town in Cilicia, Asia Minor, on the Pyramus (present-day Anavarza, Turkey), *p.* 62.

ANDERIN (EL-). Ancient town in Syria, south of Aleppo, *p.* 42.

ANKH. Egyptian hieroglyph meaning *life*, *p.* 172.

ANN ARBOR, see MICHIGAN.

ANNE (St). Mother of the Virgin Mary, *p.* 170.

ANTHEMIOS OF TRALLES. Mathematician and engineer (died 534), principal architect of St Sophia, Constantinople, *p.* 86.

ANTINOE. Ancient town in Egypt, capital of the Thebaid, *p.* 172, 326, 332; *fig.* 185, 389.

ANTIOCH. Capital of the Seleucid Empire, then of the Roman and Byzantine province of Syria. Present-day Antakya, in Turkey, *p.* 52, 53, 57, 61, 64, 105, 106, 115, 121, 128, 236, 264, 278; *fig.* 109-115, 266, 268, 301, 302, 360. *Megalopsychia mosaic*, *p.* 106; *fig.* 109-112, 114.

APAMEA. Ancient town in Syria, *p.* 52, 57, 61.

APHRODISIAS. Ancient city in Caria (present-day Geyre, in Turkey), *fig.* 252, 254.

APHRODISIOS. According to an apocryphal book of the New Testament, an Egyptian governor of Sotima who came to worship the Christ Child, *p.* 148.

APHRODITE. Greek goddess (called Venus by the Romans), *p.* 239, 298; *fig.* 276, 346.

APOLLINARIS (St). Supposed to have been the first bishop of Ravenna (1st-2nd century), *p.* 141; *fig.* 148.

APOLLO or APOLLOS (St). Hermit (died c. 395) who founded a monastery near Hermopolis, Egypt, *fig.* 186-187, 189, 192, 193.

APOLLO. Greek god, *fig.* 324.

AQUILEIA. Town in north-eastern Italy, near the Adriatic, *p.* 112, 121; *fig.* 118.

AQUITAINE. Province of south-western France, *p.* 275.

ARATUS. Greek astronomer and poet (315-240 B.C.), *p.* 193.

ARCADIUS. Roman Emperor of the East (395-408), *p.* 38, 219.

ARCOSOLIUM. An arched recess used as a burial place in a catacomb, *p.* 182.

AREOBINDUS. Consul of the Eastern Empire in 506, *fig.* 320, 325.

ARIADNE. Byzantine empress (5th century), daughter of Leo I, wife of Zeno, then of Anastasius I, *fig.* 253, 318.

ARMENIA. Region and former kingdom of Asia Minor, south of the Caucasus and Black Sea, *p.* 15, 293, 337.

ASHBURNHAM PENTATEUCH. Famous manuscript purloined from the Tours library in the mid-19th century and sold to the Earl of Ashburnham, who owned it for forty years, until it was restored to France (now in the Bibliothèque Nationale, Paris), *p.* 185, 214, 217; *fig.* 207, 242, 243.

ASIA MINOR. Peninsula of western Asia, also called Anatolia, *p.* 61, 71, 101, 172, 173, 202, 236, 269.

ASPENDOS. Town in Pamphylia (Turkey), *p.* 66; *fig.* 64.

ASSYRIA. Ancient empire in Mesopotamia, *p.* 156.

ASTERIUS (St). Bishop of Amasia in Pontus, Asia Minor (died in 410), *p.* 101, 323.

ASWAN. City in Upper Egypt where the monastery of St Simeon was located, *p.* 38, 39.

ATHENS. Capital city of Greece, *p.* 76, 152. Ilissos basilica, *p.* 76.

ATRIUM. Court surrounded by porticoes and built in ancient times in front of a house, a temple, a synagogue or a church.

AUGUSTINE (St). Father and Doctor of the Church (354-430), bishop of Hippo (396-430), *p.* 29; *fig.* 239-241.

BABYLAS (St). Bishop of Antioch, martyred in 250, *p.* 51.

BACCHUS (St). Martyred with St Sergius at Resafa, Syria, about 303, *p.* 47, 186, 189; *fig.* 201.

BAGAWAT. Group of Early Christian hypogea and shrines in an Egyptian oasis, *p.* 38.

BAGHDAD. City in Mesopotamia (Iraq), *p.* 59, 337, 340.

BAKIRHA. Ancient town in North Syria, in the Jebel Barisha, *p.* 42; *fig.* 42.

BARA (EL-). Ancient town in North Syria, south-west of Aleppo, *p.* 42.

BARABBAS. The prisoner released by Pilate instead of Christ (Matthew XXVII), *fig.* 232.

BARBERINI IVORY, *p.* 278; *fig.* 319, 322.

BARLAAM (St). Martyr, *p.* 101.

BARLETTA STATUE. Colossal bronze statue of the Emperor Valentinian I (364-374) at Barletta (province of Bari), Italy, *p.* 220; *fig.* 247.

BASIL (St). Father and Doctor of the Church (c. 330-379), bishop of Caesarea in Cappadocia (370-379), *p.* 101.

BATNA. Town in Algeria, some 50 miles south of Constantine, *p.* 29.

BAWIT. Early Christian monastery in Egypt, *p.* 38, 39, 168, 172-174, 180, 186, 189, 236, 266, 273, 336; *fig.* 184, 186, 187, 189, 192, 193, 199, 204, 278, 303.

BEHNAM. Site with ancient ruins in Syria, *p.* 60.

BEIT ALPHA. Synagogue discovered in 1928, six miles south of Bethshan (Palestine), *p.* 57, 58, 115; *fig.* 122.

BEL. Mesopotamian god corresponding to the Semitic god Baal, *p.* 263.

BELL (Miss Gertrude). English author and traveller (1868-1926), *p.* 62.

BETHLEHEM. Town in Palestine just south of Jerusalem, the early home of David and the birthplace of Christ, *p.* 53, 54, 59, 99, 339.

BIANCHI-BANDINELLI (Ranuccio). Italian archaeologist and art critic (born 1900), *p.* 185, 196, 217.

BIN BIR KILISSEH. The 'Valley of the Thousand and One Churches' at the foot of the Kara Dagh range, 10 miles from Karaman (Turkey), *p.* 67, 71; *fig.* 65-67, 70.

BITHYNIA. Ancient kingdom in north-western Asia Minor, along the Sea of Marmara and the Black Sea, *p.* 232.

BIZZOS. Personage interred near the cathedral of Ruweiha (Syria), *p.* 44.

BOBBIO. Town in Emilia (Central Italy), famous for the monastery founded there by St Columban in 612, *p.* 313.

BOSRA. Ruined village about 80 miles south of Damascus (Syria), once a populous city and seat of a bishopric, *p.* 52.

BRAD. Ruined village in Syria, 12 miles from Deir Seman, *p.* 53.

BRESCIA. City in Lombardy (northern Italy), *p.* 286, 287.

BUDRUM, in Greek HIERAPOLIS. Ancient town in Cilicia, six miles north-west of the ruins of Laodicea (present-day Ecirli, in Turkey), *p.* 62.

BYZANTIUM, see CONSTANTINOPLE.

CAMBRIDGE GOSPELS, *p.* 212; *fig.* 239-241.

CAMPANIA. Region in southern Italy (capital Naples), *p.* 25.

CANA. Village in Galilee where Christ performed His first miracle (John II), *fig.* 130.

CAPERNAUM. Town in Palestine, on the north-west shore of the Sea of Galilee, *p.* 57.

CAPPADOCIA. Ancient region of central Asia Minor (now Turkey), *p.* 61, 182.

CAROLINGIANS. Dynasty of French kings (751-987), *p.* 275.

CARTHAGE. Ancient city of North Africa, near Tunis, *p.* 29, 121, 170, 217; *fig.* 183.

CARTHAGE-DERMESH. Ruins about a third of a mile from Carthage, on the Mediterranean coast, 11 miles from Tunis, *p.* 29.

CASTELSEPRIO. Locality about 20 miles north of Milan, near Castiglione d'Olona, where an important group of early medieval frescoes were discovered in the church in 1944, *p.* 340.

CAVALLINI (Pietro). Roman painter and mosaicist (1250-1330), *p.* 101.

CHOISY (Auguste). French engineer and archaeologist (1841-1909), *p.* 85.

CHOSROES I. Sassanid king of Persia (531-579), *fig.* 382.

CILICIA. Ancient region of south-east Asia Minor, on the Mediterranean, *p.* 61, 62, 71.

CIMIEZ. Ancient locality on the French Riviera, now part of Nice, *p.* 28.

CIMITILE. Small town in southern Italy, near Nola, about 20 miles from Naples, *p.* 25.

CIVIDALE DEL FRIULI. Town north-east of Venice, *p.* 340.

CLAIR. Bishop of Eauze (died 510) in south-western France, *p.* 260.

CLASSIS. Port on the Adriatic, 3 miles frum Ravenna, *p.* 153.

CLEMENT OF ALEXANDRIA (St). Father of the Church (c. 150-215), *p.* 202.

CODEX SINOPENSIS, see SINOPE.

COLLUTHUS (St). Martyr in the Thebaid, *fig.* 185.

CONQUES. Village in south-central France, near Rodez, with a fine Romanesque church, *p.* 226.

CONSTANTINE I. Roman Emperor (306-337), founder of Constantinople, *p.* 6, 11, 12, 51, 53, 60, 81, 82, 102, 219, 339.

CONSTANTIA or CONSTANTINA. Daughter of Constantine I (c. 318-354), *p.* 11.

CONSTANTINOPLE. City built from 324 to 330 by Constantine I on the site of ancient Byzantium, *p.* 2, 27, 35, 38, 54, 60, 71, 80-99, 102, 105, 128, 172, 219, 246, 248, 269, 278, 289, 293, 337, 338, 340; *fig.* 255-262, 285, 287, 310, 318-322.
*Churches:*
Holy Apostles (on the site of the present-day mosque of Fatih), *p.* 80, 81, 96.
SS. Carpos and Babylas, *p.* 82.
St Irene, *p.* 81, 98.
St John of Studion, *p.* 84, 86.
St Mary Chalcoprateia, *p.* 81.
St Mary of the Blachernae, *p.* 81.
SS. Sergius and Bacchus, *fig.* 84, 96.
St Sophia, *p.* 81, 82, 272, 320, 334; *fig.* 1, 87, 91-103, 312, 314.
*Cisterns:*
Bin Bir Derek, *p.* 83, 273.
Yeri Batan Serai, *p.* 83.
*Obelisk:*
Obelisk of Theodosius, *p.* 319; *fig.* 245, 246.
*Palace:*
Great Palace of the Emperors, *p.* 102, 105, 129; *fig.* 105-108.
*Walls:*
Wall of Theodosius II, *p.* 84; *fig.* 88-90.

CONSTANTIUS II. Roman Emperor (357-361), son of Constantine, *p.* 81, 298; *fig.* 347.

CORINTH. City in Greece, *p.* 74.

COTTON (Sir Robert Bruce). English antiquary (1571-1631), *p.* 202; *fig.* 224.

CRUX ANSATA. Cross in the shape of the ankh (q.v.), *p.* 172.

CTESIPHON. City in Mesopotamia, *p.* 59, 61.

CYBELE. Roman goddess whose cult originated in Asia Minor, *p.* 214.

CYPRUS. Island in the Eastern Mediterranean, *p.* 53, 135, 173, 178, 236; *fig.* 144.

**GEORGIA.** Ancient land of Transcaucasia, *p.* 337.

**GERASA.** City in Palestine, east of the Jordan, *p.* 53, 57, 112, 125; *fig.* 57-59.

**GERVASIUS (St).** Martyred in Milan with his brother St Protasius, *p.* 15.

**GETHSEMANE.** Garden east of the Kidron on the lower slope of the Mount of Olives, near Jerusalem, scene of the agony and betrayal of Christ, *p.* 24.

**GOLGOTHA.** Hill outside the walls of Jerusalem where Christ was crucified, *p.* 59.

**GOLIATH.** Philistine giant slain by David with a sling (I Samuel XVII), *p.* 234; *fig.* 268.

**GREGORY OF NYSSA (St).** Father of the Eastern Church (335-395), brother of St Basil and bishop of Nyssa in Cappadocia, *p.* 101.

**GUYER (S.).** Swiss archaeologist, *p.* 62, 69.

**HABAKKUK.** Old Testament prophet, *p.* 131; *fig.* 141.

**HAH.** Locality in northern Mesopotamia, *p.* 61.

**HAMMEH (EL-).** Village in Palestine on the right bank of the Yarmuk, 4 miles from Samakh, *p.* 58.

**HARPOCRATES or HORUS.** Egyptian god, *fig.* 190.

**HATHOR.** Egyptian goddess, *p.* 35.

**HELENA (St).** Mother of Constantine I (c. 250-330), *p.* 11, 53.

**HENSHIR GOUSSA.** Ancient town in North Africa, *p.* 29; *fig.* 403.

**HENSHIR RHIRIA.** Locality in Tunisia, *p.* 29, 30.

**HEPTAPEGON, see TABGHA (EL-).**

**HERACLIUS I.** Emperor of the East (610-641), *p.* 189, 298.

**HERCULES or HERACLES.** Legendary Greek hero, *p.* 189, 239; *fig.* 269.

**HERMONTHIS.** Ancient city of Upper Egypt (present-day Armant), on the left bank of the Nile, 15 miles from Luxor, *p.* 38.

**HERMOPOLIS.** Ancient city of Upper Egypt (present-day Ashmunein), 4 miles from Roda, *p.* 38, 200.

**HEROD I.** King of the Jews (1st century B.C.), *p.* 148.

**HEROD ANTIPAS.** Tetrarch of Galilee, *p.* 203; *fig.* 227.

**HEROON.** Sepulchral monument built in the form of a small temple, *p.* 80.

**HERZFELD (Ernst).** German orientalist and archaeologist (1879-1948), *p.* 62.

**HESTIA.** Greek goddess of the hearth, *p.* 326.

**HIERAPOLIS, see BUDRUM.**

**HIEROPOLIS.** Ancient town in Phrygia (Asia Minor), *p.* 62.

**HILANI.** Architectural element of Syro-Hittite palaces: a two-storied building with portico, approached by a flight of steps, *p.* 71.

**HIPPO.** Ancient city of Numidia (North Africa), seat of the bishopric of St Augustine, *p.* 29, 33.

**HIRAH (AL-).** Ancient town in Iraq, south-east of An-Najaf, *p.* 59.

**HOMS or EMESA.** Town in Syria, *p.* 316; *fig.* 366, 367.

**HONORIUS.** Second son of Theodosius I and Emperor of the West (395-423), *p.* 17.

**HOSN (EL-).** Ancient town in Syria (present-day Niha, in Lebanon), 20 miles south-west of Baalbek, *p.* 42.

**IBRIHIN or IBRIM.** Village in Upper Egypt on the left bank of the Nile, about 14 miles south of Aswan, *p.* 38.

**ILIAD.** Homeric epic, *p.* 196; *fig.* 213.

**ILLYRICUM or ILLYRIA.** Roman province on the northern coast of the Adriatic, *p.* 2.

**IMAGO CLIPEATA.** Portrait engraved or painted on a *clipeus* (i.e. a shield or round metal plate), *p.* 167.

**IR-RUHAIYEH.** Place in north-eastern Syria, south of Kasr Ibn Wardan, *p.* 42.

**ISAAC.** Old Testament patriarch, *p.* 156; *fig.* 200.

**ISAIAH.** Hebrew prophet, *p.* 115.

**ISAURIA.** Region in Asia Minor (south-central Turkey), north of the Taurus range, *p.* 61, 66, 71.

**ISIDOROS OF MILETUS.** Byzantine architect (5th-6th century), one of the builders of St Sophia, Constantinople, *p.* 86.

**ISIDOROS THE YOUNGER.** Byzantine architect (6th century), nephew of Isidoros of Miletus, who rebuilt the dome of St Sophia (558), *p.* 47.

**ISIS.** Egyptian goddess, *fig.* 190.

**ISTANBUL, see CONSTANTINOPLE.**

**IUNCA.** Place in Tunisia, *p.* 115.

**JACOB.** Old Testament patriarch, *p.* 145; *fig.* 207, 221, 337.

**JAMES OF NISIBIS (St).** Bishop of Nisibis in northern Mesopotamia (270-338), *p.* 60.

**JEMILA.** Ancient Roman town in Algeria, some 30 miles from Setif, *p.* 30; *fig.* 27, 28.

**JERICHO.** Ancient town in Palestine in the Jordan valley, *p.* 57, 58, 146; *fig.* 160, 226.

**JERPHANION (Guillaume de).** French archaeologist (1877-1948), *p.* 289.

**JERUSALEM.** Ancient capital of Judaea, then of Palestine, *p.* 53, 59-61, 204, 269, 312, 339; *fig.* 117, 228.
Church of the Ascension, *p.* 54.
Church of the Holy Sepulchre, *p.* 12.
Church of St John the Baptist, *p.* 60.
Mount of Olives, *p.* 54, 59.

**JOHN THE BAPTIST (St).** The 'forerunner' of Christ in the Gospels, son of Zacharias and Elizabeth, *p.* 231, 232, 289; *fig.* 262, 340.

**JOHN THE EVANGELIST (St).** One of the twelve Apostles, *p.* 73, 320.

**JORDAN.** River in Palestine, *p.* 59, 131, 231.

**JOSEPH.** Favourite son of Jacob whose story is told in Genesis, *p.* 289; *fig.* 267, 336, 337.

**JOSHUA.** Successor of Moses as leader of the Hebrews and judge of Israel, *p.* 59, 145.

**JUDE (St).** One of the twelve apostles, *fig.* 131.

**JULIANA ANICIA.** Byzantine patrician lady, *p.* 197; *fig.* 214.

**JULITTA (St).** Martyred with her child St Cyr (q.v.), *p.* 183.

**JUNIUS BASSUS.** Roman consul in 317, *p.* 248.

**JUSTIN II.** East Roman Emperor (565-578), *p.* 306; *fig.* 359.

**JUSTINIAN I.** East Roman Emperor (527-565), *p.* 1, 47, 53, 54, 57, 60, 81-83, 85, 86, 96, 99, 153, 157, 278, 290, 298, 334, 337, 338; *fig.* 170, 171.

**KABR HIRAM.** Ancient place in Phoenicia, *p.* 112; *fig.* 116.

**KALAT KALOTA.** Ancient town in North Syria, some 20 miles north-west of Aleppo, *p.* 53; *fig.* 39, 41.

**KALAT SEMAN.** Monastery in Syria, built round the pillar of St Simeon Stylites, *p.* 27, 48, 51, 53, 269 ; *fig.* 49-51, 53-56.

**KALB LAUZEH.** Village in Syria, *p.* 44, 51, 53, 264; *fig.* 43-48.

**KANAKARIA.** Locality in Cyprus, *p.* 135.

KANYTELIDEIS. Monastery in Cilicia (Turkey), near Korykos, *p.* 62.

KAOUSSIEH. Suburb of Antioch, *p.* 51, 53, 69.

KARA DAGH. Mountain range in Asia Minor, between Karaman and Konya, *p.* 61, 67.

KARANIS. Town in the Fayum, Lower Egypt, *p.* 39, 186; *fig.* 190.

KARNAK. Town in Upper Egypt, near Luxor, *p.* 38.

KARTAMIN. Monastery in northern Mesopotamia, *p.* 48, 60, 61.

KASR IBN WARDAN. Ruined village in North Syria, *p.* 47, 53, 99.

KFER. Village in Syria, *p.* 42; *fig.* 38.

KHARAB SHEMS. Ancient town in North Syria, *p.* 42.

KHERBET BOU ADDOUFAN. Ruined village in Algeria, near Setif, *p.* 54.

KHIRBET EL-MAFJAR. Site in Transjordan, *p.* 269, 289.

KHODJA KALESSI, see ALAHAN.

KITI. Place in Cyprus, near Larnaca, *p.* 135; *fig.* 144.

KÖHLER (Wilhelm). German art historian, *p.* 101.

KONJUH. Locality near Kumanovo (Yugoslavia), *p.* 98.

KORYKOS. Ancient town of Cilicia (Turkey), *p.* 61, 62, 64, 269; *fig.* 71.

KOUCHAKJI. American collector, *p.* 313.

LAMPADII. Roman senatorial family, *p.* 282.

LANCKORONSKI (Count). Nineteenth-century traveller and explorer in Asia Minor, *p.* 66.

LASSUS (Jean). Contemporary French archaeologist, *p.* 47.

LAURA. Term used in the Eastern Church to designate a monastery, *p.* 33.

LEDA. Wooed by Zeus in the form of a swan, *p.* 239.

LEO I (St). Pope (440-461), *p.* 1, 101.

LESBOS. Greek island in the Aegean Sea, *p.* 76.

LIBERIUS (St). Pope (352-356), *p.* 9.

LOMBARDS. Germanic peoples who founded several states in Italy from the 6th to the 8th century, *p.* 275.

LOT. Nephew of Abraham, *fig.* 156.

LUKE (St). Evangelist, *p.* 167, 212; *fig.* 177, 239.

MACEDONIAN DYNASTY. Dynasty of Byzantine emperors from Basil I (867) to Michael VI (1056-1057), *p.* 337.

MADABA. Town in Transjordan, *p.* 112, 115; *fig.* 117, 120.

MAGI. The three Wise Men of the East who came to worship the Christ Child (Matthew II), *p.* 172, 234.

MAGNUS (Flavius Moschianus Probus). Consul in 518, *fig.* 326.

MAMRE. Beneath the sacred oak of Mamre the three angels appeared to Abraham, *p.* 53, 59.

MARDIN. Small town in Turkey, *p.* 211.

MAREOTIS (Lake). Lagoon in the Nile Delta, *p.* 38.

MARIANA. Site in Corsica, *p.* 27.

MARSEILLES. Second largest city and chief Mediterranean port of France (ancient Massilia), *p.* 25.

MARTYRIUM. Shrine built over the relics of a martyr or on a holy place, *p.* 11, 12, 15, 41, 48, 51, 338.

MARY OF EGYPT (St). Saint of the Thebaid, *fig.* 185.

MATRONA (St). Coenobite at Capua (5th century), *p.* 117; *fig.* 127.

MATTHIAS. Apostle chosen by lot to replace Judas Iscariot (Acts I), *p.* 210.

MAXIMIAN (St). Archbishop of Ravenna (546-556), *p.* 20, 289, 290, 293; *fig.* 334-337.

MECCA. Holy city of the Moslems, in Arabia, *p.* 339.

MEGAW (A.H.S.). Contemporary English archaeologist, *p.* 38.

MELCHIZEDEK. Priest and king of Salem who blessed Abraham (Genesis XIV), *p.* 156; *fig.* 155, 168.

MELEAGER. Hero in Greek mythology, *p.* 298.

MELITENE. Ancient city of Cappadocia, *p.* 59, 61.

MEMORIA. Shrine, chapel or church erected in memory of a martyr or confessor.

MENAS (St). Martyred under Diocletian, *p.* 295; *fig.* 342.

MENAS. Abbot of the monastery of Bawit, *fig.* 204.

MERIAMLIK. Ancient city of Cilicia, *p.* 61, 62, 64.

MERIDA. Town in south-western Spain (Estremadura), *p.* 30.

MERSEBURG. Town in East Germany, south of Halle, *p.* 194.

MESOPOTAMIA. Ancient land between the Tigris and Euphrates (now Iraq), *p.* 1, 59-61.

MICHIGAN (University of). Excavations at Karanis, Egypt, *p.* 39, 186.

MIDIDI. Ancient town in North Africa, *p.* 29; *fig.* 407.

MILAN. City in northern Italy (ancient Mediolanum), *p.* 2, 15, 16, 69, 102, 131, 260, 278, 306.
Sant'Ambrogio, *p.* 15, 121, 164; *fig.* 128, 175.
Santi Apostoli, *fig.* 401.
San Lorenzo, *p.* 15, 16, 102, 131, 165; *fig.* 174.
San Nazzaro, *p.* 16.; *fig.* 361
San Simpliciano, *p.* 16.
Santa Tecla, *p.* 76.
San Vittore (in Sant'Ambrogio), *p.* 121; *fig.* 128, 175.

MILETUS. Ancient city on the west coast of Asia Minor, *p.* 73, 85, 98.

MISSORIUM. Large dish for the service of the table, *p.* 298.

MOALLAKA (EL-). Coptic church in Old Cairo, *p.* 245.

MONZA. City in Lombardy, a few miles north of Milan, *p.* 313.

MORSOTT. Village in Algeria, *p.* 29.

MOSES. Lawgiver, prophet and leader of the Israelites, *p.* 38, 54, 59, 132, 145, 156, 214; *fig.* 159, 196.

MOUASSAT (EL-). Locality in Tunisia, *p.* 112.

MUSTAIR. Village in the Grisons (Switzerland), *p.* 340.

NABATAEAN KINGDOM. Ancient kingdom to the east and south-east of Palestine (capital Petra), *p.* 263.

NAHOR. Ancient town near Haran (Mesopotamia), *fig.* 219.

NAPLES. City of southern Italy, capital of Campania, *p.* 25.
Baptistery of San Giovanni in Fonte, *p.* 167; *fig.* 129, 130.

NEBO (Mount). Mountain in Transjordan where the tomb of Moses is venerated, *p.* 38, 54, 59, 112, 115.

NEBUCHADNEZZAR. King of Babylonia (605-562 B.C.) who captured Jerusalem (597), then destroyed it (586), *p.* 172.

NEON. Bishop of Ravenna (451-460), *p.* 19.

NERO. Roman Emperor (54-68), *p.* 197.

NICOMACHI. Roman senatorial family, *p.* 282.

# Bibliography

## GENERAL WORKS

### 1. Handbooks, Dictionaries, Bibliography.

L. BRÉHIER, *L'Art chrétien. Son développement iconographique, des origines jusqu'à nos jours*, Paris, 1918; 2nd edition, 1928.

L. BRÉHIER, *L'Art byzantin*, Paris, 1924.

F. CABROL, H. LECLERCQ AND H.-I. MARROU, *Dictionnaire d'archéologie chrétienne et de liturgie*, 15 vols., Paris, 1908-1953.

O. M. DALTON, *Byzantine Art and Archaeology*, Oxford, 1911.

O. M. DALTON, *East Christian Art. A Survey of the Monuments*, Oxford, 1925.

C. DIEHL, *Manuel d'art byzantin*, Paris, 1910; 2nd edition, 1925-1926, 2 vols.

F. J. DÖLGER, *Antike und Christentum*, 6 vols., Münster (Westphalia), 1929-1950.
Surveys of monuments and of writings on early Christianity and its art. *Cf.* Klauser.

R. GARRUCCI, *Storia dell'arte cristiana nei primi otto secoli della Chiesa*, 6 vols., Prato, 1873-1880.

J. HUBERT, *L'Art pré-roman*, Paris, 1938.

J. HUBERT, *L'Architecture religieuse du haut Moyen Age en France*, Paris, 1951. Collection of plans.

K. M. KAUFMANN, *Handbuch der christlichen Archäologie*, Paderborn, 3rd edition, 1922.

T. KLAUSER, *Reallexikon für Antike und Christentum* (in course of publication since 1950, 4 vols. available to date).

F. X. KRAUS, *Geschichte der christlichen Kunst*, I, Freiburg-im-Breisgau, 1896.

H. LECLERCQ, *Manuel d'archéologie chrétienne depuis les origines jusqu'au VIIIᵉ siècle*, 2 vols., Paris, 1907.

*Lexikon für Theologie und Kirche*, edited by M. BUCHBERGER, 10 vols., Freiburg-im-Breisgau, 1930-1938.

G. MILLET, *L'Art byzantin*, in André Michel, *Histoire de l'art*, I, Paris, 1905.

C. R. MOREY, *Early Christian Art. An Outline of the Evolution of Style and Iconography in Sculpture and Painting from Antiquity to the Eighth Century*, Princeton, 1941.

W. NEUSS, *Die Kunst der alten Christen*, Augsburg, 1926.

H. PEIRCE and R. TYLER, *Byzantine Art*, London, 1926; *L'Art byzantin*, 2 vols., Paris, 1932-1934.

J. PIJOAN, *Arte cristiano primitivo. Arte bizantino*, in Summa Artis. *Historia general del Arte*, VII, Madrid, 1940; 3rd edition, 1954.

*Reallexikon für Antike und Christentum*, edited by T. Klauser. *Cf.* Klauser.

*Reallexikon zur deutschen Kunstgeschichte*, founded by O. Schmitt, edited by L. H. Heydenreich (in course of publication since 1937).

D. T. RICE, *The Beginnings of Christian Art*, London, 1957.

J. P. RICHTER, *Quellen der byzantinischen Kunstgeschichte*, Vienna, 1897.
The source-books of Unger and Richter complement each other. They bring together extracts from texts relating to the monuments of Constantinople (in German translation).

A. RIEGL, *Die spätrömische Kunstindustrie nach den Funden in Oesterreich*, 2 vols., Vienna, 1901-1923.

A. RUMPF, *Stilphasen der spätantiken Kunst*, Cologne, 1957.

H. SCHLUNK, *Kunst der Spätantike im Mittelmeerraum*, Berlin, 1939.
Collections of the Kaiser Friedrich Museum, Berlin.

J. STRZYGOWSKI, *Der Ursprung der christlichen Kirchenkunst*, Leipzig, 1920; *Origin of Christian Church Art*, Oxford, 1923.

L. VON SYBEL, *Christliche Antike, Einführung in die altchristliche Kunst*, 2 vols., Marburg, 1906-1909.

P. TOESCA, *Storia dell'arte italiana : I, Il Medioevo*, Turin, 1927.

W. UNGER, *Quellen der byzantinischen Kunstgeschichte*, Vienna, 1878.

A. VENTURI, *Storia dell'arte italiana*, 22 vols., Milan, 1901-1936.

W. F. VOLBACH and M. HIRMER, *Frühchristliche Kunst. Die Kunst der Spätantike in West- und Ostrom*, Munich, 1958.
The English edition of this book (*Early Christian Art*, Thames and Hudson, London) is to be recommended for its wealth of illustrations and its concise, informative text.

K. WESSEL, *Reallexikon zur byzantinischen Kunst*, Stuttgart, 1963.

O. WULFF, *Altchristliche und byzantinische Kunst*, in Handbuch der Kunstwissenschaft, 2 vols., Berlin, 1914-1915.

Bibliographical information is given regularly in the following periodicals:
*Bonner Jahrbücher,*
*Byzantinische Zeitschrift,*
*Revue des études byzantines,*
*Rivista di archeologia cristiana,*
*Theologische Literaturzeitung.*

For the war years and the post-war period up to 1952, a bibliographical survey with commentaries is given by A. M. SCHNEIDER, in: F. DÖLGER and A. M. SCHNEIDER, *Byzanz*, Berne, 1952 (this bibliography covers all Early Christian art).

### 2. Catalogues and Inventories.

*Actes du Vᵉ Congrès international d'archéologie chrétienne à Aix-en-Provence, 1954*, Vatican City, 1957.
Miscellany of articles constituting an inventory of Early Christian monuments in all countries.

*Atti del III (and del IV) Congresso internazionale di archeologia cristiana* (in 1932 and 1938), Vatican City, 1934-1940.
Same remark as for the previous item.

R. DE LA BLANCHÈRE and P. GAUCKLER, *Catalogue du musée Alaoui* [Carthage], 2 vols., Paris, 1891-1910.

O. M. DALTON, *Catalogue of Early Christian Antiquities, ...in the British Museum*, London, 1901; *A Guide to the Early Christian and Byzantine Antiquities*, British Museum, London, 1921.

C. DIEHL, *L'Afrique byzantine. Histoire de la domination byzantine en Afrique (533-709)*, Paris, 1896.

*Early Christian and Byzantine Art at the Walters Art Gallery*, Baltimore, 1947.
Illustrated catalogue of the largest exhibition ever held of Early Christian and Byzantine works in American collections.

*Forschungen in Ephesos*, IV, fasc. 1-3, Vienna, 1932, 1937 and 1951.
Description of the great Christian foundations of Ephesus (excavated by the Austrian Archaeological Institute), which number among the most important monuments of Early Christian and Byzantine art: episcopal church of the Mother of God, funerary church of the Seven Sleepers, and the martyry church of St John.

S. GSELL, *Les Monuments antiques de l'Algérie*, 2 vols., Paris, 1901.

S. GSELL, *Atlas archéologique de l'Algérie*, Paris, 1912.

*Inventaire des mosaïques de la Gaule et de l'Afrique :* Vol. II : *Afrique proconsulaire (Tunisie)*, by P. GAUCKLER, Paris, 1910.
Vol. II, Supplement: *Afrique proconsulaire (Tunisie)*, by A. MERLIN, Paris, 1915.
Vol. III : *Afrique proconsulaire, Numidie, Maurétanie (Algérie)*, by F.-G. de PACHTÈRE, Paris, 1911.
See under the authors' names.

S. LAMBROS, *Empereurs byzantins. Catalogue illustré de la collection de portraits*, Athens, 1911.

G. MENDEL, *Catalogue des sculptures grecques, romaines et byzantines du musée de Brousse*, Athens, 1908.

G. MENDEL, *Catalogue des sculptures grecques, romaines et byzantines des musées impériaux ottomans*, I-III, Constantinople, 1912-1914.

M. C. ROSS, *Catalogue of the Byzantine and Early Medieval Antiquities in the Dumbarton Oaks Collection*, Washington, I, 1962; II, 1965.

W. F. VOLBACH, G. SALLES and G. DUTUIT, *Art byzantin*, Paris (1933). Album of fine reproductions of objects shown at the Byzantine exhibition of 1931 in Paris.

O. WULFF, *Beschreibung der Bildwerke der christlichen Epochen*, III, Berlin, Königliches Museum, 1909-1910.

*Cf.* also the catalogues of works given below in the special bibliographies, under: Ivories, Miniatures, Mosaics, Goldsmiths' Work, Painting, Sculpture, Textiles.

### 3. Travellers' Accounts

O. BENNDORF and G. NIEMANN, *Reisen in Lykien und Karien*, Vienna, 1884.

N. P. KONDAKOV, *Archaeological Journey to Syria* (in Russian), St. Petersburg, 1904.

K. G. LANCKORONSKI, *Städte Pamphyliens und Pisidiens*, Vienna, 1890-1892.

A. MATTERN, *A travers les villes mortes de Haute-Syrie*, Mélanges de l'université Saint-Joseph, XVII, Beirut, 1934.

E. von PETERSEN and F. von LASCHAN, *Reisen in Lykien*, Vienna, 1889.

A. POIDEBARD, *La Trace de Rome dans le désert de Syrie. Le limes de Trajan à la conquête arabe. Recherches aériennes.* Text and atlas. Bibliothèque du Haut-Commissariat de Syrie et du Liban, XXIII, Paris, 1934.

### 4. Monuments by Countries.

*Asia Minor.*

E. HERZFELD and S. GUYER, *Monumenta Asiae Minoris Antiqua*, II-III, The Manchester University Press, 1928-1931.

*Austria.*

R. NOLL, *Frühes Christentum in Oesterreich*, Vienna, 1954.

*Bulgaria.*

V. IVANOVA, *Anciennes Églises et couvents en terres bulgares*, in *Annuaire du Musée national bulgare pour 1922-1925* (in Bulgarian with French résumé).

*Egypt.*

L. ANTONINI, in *Aegyptus*, 20, 1940. Papyrus texts relating to monuments.

W. DE BOCK, *Matériaux pour servir à l'archéologie de l'Égypte chrétienne*, 2 vols., St. Petersburg, 1901.

J. CLÉDAT, *Le Monastère et la Nécropole de Baouît*, in Mémoires publiés par les membres de l'Institut français d'archéologie orientale, XII, XVI, XXXIX, Cairo, 1904, 1906, 1916.

U. MONNERET DE VILLARD, in *Atti del IV Congresso di archeologia cristiana*, Vatican City, 1940, and in *Orientalia christiana periodica*, VII, 1941.

J. E. QUIBELL, *Excavations at Saqqara (1908-1909, 1909-1910)*, Cairo, 1912.

K. WESSEL, *Coptic Art*, London 1966.

*England.*

G. B. BROWN, *The Early Arts in England*, 6 vols., London, 1903.

A. W. CLAPHAM, *English Romanesque Architecture before the Conquest*, Oxford, 1930.

T. D. KENDRICK, *Anglo-Saxon Art to A.D. 900*, London, 1938.

F. SAXL and R. WITTKOWER *British Art and the Mediterranean*, Oxford, 1947.

*France.*

J. BOUBE, *Les Sarcophages paléochrétiens de Martres-Tolosane*, in *Cahiers archéologiques*, IX, 1957, pp. 33-72.

L. BRÉHIER, *L'Art en France, des invasions barbares à l'époque romane*, Paris, 1930.

J. HUBERT, *L'Art pré-roman*, Paris, 1938.

*Greece.*

E. DYGGVE, in *Dissertationes Pannonicae*, series II, Budapest, 1941, and in *Rivista di archeologia cristiana* XVII, 1940. St George, Salonica.

E. DYGGVE, F. POULSEN and K. RHOMAIOS, *Das Heroon von Kalydon*, Copenhagen, 1934. A Hellenistic heroon.

G. SOTIRIOU, *The Early Christian Churches of Greece* (in Greek), Athens, 1931.

G. SOTIRIOU, *Christian and Byzantine Archaeology* (in Greek), Athens, 1942.

*Italy.*

E. BERTAUX, *L'Art dans l'Italie méridionale. De la fin de l'Empire romain à la conquête de Charles d'Anjou*, Paris, 1904 [1903].

G. BRUSIN and P. L. ZOVATTO, *Monumenti paleocristiani di Aquileia e di Grado*, Udine, 1957.

A. COLASANTI, *L'Arte bizantina in Italia*, Milan, 1912.

Milan :

E. ARSLAN, in *Archivio storico lombardo*, new series, X, 1947, pp. 5 ff., and in *Rivista di archeologia cristiana*, XXIII-XXIV, 1947-1948, pp. 367-382. On S. Simpliciano, Milan.

U. MONNERET DE VILLARD, in *Orientalia christiana periodica*, XII, 1946, pp. 374-380. On S. Lorenzo, Milan.

E. VILLA, *La basilica degli Apostoli* [in Milan], in *Ambrosius*, 1942.

Naples :

H. ACHELIS, *Die Katakomben von Neapel*, Leipzig, 1936.

Nola :

C. CHIERICI, in *Rivista di archeologia cristiana*, XV, 1938, pp. 59-72.

R. G. GOLDSCHMIDT, *Paulinus' Churches at Nola*, Amsterdam, 1940. After the writings of St Paulinus.

Ravenna :

F. W. DEICHMANN, *Frühchristliche Bauten und Mosaiken in Ravenna*, Baden-Baden, 1958.

C. RICCI, *Guida di Ravenna*, Bologna, new edition, 1923.

Rome :

C. CECCHELLI, *La vita di Roma nel Medio Evo*, Rome, 1951-1952. A wealth of information on the arts and crafts in Rome both in medieval and pre-medieval times.

F. W. DEICHMANN, *Frühchristliche Kirchen in Rom*, Basel, 1948.

W. DE GRÜNEISEN, *Sainte-Marie-Antique*, Rome, 1911.

O. MARUCCHI, *Le catacombe romane*, Rome, 1933.

P. STYGER, *Die römischen Katakomben*, Berlin, 1933. One of the few books on the catacombs which have filled in the historical background and advanced the study of the subject.

*Palestine.*

J. W. CROWFOOT, *Early Churches in Palestine*, Schweich Lectures 1937, London, 1941.

*Russia.*

N. KONDAKOV and I. TOLSTOJ, *Antiquités russes par les œuvres d'art*, St. Petersburg, 1905 ff. Volumes III to V deal with the period that concerns us here.

*Spain.*

P. BATTLE HUGUET, *Arte paleocristiano*, in *Ars Hispaniae*, II, Madrid, 1947.

H. SCHLUNK, in *Cronica del III Congreso Archeologico del Sudesto Espanol*, Murcia, 1942.
On a martyrium near Albera.

H. SCHLUNK, *Arte visigodo...*, in *Ars Hispaniae*, II, Madrid, 1947.

*Syria.*

R. DUSSAUD, P. DESCHAMPS and H. SEYRIG, *La Syrie antique et médiévale illustrée*, Bibliothèque archéologique du Haut-Commissariat de Syrie et du Liban, XVII, Paris, 1931.

J. KOLLWITZ, in *Neue deutsche Ausgrabungen im Mittelmeergebiet und im Vorderen Orient*, Berlin, 1959.

J. MATTERN, R. MOUTERDE and A. BEAULIEU, *Deir Solaib : I, Les Deux Églises; II, Mosaïques prophylactiques*, in Mélanges de l'université Saint-Joseph, XXII, Beirut, 1939.

E. RENAN, *Mission de Phénicie*, 2 vols., Paris, 1865-1874.

J. SAUVAGET, *Les Monuments historiques de Damas*, Beirut, 1932, and Paris, 1937.

G. TCHALENKO, *Villages antiques de la Syrie du Nord, la région de Bélus à l'époque romaine*, 3 vols., Paris, 1957-1959.

*Tripolitania.*

J. B. WARD PERKINS and R. G. GOODCHILD, *The Christian Antiquities of Tripolitania*, in *Archaeologia*, XCV, Oxford, 1953, pp. 1-82.

*Turkey.*

H. ROTT and K. MICHEL, *Kleinasiatische Denkmäler*, Leipzig, 1908.

Constantinople :

G. BRETT and others, *The Great Palace of the Byzantine Emperors*, I-II, London, 1947.

R. DEMANGEL and E. MAMBOURY, *Le Quartier des Manganes et la première région de Constantinople*, Paris, 1939.

R. JANIN, *Constantinople byzantine. Développement urbain et répertoire topographique*, Paris, 1950.

B. MEYER-PLATH and A. M. SCHNEIDER, *Die Landmauer von Konstantinopel*, Berlin, 1943.

MUZAFFER and A. RAMAZANOGLOU, *L'Ensemble de Sainte-Irène et des diverses Sainte-Sophie*, Istanbul, 1946.

D. T. RICE, *The Great Palace of the Byzantine Emperors, Second Report*, Edinburgh, 1958.

A. M. SCHNEIDER, *Byzanz*, Berlin, 1936.

A. M. SCHNEIDER, in *Archäologischer Anzeiger*, 1941, pp. 296-318, and 1943, pp. 251-256, and in *Byzantinische Zeitschrift*, 42, 1942, pp. 178-185.

*Yugoslavia.*

E. KITZINGER, in *Dumbarton Oaks Papers*, III, 1946, pp. 81-162.
On the monuments at Stobi.

D. J. MANO-ZISSI, in *Starinar*, V-VI, Belgrade, 1956, pp. 155-180.
On the monuments at Tsaritchin Grad.

M. VASIC, *Architecture and Sculpture in Dalmatia* (in Serbian), Belgrade, 1922.

Konjuh :

S. RADOJCIC, *The Church of Konjuh*, in Proceedings of the Institute of Byzantine Studies (Serbian Academy of Sciences). I, 1952, pp. 148-168.

Salona :

E. DYGGVE, *History of Salonitan Christianity*, Oslo, 1951.

Tsaritchin Grad :

V. PETKOVIC and A. GRABAR, in *Cahiers archéologiques*, III, 1948, pp. 39-48 and 49-63.

## 5. General Studies bearing on Art Forms and Techniques.

D. V. AJNALOV, *The Hellenistic Basis of Byzantine Art* (in Russian), St. Petersburg, 1900-1901.

A. ALFÖLDI, *Zur Ausgestaltung des monarchischen Zeremoniells am römischen Kaiserhofe*, in *Römische Mitteilungen*, XLIX, 1934, pp. 1-118.

C. BAYET, *Recherches pour servir à l'histoire de la peinture et de la sculpture chrétiennes en Orient avant la querelle des Iconoclastes*, Paris, 1879.

H. DÜTSCHKE, *Ravennatische Studien*, Leipzig, 1909.

R. EISLER, *Weltenmantel und Himmelszelt. Religionsgeschichtliche Untersuchungen zur Urgeschichte des antiken Weltbildes*, Munich, 1910.

J. GAGÉ, *La Victoire impériale dans l'empire chrétien*, in *Revue d'histoire et de philosophie religieuses*, XIII, Strasbourg, 1933, pp. 370-400.

F. GERKE, *Ideengeschichte der ältesten christlichen Kunst*, in *Zeitschrift für Kirchengeschichte*, LIX, 1940, pp. 1-102.

A. GRABAR, *L'Empereur dans l'art byzantin. Recherches sur l'art officiel de l'Empire d'Orient*, Paris, 1936.

A. GRABAR, *Martyrium. Recherches sur le culte des reliques et l'art chrétien antique*, 2 vols. and album, Paris, 1943-1946.

W. DE GRÜNEISEN, *Le Portrait (études comparatives). Traditions hellénistiques et influences orientales*, Rome, 1911.

W. DE GRÜNEISEN, *La Perspective. Esquisse de son évolution des origines jusqu'à la Renaissance*, in *Mélanges d'archéologie et d'histoire*, XXXI, 1911, pp. 393-434.
With many illustrations of buildings and paintings.

A. HEISENBERG, *Grabeskirche und Apostelkirche*, 2 vols., Leipzig, 1908.
Studies of two famous churches no longer in existence: the Holy Sepulchre at Jerusalem and the Holy Apostles in Constantinople.

E. MALE, *Rome et ses vieilles églises*, Paris, 1942.

E. MALE, *La Fin du paganisme en Gaule et les plus anciennes basiliques chrétiennes*, Paris, 1950.

E. MÜNTZ, *Études sur l'histoire de la peinture et de l'iconographie chrétiennes*, Paris, 1882.

C. ROHAULT DE FLEURY, *La Messe; études archéologiques sur ses monuments*, 3 vols., Paris, 1882-1883.

P. E. SCHRAMM, *Das Herrscherbild in der Kunst des Mittelalters*, in *Bibliothek Warburg, Vorträge 1922-1923*, I, 1924.

## ARCHITECTURE

### 1. The Monuments.

D. AJNALOV, *Christian Monuments of the Chersonese* [Crimea] (in Russian), Moscow, 1905.

Y. ALLAIS, *Djemila*, Paris, 1938.

E. ANTONIADES, *Description of St Sophia* (in Greek), 3 vols., Athens, 1907-1909.

B. M. APOLLONJ-GHETTI, A. FERRUA, S.J., E. JOSI and E. KIRSCHBAUM, S.J., with preface by Mgr L. KAAS, *Esplorazioni sotto la Confessione di San Pietro in Vaticano*, I-II, Vatican City, 1951.
On the excavations carried out under St. Peter's during the war.

A. BADAWY, *Les Premières Églises d'Égypte* in *Kyrilliana*, Seminarium Franciscanum Orientale, Cairo, 1947
Texts.

P. B. BAGATTI, *Gli antichi edifici sacri di Betlemme*, Jerusalem, 1952.

A. BALLU, *Les Ruines de Timgad (antique Thamugadi)*, Paris, 1897.

A. BALLU, *Le Monastère byzantin de Tébessa*, Paris, 1898.

A. BALLU, *Les Ruines de Timgad. Nouvelles découvertes*, Paris, 1903.

A. BALLU, *Guide illustré de Timgad (antique Thamugadi)*, Paris, 2nd edition, 1911.

A. BALLU, *Guide illustré de Djemila (antique Cuicul)*, Algiers, 1926.

G. L. BELL, *Churches and Monasteries of the Tûr Abdîn and Neighbouring Districts*, in *Zeitschrift für Geschichte der Architektur*, Beiheft 9, Heidelberg, 1913.

F. BENOIT, *L'Abbaye de Saint-Victor et l'église de la Major à Marseille*, Petites monographies des grands édifices de la France, Paris, 1936.

W. DE BOCK, *Matériaux pour servir à l'archéologie de l'Égypte chrétienne*, 2 vols., St. Petersburg, 1901.

A. J. BUTLER, *The Ancient Coptic Churches of Egypt*, Oxford, 1884.

H. C. BUTLER, *American Archaeological Expedition to Syria in 1899-1900. Part II : Architecture and Other Arts*, New York-London, 1903.

H. C. BUTLER, *The Tychaion at es-Sanamein and the Plan of the Early Christian Churches*, in *Revue archéologique*, VIII, 1906.

H. C. BUTLER, *Syria. Publications of the Princeton University. Archaeological Expeditions to Syria in 1904-1905 and 1909. Part II : Architecture. — Section A : Southern Syria. Section B : Northern Syria*. Leyden, 1910-1920.

H. C. BUTLER, *Early Churches in Syria, Fourth to Seventh Centuries*, edited and completed by P. BALDWIN SMITH, Princeton, 1929.

R. CAGNAT, *Carthage, Timgad, Tébessa et les villes antiques de l'Afrique du Nord*, Paris, 1909.

A. CALDERINI, *La zona monumentale di S. Lorenzo in Milano*, Milan, 1934.

A. CALDERINI, G. CHIERICI and C. LECCHELLI, *La Basilica di S. Lorenzo Maggiore in Milano*, Milan, 1951.

W. A. CAMPBELL, *Martyrion in Seleucia-Pieria*, 1941.

F. CHIESA and others, *Il battistero di Riva San Vitale*, Bellinzona, 1955.

K. J. CONANT, *The First Dome of St. Sofia and its Rebuilding*, in *The Bulletin of the Byzantine Institute*, I, 1946, pp. 71-78.

C. COURTOIS, *Timgad (antique Thamygadi)*, Algiers, 1951, and Paris, 1955.

J. W. CROWFOOT, *Churches at Bosra and Samaria*, British School of Archaeology in Jerusalem, 1937.

A. DE CAPITANI D'ARZAGO, *Architettura dei secoli quarto e quinto in alta Italia*, Milan, 1944.

C. DELVOYE, *Recherches récentes sur les origines de la basilique paléochrétienne*, in *Annuaire de l'Institut de philologie et d'histoire orientale et slave*, XIV, Brussels, 1954-1957, pp. 205-228.

R. DEMANGEL and E. MAMBOURY, *Le Quartier des Manganes et la première région de Constantinople*, Paris, 1939.
Excavations at Constantinople.

C. DIEHL, M. LE TOURNEAU and H. SALADIN, *Les Monuments chrétiens de Salonique*, 2 vols., Paris, 1918.

E. DYGGVE, *Forschungen in Salona*, III, Vienna, 1939.

J. EBERSOLT, *Monuments d'architecture byzantine*, Paris, 1934.

J. EBERSOLT and A. THIERS, *Les Églises de Constantinople*, Paris, 1913.

M. ECOCHARD, *Le Sanctuaire de Qal'at Sem'ân*, in *Bulletin d'Études orientales*, VI (1936), Institut français de Damas, Damascus, 1937.

R. EGGER, *Frühchristliche Kirchenbauten im südlichen Norikum*, Vienna, 1916.

W. EMERSON and R. L. VAN NICE, *Haghia Sophia, Istanbul: Preliminary Report of a Recent Examination of the Structure*, in *American Journal of Archaeology*, XLVII, 1943, pp. 401-436.

E. H. FRESHFIELD, *Cellae trichorae*, I-II, London, 1913-1918.

G. GALASSI, *L'Architettura protoromanica nell' Esarcato*, Ravenna, 1928.

P. GAUCKLER, *Basiliques chrétiennes de Tunisie*, Paris, 1913.

W. GERBER and R. EGGER, *Forschungen in Salona*, I-II-III, Vienna, 1917, 1926, 1939.

C. GURLITT, *Die Baukunst Konstantinopels*, Berlin, 1908-1912.

W. HARVEY and others, *The Church of the Nativity at Bethlehem*, London, 1910.

R. HEYDENREICH, *Das Grabmal Theoderichs zu Ravenna*, Bonn, 1941.

C. HUELSEN, *Le Chiese di Roma nel medio evo*, Rome, 1927.

A. L. JAKOBSON, *The Chersonese at the Beginning of the Middle Ages* (in Russian), Moscow-Leningrad, 1959.

K. M. KAUFMANN, *Die Ausgrabung der Menasheiligtümer...*, 3 vols., Cairo, 1906-1908.

K. M. KAUFMANN, *Die Menasstadt....* Leipzig, 1910.

H. KNACKFUSS, *Didyma*, Berlin, 1941.

C. KRAELING and others, *Gerasa*, New Haven, 1938.
Several churches of the 4th-7th centuries.

R. KRAUTHEIMER, *Corpus basilicarum christianarum Romae*, I et seq., Vatican City (in course of publication since 1937).

R. KRAUTHEIMER, *Mensa-Coemeterium-Martyrium* in *Cahiers archéologiques*, XI, 1960, pp. 15-40.

D. KRENCKER, *Die Wallfahrtskirche des Symeon Stylites in Kal'at Sim'an*, in *Abhandlungen der Preussischen Akademie der Wissenschaften zu Berlin*, 1918, Philologisch-historische Klasse, 4, Berlin, 1939.

K. G. LANCKORONSKI, *Der Dom von Aquileia*, Vienna, 1906.

J. LASSUS, *Sanctuaires chrétiens de Syrie*, Paris, 1947.

P. LAUER, *Le Palais de Latran, étude historique et archéologique*, Paris, 1912.

P. LEMERLE, *Philippes et la Macédoine orientale à l'époque chrétienne et byzantine*, Paris, 1945.

L. LESCHI, *Tipasa de Maurétanie*, Algiers, 1951.

L. LESCHI, *Djemila (antique Cuicul)*, Algiers, 1954.

W. R. LETHABY and H. SWAINSON, *The Church of Sancta Sophia at Constantinople*, London, 1894.

H. H. LEWELL and F. W. MASLUCK, *The Church of Our Lady at the Hundred Gates in Paros*, London, 1920.

A. MADER, *Altchristliche Basiliken und Lokaltraditionen in Süd-Judäa*, Paderborn, 1918.

B. MALAJOLI, *La basilica eufrasiana di Parenzo*, 2nd edition, Padua, 1943.

E. MAREC, *Monuments chrétiens d'Hippone*, Paris, 1958.

F. MAYENCE, *La Première Campagne de fouilles à Apamée*, in *L'Antiquité classique*, I (1931), IV (1935), V (1936).

J. MÉCÉRIAN, *Sur le martyrium de saint Syméon le Jeune, sur le Mont-Admirable*, in *Comptes rendus de l'Académie des Inscriptions et Belles-Lettres*, Paris, 1936.

386

J. MÉCÉRIAN, *Expédition archéologique*, in *L'Antiochène occidentale*, Beirut, 1964.

A. H. S. MEGAW, in *Proceedings of the IXth Congress of Byzantine Studies at Salonica*, I (in Greek), pp. 287-295. On the church of Hermopolis in Egypt.

M. MESNARD, *La Basilique de Saint-Chrysogone à Rome*, Rome-Paris, 1935.

G. MILLET, *Sainte-Sophie avant Justinien*, in *Orientalia christiana periodica*, XIII, 1947, pp. 597-612.

F. MILTNER, *Ephesos, Stadt des Artemis und des Johannes*, Vienna, 1958.

P. MONCEAUX, *Timgad chrétien*, Paris, Annual Reports of the Ecole Pratique des Hautes Etudes, 1910-1911.

U. MONNERET DE VILLARD, *Les Couvents près de Sohâg*, Milan, I, 1925; II, 1926.

U. MONNERET DE VILLARD, *Le chiese della Mesopotamia*, in *Orientalia christiana Analecta*, 128, Rome, 1940.

U. MONNERET DE VILLARD, *La Nubia romana*, Rome, 1941.

R. NETZHAMMER, *Die christlichen Altertümer der Dobrudscha*, Bucarest, 1918.

P. DE PALOL SALELLAS, *Tarraco hispanovisigoda*, Tarragona, 1953.

V. PARVAN, *Cetatea Tropaeum*, Bucarest, 1912.

M. PRELOG, *Porec (Parenzo) and its Monuments* (in Serbian), Belgrade, 1957.

C. PREUSSER, *Nordmesopotamische Baudenkmäler altchristlicher und islamischer Zeit*, Leipzig, 1911.

W. M. RAMSAY and G. L. BELL, *The Thousand and One Churches*, London, 1909. Group of ancient churches in Asia Minor.

F. REGGIERI, *Dieci battisteri lombardi dal secolo V al XII* (Series "I monumenti italiani", IV), Rome, 1935.

F. ROUSTAN, *La Major et le premier baptistère de Marseille*, Marseilles, 1905.

S. SALLER, *The Memorial of Moses on Mount Nebo*, Jerusalem, 1941.

M. SALMI, *La Basilica di S. Salvatore di Spoleto*, Florence, 1951. I do not deal with this church in the present work because I believe it to date from a later period.

F. SARRE and E. HERZFELD, *Archäologische Reise im Euphrat- und Tigrisgebiet*, 2 vols., Berlin, 1911-1920. Description of the church of St. Sergius at Resafa.

A. M. SCHNEIDER, *Die Grabung im Westhof der Sophienkirche zu Konstantinopel*, Berlin, 1941.

A. M. SCHNEIDER, *Das Architektursystem der Hagia Sophia*, in *Oriens christianus*, XXXVI, 1941.

A. M. SCHNEIDER, *Die Hagia Sophia zu Konstantinopel*, Berlin, 1939, 2nd edition, 1942.

A. SCHUCHERT, *Santa Maria Maggiore zu Rom*, Vatican City, 1939.

G. SOTIRIOU, *Christian Thebes* [Thessaly] (in Greek), in ’Αρχαιολογικη ’Εφημερισ, 1929 (in 1931), pp. 1-158.

H. SPANNER and S. GUYER, *Rusafa. Die Wallfahrtsstadt des heiligen Sergios*, Berlin, 1926.

O. H. STRUB-RÖSSLER, *Die Hagia Sophia... eine generelle Untersuchung ihrer Konstruktion*, in *Byzantinische Zeitschrift*, XLII, 1942, pp. 158-177.

J. STRZYGOWSKI, *Kleinasien, ein Neuland der Kunstgeschichte*, Leipzig, 1903.

E. H. SWIFT, *Hagia Sophia*, New York, 1940.

G. TCHALENKO, *Villages antiques de la Syrie du Nord, la région de Blus à l'époque romaine*, 3 vols., Paris, 1957-1959.

P. A. UNDERWOOD, *Some Principles of Measure in the Architecture of the Period of Justinian*, in *Cahiers archéologiques*, III, 1948.

E. VALLET, E. ALBERTINI and M. HUTTNER, *Guide pratique illustré pour visiter les ruines de l'antique Cuicul (actuellement Djemila)*, Algiers, 1924.

M. VAN BERCHEM and J. STRZYGOWSKI, *Amida*, Heidelberg, 1910. Churches of northern Mesopotamia.

A. VAN MILLINGEN, *Byzantine Churches in Constantinople*, London, 1912.

J. VAULTRIN, *Les Basiliques chrétiennes de Carthage*, in *Revue africaine*, LXXIII, 1932.

P. VERZONE, *L'Architettura religiosa dell'alto medio evo nell'Italia settentrionale*, Milan, 1942.

P. VERZONE, *Alahan Monastir*, Vigliongo, 1956.

L. H. VINCENT, *Bethléem, le sanctuaire de la Nativité*, Paris, 1914.

L. H. VINCENT and F. M. ABEL, *Jérusalem : II, Jérusalem nouvelle*, Paris, 1914.

M. DE VOGÜÉ, *Syrie centrale, Architecture civile et religieuse du Ier au VIIe siècle*, 2 folio vols., Paris, 1865-1877.

J. B. WARD PERKINS, *The Shrine of Maryût*, in *Papers of the British School at Rome*, XVII, 1949, pp. 26-71.

J. B. WARD PERKINS and M. H. BALLANCE, *The Caesareum at Cyrene and the Basilica at Cremna*, in *Papers of the British School at Rome*, XXVI, new series, XIII, 1958, pp. 137-194.

J. B. WARD PERKINS and R. G. GOODCHILD, *The Christian Antiquities of Tripolitania*, in *Archaeologia*, XCV, Oxford, 1953, pp. VIII and 1-158.

C. WATZINGER, *Denkmäler Palästinas*, II, Leipzig, 1935.

T. WIEGAND, *Sinai*, in *Wissenschaftliche Veröffentlichungen des deutschtürkischen Denkmalschutzkommandos*, Heft 1, Berlin, 1920, pp. VIII and 1-146.

## 2. Studies.

W. ALTMANN, *Die italischen Rundbauten*. Berlin, 1906.

H. C. BUTLER, *Architecture and Other Arts*, New York, 1903.

C. CECCHELLI, *Mausolei imperiali e reali di tardo impero e dell'alto medioevo*, Rome, 1940.

A. CHOISY, *L'Art de bâtir chez les Romains*, Paris, 1873.

A. CHOISY, *L'Art de bâtir chez les Byzantins*, Paris, 1883.

J. G. DAVIES, in *American Journal of Archaeology*, LXI, 1957, pp. 171-173.

G. DE ANGELIS D'OSSAT, *Romanità delle cupole paleocristiane*, Rome, 1946.

F. W. DEICHMANN, *Versuch einer Darstellung der Grundrisstypen des Kirchenbaues in frühchristlicher und byzantinischer Zeit...*, Würzburg, 1937.

F. W. DEICHMANN, *Studien zur Architektur Konstantinopels*, Baden-Baden, 1956. Observations bearing on construction technique.

C. DELVOYE, *Les Basiliques paléochrétiennes*, Ravenna, 1959. Résumé of a course, with select bibliography.

J. DURM, *Die Baukunst der Etrusker und der Römer*, Stuttgart, 1905.

N. DUVAL, *Les Origines de la basilique chrétienne*, in *l'Information d'histoire de l'art*, 1962, No. 1, pp. 1-19.

P. FRANKL, *Die frühmittelalterliche und romanische Baukunst*, in *Handbuch der Kunstwissenschaft*, Berlin, 1926.

H. GLÜCK, *Ursprung des römischen und abendländischen Wölbungsbaues*, Vienna 1933.

L. HAUTECŒUR, *Mystique et architecture. Le symbolisme du cercle et de la coupole*, Paris, 1954.

A. HEISENBERG, *Grabeskirche und Apostelkirche*, 2 vols., Leipzig, 1908.
Study of the texts relating to two famous churches (destroyed) of Golgotha and Constantinople.

J. HUBERT, *L'Art pré-roman*, Paris, 1938.

J. HUBERT, *Les églises à rotonde orientale*, in *Actes du III<sup>e</sup> Congrès international pour l'étude du Haut Moyen Age* (1951), Olten-Lausanne, 1954.

T. KLAUSER, *Vom Heroon zur Märtyrer-Basilika*, Bonn, 1942.

R. KRAUTHEIMER, *The Beginnings of Christian Architecture*, in *Review of Religion*, 1932.

R. KRAUTHEIMER, *S. Pietro and the Tripartite Transept in the Early Christian Basilica*, in *Proceedings of the American Philosophical Society*, LXXXIV, 1941, pp. 353-595.

R. KRAUTHEIMER, *Introduction to an Iconography of Mediaeval Architecture*, in *Journal of the Warburg and Courtauld Institute*, V, 1942, pp. 1-33.
The problem of typology in Christian architecture: what defined an edifice in the eyes of the Ancients?

R. KRAUTHEIMER, *Early Christian and Byzantine Architecture*, London, 1965.

E. LANGLOTZ and F. DEICHMANN, article BASILIKA, in *Reallexikon für Antike und Christentum*, I, 1950.

A. ORLANDOS, *The Timber-roofed Basilica* (in Greek), 2 vols., Athens, 1952-1954.

A. PRANDI, *Il complesso monumentale della basilica celimontana dei SS. Giovanni e Paolo*, Vatican City, 1953.

W. RAVE, *Trompe und Zwickel*, in *Festschrift für Hans Jantzen*, Berlin, 1951.

G. T. RIVOIRA, *Le origini dell'architettura lombarda*, Milan, 2nd edition, 1908; *Lombardic Architecture: Its Origin, Development and Derivatives*, London, 1910.

M. RUMPLER, *La coupole dans l'architecture byzantine et musulmane*, Strasbourg, 1956.

B. SMITH, *Architectural Symbolism of Imperial Rome and the Middle Ages*, Princeton, 1956.

P. STYGER, *Nymphäen, Mausoleen, Baptisterien*, in *Architectura*, I, 1933.

J. B. WARD PERKINS, *The Italian Element in Late Roman and Early Mediaeval Architecture*, in *Proceedings of the British Academy*, XXXIII, 1947, pp. 163-194.

J. B. WARD PERKINS, in D. T. RICE, *The Great Palace of the Byzantine Emperors*, II, Edinburgh, 1958.
Important study of the construction of Byzantine walls.

W. R. ZALOZIECKY, *Die Sophienkirche in Konstantinopel und ihre Stellung in der Geschichte der abendländischen Architektur*, Rome-Fribourg, 1936.

### 3. Secular Architecture.

E. DYGGVE, *Ravennatium Palatium Sacrum*, in *Medd. Dansk. Vid. Selsk.*, III, No. 2, Copenhagen, 1941, p. 63.

J. EBERSOLT, *Le Grand Palais de Constantinople et le Livre des cérémonies*, Paris, 1910.

F. KRISCHEN, *Die Landmauer von Konstantinopel*, I, Berlin, 1938.

H. LEITZMANN, *Die Landmauer von Konstantinopel*, Berlin, 1929.

B. MEYER-PLATH and A. M. SCHNEIDER, *Die Landmauer von Konstantinopel*, II, Berlin, 1943.

J. STRZYGOWSKI and P. FORSCHHEIMER, *Die byzantinischen Wasserbehälter von Konstantinopel*, Vienna, 1893.

K. M. SWOBODA, *Römische und romanische Paläste*, Vienna, 1919.

T. WIEGAND and E. MAMBOURY, *Die Kaiserpaläste von Konstantinopel*, Berlin, 1934.

### PAINTING

#### 1. Mosaics and Wall Paintings. Mosaic Pavements. Icons.

In addition to works of a general character listed above under General Works (Garrucci, Peirce and Tyler, Volbach and Hirmer, Grabar, *Martyrium*, II), consult the following:

a) *Surveys*:

*Frühe Ikonen*, Vienna-Munich, 1965.

M. VAN BERCHEM and E. CLOUZOT, *Mosaïques chrétiennes du IV<sup>e</sup> au X<sup>e</sup> siècle*, Geneva, 1924.

J. WILPERT, *Die Römischen Mosaiken und Malereien der kirchlichen Bautem vom IV. bis XIII. Jahrhundert*, I-IV, Freiburg-im-Breisgau, 1916.

b) *Monographs* (listed by localities):
Antinoe, Egypt (wall paintings).
M. SALMI, *I dipinti paleocristiani di Antinoe*, in *Scritti dedicati alla memoria di Ippolito Rosellini*, Florence, 1945, pp. 159-169.

Antioch (mosaic pavements).
DORO LEVI, *Antioch Mosaic Pavements*, I-II, Princeton, 1957.

Aquileia, Italy (mosaic pavements).
G. BRUSIN and P.L. ZOVATTO, *Monumenti paleocristiani di Aquileia e di Grado*, Udine, 1957.

Bagawat, Egypt (wall paintings).
W. DE BOCK, *Matériaux pour servir à l'archéologie de l'Égypte chrétienne*, I-II, St. Petersburg, 1901.

A. FAKHRY, *The Necropolis of El-Bagawat in Kharga Oasis*, Cairo, 1951.

Bawit, Egypt (wall paintings).
J. CLEDAT, *Le monastère et la nécropole de Baouît*, in *Mémoires publiés par les membres de l'Institut français d'archéologie orientale*, XII, XVI, XXXIX, Cairo, 1904, 1906, 1916.

J. MASPERO and E. DRIOTON, *Fouilles exécutées à Baouît*, in the same *Mémoires*, LIX, Cairo, 1943.

Constantinople (mosaic pavements).
*The Great Palace of the Byzantine Emperors*, I-II, Oxford, 1947, 1958.

Gerasa, Palestine.
C. KRAELING and others, *Gerasa, City of the Decapolis*, New Haven, 1938.

Kiev (icons).
N. PETROV, *Album of Masterpieces of the Museum of the Kiev Academy* (in Russian), Kiev, 1912.

Milan (mosaics).
A. CALDERINI, G. CHIERICI and C. LECCELLI, *La basilica di San Lorenzo Maggiore in Milano*, Milan, 1951. See also Wilpert, *Römische Mosaiken...*, cited above.

Mount Nebo, Palestine (mosaic pavements).
S. SALLER, *The Memorial of Moses on Mount Nebo*, Jerusalem, 1941.

S. SALLER, *The Town of Nebo*, Jerusalem, 1949.

Mount Sinai (mosaics and icons).
G. SOTIRIOU, in *Atti dello VIII Congresso internazionale di studi bizantini*, Palermo, 1951, Vol. II, pp. 246-252.

G. SOTIRIOU, *Icônes du monastère de Sinaï*, I-II, Athens, 1956.

Naples (mosaics, wall paintings).

H. ACHELIS, *Die Katakomben von Neapel*, Leipzig, 1936.

J. L. MAIER, *Le Baptistère de Naples et ses mosaïques*, Fribourg (Switzerland), 1964.

Parenzo (mosaics).
I. MAXIMOVIC, in *Sbornik Radova Viz. Inst.*, No. VIII-2, Belgrade, 1964, pp. 247-262.

B. MOLAJOLI, *La basilica eufrasiana di Parenzo*, Padua, 1943.

Ravenna (mosaics).
G. BOVINI, various articles in *Felix Ravenna*, 1950 et seq.

F. W. DEICHMANN, *Frühchristliche Bauten und Mosaiken in Ravenna*, Baden Baden, 1958.

E. DINKLER, *Die Apsismosaik von S. Apollinare in Classe*, Cologne, 1964.

C. O. NORDSTRÖM, *Ravennastudien*, Stockholm, 1953.

Rome (mosaics, wall paintings, icons).
C. BERTELLI, *La Madonna di Santa Maria in Trastevere*, Rome, 1961.

C. CECCHELLI, *I mosaici della basilica di S. Maria Maggiore*, Turin, 1956.

P. CELLINI, *Una Madonna molto antica*, in *Proporzioni*, III, 1950.

W. de GRÜNEISEN, *Sainte-Marie-Antique*, Rome, 1911.

E. KITZINGER, *Römische Malereien vom Beginn des 7. bis zur Mitte des 8. Jahrhunderts*, no place, no date.

G. MATTHIAE, *Pittura romana del medioevo*, Rome, 1965.

J. WILPERT, *Die Römischen Mosaiken und Malereien der kirchlichen Bauten vom IV. bis XIII. Jahrhundert*, I-IV, Freiburg-im-Breisgau, 1916.

Salonica (mosaics).
C. DIEHL, M. LE TOURNEAU and H. SALADIN, *Les Monuments chrétiens de Salonique*, 2 vols., Paris, 1918.

H. TORP, *Mosaikkene i St. Georg-Rotunden*, Oslo, 1963.

F. I. USPENSKY, in the *Izvestija* of the Russian Archaeological Institute of Constantinople (in Russian), Vol. XIV.

A. XYNGOPOULOS, in *Archeologikon Deltion* (in Greek), Athens, 1929.

Sakkara, Egypt (wall paintings).
J. E. QUIBELL, *Excavations at Saqqara (1908-1909, 1909-1910)*, Cairo, 1912.

Sofia, Bulgaria (wall paintings).
K. MIATEV, *The Decorative Painting of the Necropolis of Sofia* (in Bulgarian), Sofia, 1925.

Stobi and Tsaritchin Grad, Yugoslavia (mosaic pavements).

E. KITZINGER, in *Dumbarton Oaks Papers*, III, 1946, pp. 81-162.

D. MANO-ZISSI, in *Starinar*, V-VI, Belgrade, 1956, pp. 155-188.

## 2. Miniatures.

*General.*

E. BETHE, *Buch und Bild im Altertum*, edited by E. Kirsten, Leipzig, 1945.

T. BIRT, *Die Buchrolle in der Kunst*, Leipzig, 1907.

P. BUBERL, *Die byzantinischen Handschriften*, I. Leipzig, 1937.
Description of the oldest illustrated Greek manuscripts preserved in Austria.

A. BYVANCK, *Antike Buchmalerei*, Leyden, 1938-1940.

S. J. GASIOROWSKI, *Malarstwo Minjaturowe Grecko-Rzymske*, Cracow, 1928.

R. KOEMSTEDT, *Vormittelalterliche Malerei*, Augsburg, 1929.

N. P. KONDAKOFF, *Histoire de l'art byzantin considéré principalement dans les miniatures*, 2 vols., Paris, 1886-1891.

G. MILLET, *Recherches sur l'iconographie de l'Évangile*, Paris, 1916.

C. NORDENFALK, in A. GRABAR and C. NORDENFALK, *Early Medieval Painting*, The Great Centuries of Painting, Skira, Geneva, 1957.

L. RÉAU, *Histoire de la peinture au Moyen Age. La miniature*, Melun, 1946.

W. SCHUBART, *Das Buch bei den Griechen und Römern*, Berlin, 2nd edition, 1921.

K. WEITZMANN, *Illustrations in Roll and Codex. A Study of the Origin and Method of Text Illustration*, Princeton, 1947.

K. WEITZMANN, *Greek Mythology in Byzantine Art*, Princeton, 1951.

K. WEITZMANN, *Ancient Book Illumination*, Cambridge, Mass., 1959.

*Scientific and Historical Works and Classical Authors.*

R. BIANCHI-BANDINELLI, *Ilias Ambrosiana*, Bern-Olten, 1948 (facsimile).

R. BIANCHI-BANDINELLI, *Hellenistic Byzantine Miniatures of the Iliad (Ilias Ambrosiana)*, Olten, 1955.

B. BISCHOFF and W. KOEHLER, *Eine illustrierte Ausgabe der spätantiken Ravennater Annalen*, in *Medieval Studies in Memory of A. K. Porter*, I, Cambridge, Mass., 1939, p. 125 ff.

K. BULAS, *Les Illustrations antiques de l'Iliade*, Lvov, 1929, and in *American Journal of Archaeology*, LIV, 2, 1950, p. 112 ff.

*Codices e Vaticanis selecti* : Vol. I, *Vergilius Vaticanus;* Vol. II, *Vergilius Romanus*, Rome, 1943 (3rd edition) and 1902.

O. JAHN, *Griechische Bildchroniken*, Bonn, 1873.

L. W. JONES and C. R. MOREY, *The Miniatures of the Manuscripts of Terence prior to the Thirteenth Century*, 2 vols., Princeton, 1931.

J. LEROY, *Les Manuscrits syriaques à peintures conservés dans les bibliothèques d'Europe et d'Orient. Contribution à l'étude de l'iconographie des églises de langue syriaque*, text and plates, Paris, 1964.

E. NAVILLE, *Das ägyptische Totenbuch der XVIII-XX. Dynastie*, 3 vols., Berlin, 1886.

A. von PREMERSTEIN, K. WESSELY and J. MANTUANI, *Dioscorides. Codex Aniciae Julianae picturis illustratus...*, Leyden, 1900.

A. REHM and E. SCHRAMM, *Herons und Philons Bellipoüka*, in *Abhandlungen der Preussischen Akademie der Wissenschaften, Philologisch-historische Klasse*, 1918, Abh. 2 and 16, 1918-1919. *Cf.* the same authors, in *Abhandlungen der bayerischen Akademie, Philologisch-historische Klasse*, neue Folge, 2, 1929.

F. SAXL and H. MEIER, *Verzeichnis astrologischer und mythologischer illustrierter Handschriften des lateinischen Mittelalters* : III, *Handschriften in englischen Bibliotheken*, edited by H. Bober, London, 1953.

H. STERN, *Le calendrier de 354*, Paris, 1953.

R. STETTINER, *Die illustrierten Prudentius Handschriften*, Berlin, 1895 and 1905. *Cf.* H. WOODRUFF, in *Art Studies*, VII, 1929, pp. 33-79.

J. STRZYGOWSKI, *Eine Alexandrinische Weltchronik*, Vienna, 1906.

*Christian Texts.*

O. L. von GEBHARDT, *The Miniatures of the Ashburnham Pentateuch*, London, 1883.

H. GERSTRINGER, *Die Wiener Genesis*, Vienna, 1931.

A. GRABAR, *Les Peintures de l'Évangéliaire de Sinope*, Paris, 1948.

A. HASELOFF, *Codex Purpureus Rossanensis*, Berlin-Leipzig, 1898.

A. MUNOZ, *Il codice purpureo di Rossano e il frammento Sinopense*, Rome, 1907.

C. NORDENFALK, *Die spätantiken Kanontafeln*, 2 vols., Göteborg, 1938.

H. OMONT, *Fac-similés des miniatures des plus anciens manuscrits grecs de la Bibliothèque nationale*, Paris, 2nd edition, 1929.

F. WICKOFF, *Die Wiener Genesis*, Vienna, 1895.

F. WORMALD, *The Miniatures in the Gospels of Saint Augustine Corpus Christi*, Cambridge, 1954.

## SCULPTURE

J. BAUM, *La Sculpture figurale en Europe à l'époque mérovingienne*, Paris, 1937.

G. BECATTI, *La colonna coclide istoriata*, Rome, 1960.

C. DELVOYE, *La Sculpture byzantine*, in *Corsi*, Ravenna, 1961.
Résumé of a course, with select bibliography.

E. GERKE, *La scultura paleobizantina in Oriente*, in *Corsi* [sull'arte ravennate e bizantina], Ravenna, 1959, fasc. II.

A. GRABAR, *Sculptures byzantines de Constantinople (IVe-Xe s.)*, Paris, 1963.

J. KOLLWITZ, *Die oströmische Plastik der Theodosianischen Zeit*, Berlin, 1941.

H. PEIRCE and R. TYLER, *Byzantine Art*, London, 1926; *L'Art byzantin*, 2 vols., Paris, 1932-1934.

O. WULFF, *Altchristliche und mittelalterliche byzantinische und italienische Bildwerke*, Berlin Museum, 1909.

O. WULFF and W. F. VOLBACH, *Beschreibung der Bildwerke der christlichen Epochen: III, Ergänzungsband*, Berlin, 1923.

### Sarcophagi.

J. BOUBE, *Les Sarcophages paléochrétiens de Martres-Tolosane*, in *Cahiers archéologiques*, IX, 1957, pp. 33-72.

M. LAWRENCE, *The Sarcophagi of Ravenna*, College Art Association, *Studies*, No. 2, New York, 1945.

E. LE BLANT, *Les Sarcophages chrétiens de la Gaule*, Paris, 1886.

J. B. WARD PERKINS, in *Archaeologia*, LXXXVII, London, 1938, pp. 79-128.
Aquitanian sarcophagi.

J. WILPERT, *I sarcofagi cristiani antichi*, 5 vols., Vatican City, 1929-1936.

### Coptic Sculpture.

J. BECKWITH, *Coptic Sculpture*, London, 1963.

E. CHASSINAT, *Fouilles à Baouit*, I, Cairo, 1911, and Paris, 1912.

W. E. CRUM, *Catalogue général des antiquités égyptiennes du musée du Caire, Coptic Monuments*, Cairo, 1902.

G. DUTHUIT, *La Sculpture copte*, Paris, 1931.
Detailed survey and study, an essential work.

A. GAYET, *Les Monuments coptes du musée de Boulaq. Catalogue des sculptures et stèles ornées de la salle copte du musée*, Cairo-Paris, 1889.

A. GAYET, *La Sculpture copte*, in *Gazette des Beaux-Arts*, 7, 3e période, p. 422, and 8, 4e période, pp. 80-88 and 145-153, Paris 1892.

E. KITZINGER, in *Archaeologia*, LXXXVII, London, 1937, pp. 181-215.
Thorough study of ornamental sculpture.

J. STRZYGOWSKI, *Catalogue général des antiquités égyptiennes du musée du Caire. Koptische Kunst*, Vienna, 1904.

## IVORIES

G. BOVINI and L. B. OTTOLENGHI, *Catalogo della mostra degli avori dell'alto medioevo*, Ravenna, 2nd edition, 1956.

L. BRÉHIER, *La Sculpture et les arts mineurs byzantins*, Paris, 1936.

C. CECCHELLI, *La cattedra di Massimiano ed altri avori romano-orientali*, Rome, 1936-1944.

O. M. DALTON, *Catalogue of Early Christian Antiquities ...in the British Museum*, London, 1901.

O. M. DALTON, *Catalogue of the Ivory Carvings of the Christian Era... of the British Museum*, London, 1909.

R. DELBRÜCK, *Die Consulardiptychen und verwandte Denkmäler*, Berlin-Leipzig, 2 vols., 1926-1929.

H. GRAEVEN, *Frühchristliche und mittelalterliche Elfenbeinwerke in photographischer Nachbildung*, 2 vols., Rome, 1898-1900.
Collections in England and Italy.

M. LAURENT, *Les Ivoires prégothiques conservés en Belgique*, Brussels-Paris, 1912, new edition, 1927.

M. H. LONGHURST, *Victoria and Albert Museum. Catalogue of Carvings in Ivory*, London, 1927.

E. P. DE LOOS-DIETZ, *Vroeg-christelijke ivoren*, Assen, 1947.

E. MOLINIER, *Catalogue des ivoires du Musée national du Louvre*, Paris, 1896.

C. R. MOREY, *Gli oggetti di avorio e di osso. Catalogo del Museo Sacro Vaticano*, I, Vatican City, 1936.

C. R. MOREY, *Early Christian Ivories of the Eastern Empire*, in *Dumbarton Oaks Papers*, I, Washington, 1941.

J. NATANSON, *Early Christian Ivories*, London, 1953.

W. NEUSS, *Die Anfänge des Christentums im Rheinlande*, Bonn, 3rd edition, 1933.

J. SAUER, *Die altchristliche Elfenbeinplastik*, Leipzig, 1922.

G. SCHLUMBERGER, *L'Ivoire Barberini*, in *Monuments Piot*, VII, Paris, 1900, pp. 79-94.

J. STRZYGOWSKI, *Das Etchmiadzin Evangeliar*, in *Byzantinische Denkmäler*, I, Vienna, 1891.

G. STUHLFAUTH, *Die altchristliche Elfenbeinplastik*, Leipzig, 1896.

W. VÖGE, *Beschreibungen der Bildwerke der christlichen Epochen. Die Elfenbeinwerke. Katalog der königlichen Museen zu Berlin*, 2nd edition, Berlin, 1900.

W. F. VOLBACH, *Elfenbeinarbeiten der Spätantike und des frühen Mittelalters*, 2nd edition, Mainz, 1952.
This fundamental work provided the basis for the choice of ivory carvings illustrated here. It includes an extensive bibliography up to 1952.

## INDUSTRIAL ARTS

In addition to the catalogues and surveys listed above under General Works (Garrucci, Peirce and Tyler, Volbach and Hirmer, Bréhier), consult the following:

C. DELVOYE, *Les Ateliers d'arts somptuaires à Constantinople*, in *Corsi*, Ravenna, 1965.
Résumé of a course, with select bibliography.

J. LABARTE, *Histoire des arts industriels au Moyen Age et à l'époque de la Renaissance*, 2nd edition, 3 vols., Paris, 1872-1875.

E. MOLINIER, *Histoire générale des arts appliqués à l'industrie, du Ve à la fin du XVIIIe siècle*, 6 vols., Paris, 1896-1912.

A. RIEGL, *Die spätrömische Kunstindustrie nach den Funden in Oesterreich-Ungarn*, 2 vols., Vienna, 1901-1923.

J. STRZYGOWSKI, *Altai-Iran und Völkerwanderung*, Leipzig, 1917.

## SILVER

G. BRUSIN and P. L. ZOVATTO, *Monumenti paleocristiani di Aquileia e di Grado*, Udine, 1957.

D. E. CRUIKSHANK, *Byzantine Silver Stamps*, Washington, 1961.

O. M. DALTON, in *Archaeologia*, 57, pp. 159-174, and 60, pp. 1-24, and in *The Burlington Magazine*, X, 1907, pp. 355-362.

C. DIEHL, in *Syria*, II, 1921, pp. 81-95.

G. A. EISEN, *The Great Chalice of Antioch*, New York, 1923 (cf. reviews of this book : J. WILPERT, in *The Art Bulletin*, IX, 1926, pp. 89-141, and G. DE JERPHANION, in *Orientalia Christiana*, VII, No. 27, 1926).

A. GRABAR, *Les Ampoules de Terre sainte, Monza, Bobbio*, Paris, 1957.

T. D. KENDRICK, *The Mildenhall Treasure*, London, 1947.

L. D. MATZULEVITCH, *Byzantinische Antike*, Berlin-Leipzig, 1929.

### GOLD AND JEWELRY

W. DENNISON, *A Gold Treasure of the Late Roman Period from Egypt*, New York, 1918.

M. C. ROSS, *Early Christian and Byzantine Art*, Baltimore, 1947.
Includes many pieces from American collections exhibited at the Walters Art Gallery, Baltimore, in 1947.

R. ZAHN, in *Amtliche Berichte aus den Kunstsammlungen*, Berlin, XXXVIII, 1916-1917.

### TEXTILES

#### 1. Classification.

JOHN BECKWITH, *Coptic Textiles*, in *Ciba Review*, Vol. II, No. 133, Basel, August 1959.

A. F. KENDRICK, *Victoria and Albert Museum. Catalogue of Textiles from Burying Grounds in Egypt*, 3 vols., London, 1920-1922.

O. WULFF and W. F. VOLBACH, *Spätantike und koptische Stoffe aus ägyptischen Grabfunden in den Staatlichen Museen*, Berlin, 1926.

#### 2. Surveys.

(In addition to works listed above.)

A. APOSTOLAKI, *Coptic Textiles in the Museum of Decorative Arts* (in Greek), Athens, 1932.

O. VON FALKE, *Kunstgeschichte der Seidenweberei*, 2 vols., Berlin, 1913. Several later editions.

M. MATIÉ and K. LIAPUNOVA, *Art Textiles of Coptic Egypt* (in Russian), Moscow-Leningrad, 1951.

R. PFISTER, *Tissus coptes du Musée du Louvre*, 4 fasc., Paris, 1931.

A. RIEGL, *Die ägyptischen Textilfunde im K. K. österreichischen Museum*, Vienna, 1889.

W. F. VOLBACH, *Catalogo del Museo Sacro della Biblioteca vaticana : III, I tessuti*, Vatican City, 1942.

A. C. WEIBEL, *Ten Thousand Years of Textiles*, The Detroit Institute of Arts, New York, 1952.

I. M. WILSON, *Ancient Textiles from Egypt in the University of Michigan Collection*, in *University of Michigan Studies*, XXXI, Ann Arbor, 1933, pp. 1-77.

#### 3. Technique.

(In addition to works listed above under 1 and 2, in particular Pfister and Beckwith.)

C. J. LAMM, *Cotton in Mediaeval Textiles of the Near East*, Paris, 1938.

R. PFISTER, in *Mélanges R. Linossier*, Paris, 1932, pp. 433-459.

R. PFISTER, in *Seminarium Kondakovianum*, VII, Prague, 1935, pp. 1-59.

R. PFISTER, *Textiles de Palmyre*, 3 fasc., Paris, 1934-1940.

R. PFISTER, *Textiles de Halabiyeh (Zénobie) découverts par le Service des antiquités de la Syrie dans la métropole de Halabiyeh sur l'Euphrate*, Paris, 1951.

R. PFISTER and L. BELLINGER, *The Excavations at Dura-Europos : IV, 2, The Textiles*, New Haven, 1945.

#### 4. Studies.

(In addition to works listed above.)

Le P. P. DU BOURGUET, in *Bulletin de la Société archéologique d'Alexandrie*, XL, 1935, pp. 1-31. Coptic textiles of the Moslem period.

E. KITZINGER, in *Dumbarton Oaks Papers*, III, Washington, 1946, pp. 1-72. Iconography.

E. KÜHNEL, in *Bulletin de la Société d'Archéologie copte*, IV, Cairo, 1938, pp. 79-89. Coptic textiles of the Moslem period.

H. SEYRIG and L. ROBERT, in *Cahiers archéologiques*, VIII, 1956, pp. 27-36. On a textile found in Egypt and thought to have been made near Constantinople.

## ICONOGRAPHY

### General Iconographic Surveys.

No special publication of this kind exists, but many books dealing with painting and sculpture, and with certain aspects of the industrial arts, offer a more or less extended treatment of iconographic imagery. See above under General Works, Painting, Sculpture, and Industrial Arts.

There are innumerable books and articles dealing with one or several iconographic themes. In the selection given below we distinguish between pagan, imperial, Jewish and Christian themes. We would also emphasize the multiplicity of the iconographic programmes—a characteristic trait of the art dealt with in this volume.

### Pagan Themes.

A. ALFÖLDI, *The Festival of Isis at Rome under the Christian Emperors of the IVth Century*, in *Dissertationes Pannoniae*, II, 7, Budapest, 1937.

A. ALFÖLDI, *Die Kontorniaten*, Budapest, 1941-1943.

F. CUMONT, *Recherches sur le symbolisme funéraire des Romains*, Paris, 1942.

F. WIRTH, *Römische Wandmalerei vom Untergang Pompejis bis ans Ende des dritten Jahrhunderts*, Berlin, 1934.

See also the works listed here under Sculpture (Kollwitz), Ivories (Bréhier), Silver (Diehl and above all Matzulevitch), and Miniatures (Stern).

### Imperial Roman and Byzantine Themes.

In addition to studies of coins, see the works by Lambros and Grabar (under General Works 2 and 5), Kollwitz (under Sculpture), Delbrück (under Ivories), and the following:

A. ALFÖLDI, two lengthy studies, in *Römische Mitteilungen*, 49, 1934, pp. 1-118, and 50, 1935, pp. 1-171.

P. G. HAMBERG, *Studies in Roman Imperial Art*, Uppsala, 1945.

H. P. L'ORANGE, *Studies in the Iconography of Cosmic Kingship in the Ancient World*, Oslo, 1952.

### Jewish Themes.

E. R. GOODENOUGH, *Jewish Symbols in the Greco-Roman Period*, 8 vols., New York, 1953 et seq.
An exhaustive and valuable corpus.

H. KOHL and C. WATZINGER, *Antike Synagogen in Galiläa*, Leipzig, 1916.

*Paintings of a religious character:*
C. KRAELING, *The Synagogue* [of Dura-Europos], in *The Excavations at Dura Europos*, VIII, New Haven, 1958.
This important but inadequately illustrated monograph does not supersede previous publications.

A. GRABAR, in *Revue de l'histoire des religions*, 123, 1941, pp. 143-192, and 124, 1941, pp. 5-35.

H. L. HEMPEL, in *Zeitschrift für die alttestamentliche Wissenschaft*, 69, 1957, pp. 103-131.

J. LEVEEN, *The Hebrew Bible in Art*, London, 1944.

Comte DU MESNIL DU BUISSON, *Les Peintures de la synagogue de Doura-Europos*, Vatican City, 1939.

C. NORDSTRÖM, *Some Jewish Legends in Byzantine Art*, in *Byzantion*, XXV-XXVII, 1955-1957, pp. 457-508.

C. ROTH, *Jewish Antecedents of Christian Art*, in *Journal of the Warburg and Courtauld Institute*, 16, 1953.

K. WEITZMANN, in *Münchener Jahrbuch der bildenden Kunst*, III-IV, 1954, pp. 96-120.

### Christian Themes.

In addition to the general surveys listed above under General Works, consult the art and archaeological journals, the monographs on various monuments and works of art (e.g. under Mosaics and Wall Paintings, Miniatures, Sculpture, Ivories and Industrial Arts), and the many studies of iconographic themes.

L. DE BRUYNE, *L'imposition des mains dans l'art chrétien ancien*, in *Rivista di archeologia cristiana*, XV, 1943, p. 113 ff.

C. CECCHELLI, *Il trionfo della croce*, Rome, 1954.

F. CUMONT, *L'Adoration des Mages et l'art triomphal de Rome*, in *Atti della Pontificia romana Accademia di archeologia, Memoria*, III, Rome, 1932.

P. A. FÉVRIER, *Les Quatre Fleuves du Paradis*, in *Rivista di archeologia cristiana*, XXXII, 1956, pp. 179-199.

J. FINK, *Noe der Gerechte in der frühchristlichen Kunst*, Münster (Westphalia), 1955.

F. GERKE, *Christus in der spätantiken Plastik*, Mainz, 1938.
Cf. K. WESSEL, in *Archäologischer Anzeiger*, 1950-1951, p. 300, 1953, p. 168 ff.; F. VAN DER MEER, *Majestas Domini*, Rome, 1938.

E. H. KANTOROWICZ, *The Kings Advent*, in *The Art Bulletin*, XXVI, 1944, p. 267 ff.

H. KEHRER, *Die heiligen drei Könige in der Literatur*, 2 col., Leipzig, 1908-1909.

N. P. KONDAKOV, *Iconography of the Mother of God* (in Russian), 3 vols., St. Petersburg, 1914-1915.

C. LEONARDI, *Ampelos. Il simbolo della vite nell'arti pagane e paleocristiana*, in *Ephemerides liturgicae, Sieto historica*, XXI, 1947.

A. G. MARTINIER, *L'Iconographie des catacombes et la catéchèse antique*, in *Rivista di archeologia cristiana*, XXV, 1949, p. 105 ff.

K. MICHEL, *Gebet und Bild*, in *Studien über christliche Denkmäler*, neue Folge, I, Strasbourg, 1902.

F. NOACK, *Die Geburt Christi in der bildenden Kunst...*, Darmstadt, 1894.

C.-H. PUECH, *Le Cerf et le serpent*, in *Cahiers archéologiques*, IV, 1949, p. 20 ff.

J. QUASTEN, *Der Gute Hirte in frühchristlicher Totenliturgie und Grabeskunst*, in *Miscellanea in honorem Giovanni Mercati : I, Studi e testi*, 121, Vatican City, 1946, p. 37 ff.

J. REIL, *Die frühchristlichen Darstellungen der Kreuzigung Christi*, Leipzig, 1904.

E. SCHLEE, *Die Ikonographie der Paradiesflüsse*, Leipzig, 1937.

M. SIMON, *Sur l'origine des sarcophages chrétiens du type Bethesda*, in *Mélanges d'archéologie et d'histoire*, LV, 1938, p. 201 ff.

B. SMITH, *Early Christian Iconography and the School of Provence*, Princeton, 1918.

Now out of date. On a similar theory put forward by Volbach, who assigns certain Early Christian ivories to Gaul, see his book on ivory carvings (listed above under Ivories).

F. SÜHLING, *Die Taube als religiöses Symbol im christlichen Altertum*, in *Römische Quartalschrift*, Suppl. 24, 1930, pp. 1-399.

J. WILPERT, *Fractio panis*, Freiburg-im-Breisgau, 1895.

### Baptismal Iconography.

L. DE BRUYNE, in *Miscellanea liturgica in honorem C. C. Mohlberg*, I, Rome, 1948.

L. DE BRUYNE, in *Actes du V⁰ Congrès international d'archéologie chrétienne*, Aix-en-Provence, 1954, Vatican City, 1957.
Cf. H. Stern, in the same volume of proceedings.

### Iconography in Churches.

*Rome.*
(In addition to monographs on churches listed above under General Works.)

K. LEHMANN, in *The Art Bulletin*, XXXVII, 1955, pp. 193-196, 291-292. On the iconography of Santa Costanza.

H. STERN, in *Dumbarton Oaks Papers*, Vol. XII, 1958, pp. 157-218. On the same subject.

*Ravenna.*
C. O. NORDSTRÖM, *Ravennastudien*, Stockholm, 1953.
Several studies in *Felix Ravenna*.

O. S. von SIMSON, *Sacred Fortress. Byzantine Art and Statecraft in Ravenna*, Chicago, 1948.

### Cycles.

(In addition to Millet, *Iconographie*, and Grabar, *Ampoules*.)

J. REIL, *Die altchristlichen Bilderzyklen des Lebens Jesu*, Leipzig, 1910.

K. SCHEFOLD, *Altchristliche Bilderzyklen*, in *Rivista di archeologia cristiana*, XVI, 1939, pp. 289-314.

# List of Illustrations

*The descriptive notices in the List of Illustrations*
*have been compiled with the assistance of Madame Clémence DUPRAT,*
*scientific advisor to the Arts of Mankind series.*

The present volume deals with a period in which many of the surviving works of art cannot be dated with precision. In the main text of the book we have indicated or suggested the chronological limits within which a given work or group of works may be situated. To do more would be to distort the evidence we have and run the risk of serious errors. For this reason, in the descriptive notices that follow, we have purposely refrained from assigning conjectural dates to works or monuments which cannot be dated with any certainty.

In many cases, too, the size of the object is not indicated in the descriptive notice. The exact measurements of a fragmentary textile or a necklace may have a certain commercial interest, but for the historical and aesthetic study of such objects—and this is the purpose of the present work—they are generally irrelevant. The reader will have no trouble imagining the approximate size of objects in common use (furniture, books, arms, vases) and of others whose scale is defined either by the dimensions of their constituent materials (ivory plaques, coloured stones and glass) or by their architectural setting (scale plans of the buildings will give a sufficient idea of the size of the mosaics and wall paintings contained in them).

A. G.

FRONTISPIECE. Rome, Santa Maria Maggiore, Mosaic on the Triumphal Arch. *Presentation in the Temple, detail.* First half of the 5th century (432-440). (Photo De Antonis)

1. Constantinople, St Sophia. ANTHEMIOS OF TRALLES AND ISIDOROS OF MILETUS. *View of the Interior looking towards the Apse.* 532-537 and 558-562. (Photo Magnum-E. Lessing)

2. Rome, San Paolo fuori le Mura. *Section.* 4th-5th century (386-c. 440).

Interior of the church: length 387 ft, width 295 ft, height 72 ft. (After André Chastel, *L'Art italien*, Collection *Arts, Styles et Techniques*, Vol. I, Paris, 1956, fig. 2, p. 42)

3. Rome, San Paolo fuori le Mura. *View of the Nave looking towards the Apse.* 4th-5th century (386-c. 440), rebuilt after the fire of 1823. (Photo Alinari)

4. Rome, Santa Maria Maggiore. *View of the Nave looking towards the Triumphal Arch.* 5th century, pontificate of Pope Sixtus III (432-440). (Photo Gabinetto Fotografico Nazionale, Rome)

5. Rome, Santa Sabina. *Exterior.* Early 5th century (after 410). (Photo De Antonis)

6. Rome, Santa Sabina. *Interior showing the Nave and Side Aisles.* Early 5th century (after 410). (Photo Alinari)

7. Rome, Santa Sabina. *Detail of the Polychrome Marble Revetment in the Nave.* Early 5th century (after 410). (Photo Scala)

8. Rome, San Giovanni in Laterano, Baptistery. *Interior showing the Octagon.* First half of the 5th century, pontificate of Pope Sixtus III (432-440). (Photo Alinari)

9. Rome, San Stefano Rotondo. *Exterior.* Second half of the 5th century, pontificate of Pope Simplicius (468-483). (Photo Alinari)

10. Rome, San Stefano Rotondo. *Interior.* Second half of the 5th century, pontificate of Pope Simplicius (468-483). (Photo De Antonis)

11. Ravenna, Sant'Apollinare in Classe. *View of the Apse.* Consecrated in 549. Mosaics above the colonnades. (Photo A. Perissinotto, Padua)

12. Ravenna, Sant'Apollinare in Classe. *Exterior.* Consecrated in 549. (Bildarchiv Foto Marburg)

13. Ravenna, Mausoleum of Galla Placidia. *Exterior.* First half of the 5th century. Brick. (Photo Alinari)

14. Ravenna, Sant'Apollinare Nuovo. *Colonnade in the Nave, south side, with Mosaics on the Wall.* Early 6th century. (Photo A. Perissinotto, Padua)

15. Ravenna, Mausoleum of Theodoric. *Exterior.* Early 6th century. Dressed stone. (Photo Villani & Figli, Bologna)

16. Ravenna, San Giovanni Evangelista. *Exterior showing the Apse.* Early 5th century (425). Brick. (Photo Villani & Figli, Bologna)

17. Ravenna, Orthodox Baptistery (also called Cathedral Baptistery or Baptistery of Neon). *Exterior.* First quarter of the 5th century. Brick. (Photo Villani & Figli, Bologna)

18. Ravenna, Arian Baptistery. *Exterior.* About 500. Brick. (Photo Alinari)

19. Ravenna, Orthodox Baptistery (also called Cathedral Baptistery or Baptistery of Neon). *Interior.* First quarter of the 5th century. (Photo A. Perissinotto, Padua)

20. Ravenna, San Vitale. *Exterior.* Begun in 532, consecrated in 547. Brick. Cf. plan fig. 400. (Photo Villani & Figli, Bologna)

21. Ravenna, San Vitale. *Side Wall of the Choir, with Mosaics.* Begun in 532, consecrated in 547. (Photo Scala)

22. Perugia, Rotunda of Sant'Angelo. *Interior.* Late 4th century. (Photo G. Franci)

23. Spoleto, San Salvatore. *Façade.* 5th-6th century. (Photo Alinari)

24. Fréjus (Var), Baptistery. *Interior.* Early 5th century. (Photo U.D.F.-La Photothèque)

25. Vienne (Isère), Church of Saint-Pierre (now the Musée Lapidaire). *View of the Nave with Arcade and Side Wall.* 5th century. (Photo Musées de Vienne)

26. Riez (Basses-Alpes), Baptistery. *Interior.* 5th-6th century. (Photo U.D.F.-La Photothèque)

27. Jemila or Djemila (Algeria), Baptistery. *Circular Vaulted Gallery with Niches.* 5th-6th century. (After Louis Leschi, *Djemila, antique Cuicul,* Algiers, 1953, fig. 41, p. 52)

28. Jemila or Djemila (Algeria), Baptistery. *Ciborium over the Baptismal Font.* 5th-6th century. (After Louis Leschi, *Djemila, antique Cuicul,* Algiers, 1953, fig. 42, p. 53)

29. Damous-el-Karita, Carthage (Tunisia). *View of the Basilica.* 5th-6th century. (Photo Roger Viollet)

30. Tebessa (Algeria). *Doorway of the Basilica.* 5th-6th century. Cf. plan fig. 410. (Photo Marcel Bovis)

395

31. Tebessa (Algeria). *View of the Basilica.* 5th-6th century. (Photo Marcel Bovis)

32. Tebessa (Algeria). *Approach to the Basilica.* 5th-6th century. (Photo Marcel Bovis)

33. Sohag (Egypt), White Monastery (Deir el-Abiad). *View of the Exterior from the South-West.* Early 5th century. (Photo Romero-Technische Hochschule, Darmstadt)

34. Sohag (Egypt), Red Monastery (Deir el-Ahmar). *Interior of the Church showing the Upper Part of the South Apse.* Early 5th century. (Photo J. Doresse, Paris)

35. Sohag (Egypt), Red Monastery (Deir el-Ahmar). *Interior of the Church showing the Lower Part of the South Apse.* Early 5th century. (Photo J. Doresse, Paris)

36. Sohag (Egypt), White Monastery (Deir el-Abiad). *Interior of the Church showing the North End of the Narthex.* Early 5th century. Cf. plan fig. 413. (Photo Costa, Cairo)

37. Sakkara (Egypt), Monastery of St Jeremiah. *Partial View of the Refectory and Chapel.* 5th century. Cf. plan fig. 414. (After J.E. Quibell, *Excavations at Saqqara, 1908-1909, 1909-1910. The Monastery of Apa Jeremias,* Cairo, 1912, pl. IX bottom)

38. Kfer (Syria), Church. *Exterior showing the Apse.* 5th century. (Photo Institut français d'archéologie, Beirut)

39. Kalat Kalota (Syria), East Church. *South Façade.* 5th century. (Photo Institut français d'archéologie, Beirut)

40. Simkhar (Syria), Chapel beside the Basilica. *Façade.* Chapel added in the 6th century to the 4th-century church. (Photo Institut français d'archéologie, Beirut)

41. Kalat Kalota (Syria), East Church. *West Façade.* 5th century. (Photo Institut français d'archéologie, Beirut)

42. Bakirha (Syria), West Church. *Exterior showing the Baptistery.* 5th-6th century. (Photo Institut français d'archéologie, Beirut)

43. Kalb Lauzeh (Syria), Basilica. *West Façade.* 6th century. (Photo Institut français d'archéologie, Beirut)

44. Kalb Lauzeh (Syria), Basilica. *View from the South-East.* 6th century. (Photo Lucien Hervé)

45. Kalb Lauzeh (Syria), Basilica. *Exterior showing the Apse.* 6th century. (Photo Institut français d'archéologie, Beirut)

46. Kalb Lauzeh (Syria), Basilica. *North Arcade of the Nave.* 6th century. (Photo Institut français d'archéologie, Beirut)

47. Kalb Lauzeh (Syria), Basilica. *View from the North-East.* 6th century. (Photo Institut français d'archéologie, Beirut)

48. Kalb Lauzeh (Syria), Basilica. *View of the Apse from the Interior.* 6th century. (Photo Institut français d'archéologie, Beirut)

49. Kalat Seman and Deir Seman (Syria). *Aerial View of the Two Monasteries.* (Photo Institut français d'archéologie, Beirut)

50. Kalat Seman (Syria), Monastery of St Simeon Stylites. *Cruciform Sanctuary: View from the Interior of the Central Apse at the East End.* 5th century (c. 480). Cf. plan fig. 423. (Photo Institut français d'archéologie, Beirut)

51. Kalat Seman (Syria), Monastery of St Simeon Stylites. *Cruciform Sanctuary: Central Shrine with the Base of the Saint's Pillar.* 5th century (c. 480). (Photo Lucien Hervé)

52. Turmanin (Syria), Basilica. *Reconstruction showing the Façade.* 5th-6th century. Basilica no longer in existence. (After the Comte de Vogüé, *Syrie centrale. Architecture civile et religieuse du Ier au VIIe siècle,* Vol. II, Paris, 1865-1877, pl. 135)

53. Kalat Seman (Syria), Monastery of St Simeon Stylites. *Cruciform Sanctuary: Exterior View of the Apses at the East End.* 5th century (c. 480). (Photo Institut français d'archéologie, Beirut)

54. Kalat Seman (Syria), Monastery of St Simeon Stylites. *Cruciform Sanctuary: Arch of the Main Doorway of the South Façade.* 5th century (c. 480). (Photo Lucien Hervé)

55. Kalat Seman (Syria), Monastery of St Simeon Stylites. *Cruciform Sanctuary: View of the South Façade.* 5th century (c. 480). (Photo Lucien Hervé)

56. Kalat Seman (Syria), Monastery of St Simeon Stylites. *Cruciform Sanctuary: North Side.* 5th century (c. 480). (Photo Lucien Hervé)

57. Gerasa (Palestine), Cathedral. *Main Doorway and Flight of Steps.* 4th century. (Photo Maurilio Sacchi)

58. Gerasa (Palestine), Cathedral. *Columns with Part of the Architrave.* 4th century. (Photo René Burri-Magnum)

59. Gerasa (Palestine), Church of Genesius. *View of the Apse and the Rudimentary Transept.* 7th century (611). (Photo Maurilio Sacchi)

60. Dag Pazarli (Asia Minor), Church. *Interior of the Apse.* 6th century. (Photo Professor G.H. Forsyth)

61. Dag Pazarli (Asia Minor), Church. *Exterior of the Apse.* 6th century. (Photo Professor G.H. Forsyth)

62. Alahan or Alahan Monastir (Asia Minor). *Main Church of the Monastery seen from the South-East.* 5th century (c. 450). (Photo Professor G.H. Forsyth)

63. Alahan or Alahan Monastir (Asia Minor). *Main Church of the Monastery: Interior View of the Apse and the Base of the Central Tower.* 5th century (c. 450). (Photo Professor G.H. Forsyth)

64. Aspendos (Asia Minor), Basilica in the Forum. *Ruins of the Forepart.* Watercolour of 1885 by G. Niemann. Cf. plan fig. 451. (After Comte C. de Lanckoronski, *Les Villes de la Pamphylie et de la Pisidie,* Paris, 1890, Vol. I, pl. XVII)

65. Bin Bir Kilisseh (Maden sehir, Asia Minor), Church I (after Strzygowski). *Side Aisle.* 4th-6th century. Cf. plan fig. 449. (Photo A. Perissinotto, Padua)

66. Bin Bir Kilisseh (Maden sehir, Asia Minor), Church VI (after Strzygowski). *Apse.* 4th-6th century. (Photo A. Perissinotto, Padua)

67. Bin Bir Kilisseh (Asia Minor). *View of Two Ruined Buildings.* Drawing by Léon de Laborde, lithograph by Freeman (1826). (After Léon de Laborde, *Voyage de l'Asie Mineure,* Paris, 1838, pl. LXVII, p. 140)

68. Daouleh (Asia Minor), Church VI. *View of the Nave and Apse.* 4th-6th century. (Photo École des Hautes Études, Paris)

69. Daouleh (Asia Minor), Church VI. *Exterior showing the Apse.* 4th-6th century. (Photo École des Hautes Études, Paris)

70. Bin Bir Kilisseh (Maden sehir, Asia Minor), Church I (after J. Strzygowski). *Exterior showing the Apse and an Aisle.* 4th-6th century. (Photo N. and M. Thierry)

71. Korykos (Asia Minor), Church 'extra muros.' *Double Bay.* 5th century. Cf. plan fig. 444. (Photo N. and M. Thierry)

72. Ephesus (Asia Minor). Church of the Virgin. *Detail of the Ruins.* 4th-6th century. Cf. plans fig. 452-453. (Photo A. Perissinotto, Padua)

73. Ephesus (Asia Minor), Church of the Virgin. *Detail of the Ruins.* 4th-6th century. (Photo A. Perissinotto, Padua)

74. Ephesus (Asia Minor), Martyrium Church of St John (first state). *General View (reconstruction).* 5th century. (After *Forschungen in Ephesos*, IV, 3, Vienna, 1951, fig. 63, p. 233)

75. Ephesus (Asia Minor), Martyrium Church of St John (first state). *Longitudinal Section (reconstruction). In the centre, Ciborium and Dome.* 5th century. (After *Forschungen in Ephesos*, IV, 3, Vienna, 1951, pl. LXXII lower right)

76. Ephesus (Asia Minor), Church of the Seven Sleepers. *Nave of the Lower Basilica, with Superimposed Arcosolia.* 5th century. Brick Vaulting. Cf. plan fig. 455. (Photo A. Perissinotto, Padua)

77. Salonica (Greece), Basilica of the Virgin Acheiropoietos (called Eski Juma by the Turks). *Colonnade in the Nave (before restoration).* 5th century. (After *Album Macédoine*, IV, *Salonique*, Mission Le Tourneau, École des Hautes Études, Paris, p. 25)

78. Salonica (Greece), Basilica of the Virgin Acheiropoietos (called Eski Juma by the Turks). *Colonnade in the Nave (as restored after the fire of 1917).* 5th century. (Photo Emile Séraf, Athens)

79. Salonica (Greece), Basilica of St Demetrios. *General View (after restoration).* 5th-7th century. Cf. plan fig. 456. (Photo Hassia)

80. Salonica (Greece), Basilica of St Demetrios. *Nave (after restoration).* 5th-7th century. (Hirmer Fotoarchiv, Munich)

81. Salonica (Greece), Church of St George. *Exterior.* Early 4th century. Cf. plan fig. 461. (Photo A. Perissinotto, Padua)

82. Salonica (Greece), Church of St George. *Dome Mosaics, detail: Martyrs in an Architectural Setting.* Early 4th century. In situ. (Photo Émile Séraf, Athens)

83. Salonica (Greece), Church of St George. *Dome Mosaics, detail: Martyr Orant.* Early 4th century. In situ. (Hirmer Fotoarchiv, Munich)

84. Constantinople, Church of Sts Sergius and Bacchus. *Exterior.* About 530. (Photo J. Powell)

85. Ephesus (Asia Minor), Martyrium Church of St John (second state). *General View in the time of Justinian (reconstruction).* 6th century. Cf. plan fig. 462. (After *Forschungen in Ephesos*, IV, 3, Vienna, 1951, fig. 44, p. 169)

86. Ephesus (Asia Minor), Martyrium Church of St John (second state). *View of the Nave in the time of Justinian (reconstruction).* 6th century. (After *Forschungen in Ephesos*, IV, 3, Vienna, 1951, fig. 42, p. 165)

87. Constantinople, Basilica of St Sophia. *Theodosian Façade with a Portico surmounted by a Pediment (reconstruction).* Early 5th century (c. 415). Basilica destroyed in the Nika riots of 532 and replaced by the present domed church of St Sophia. (After A.M. Schneider, *Die Hagia Sophia zu Konstantinopel*, Berlin, 1939, fig. 3)

88. Constantinople. *View of the Defensive Walls of Theodosius II.* 5th century (413-440). Built of alternating courses of masonry and bricks. (Photo A. Perissinotto, Padua)

89. Constantinople. *Detail of the Defensive Walls of Theodosius II, with a Tower (reconstruction).* 5th century (413-440). (After B. Meyer-Plath and A.M. Schneider, *Die Landmauer von Konstantinopel*, Berlin, 1938, pl. 3)

90. Constantinople. *Interior of a Tower on the Defensive Walls of Theodosius II (reconstruction).* 5th century (413-440). (After B. Meyer-Plath and A.M. Schneider, *Die Landmauer von Konstantinopel*, Berlin, 1938, pl. 9)

91. Constantinople, St Sophia. ANTHEMIOS OF TRALLES AND ISIDOROS OF MILETUS. *Overall View from the South-West.* 532-537 and 558-562. (Photo A. Perissinotto, Padua)

92. Constantinople, St. Sophia. ANTHEMIOS OF TRALLES AND ISIDOROS OF MILETUS. *Interior, detail.* 532-537 and 558-562. (Photo Magnum-E. Lessing)

93. Constantinople, St Sophia. ANTHEMIOS OF TRALLES AND ISIDOROS OF MILETUS. *Plan of the Church and the Atrium (destroyed).* 532-537 and 558-562. Overall width 228½ ft. Depth of the south-east apse 20 ft. Length of the central entrance porch at the extremity of the south-east apse 265½ ft. Diameter of the dome 108 ft. Height from floor level to the top of the dome 182½ft. Height from the base to the top of the dome 45 ft. (After W.F. Volbach and M. Hirmer, *Frühchristliche Kunst. Die Kunst der Spätantike in West und Ostrom*, Munich, 1958, fig. 28, p. 82)

94. Constantinople, St Sophia. ANTHEMIOS OF TRALLES AND ISIDOROS OF MILETUS. *Cross-Section.* 532-537 and 558-562. (After E.M. Antoniades, *Description of St Sophia*, Vol. I, Athens, 1907, pl. K1)

95. Constantinople, St Sophia. ANTHEMIOS OF TRALLES AND ISIDOROS OF MILETUS. *Longitudinal Section.* 532-537 and 558-562. (After E.M. Antoniades, *Description of St Sophia*, Vol. I, Athens, 1907, pl. θ)

96. Constantinople, St Sophia. ANTHEMIOS OF TRALLES AND ISIDOROS OF MILETUS. *View from the East.* 532-537 and 558-562. (Photo A. Perissinotto, Padua)

97. Constantinople, St Sophia. ANTHEMIOS OF TRALLES AND ISIDOROS OF MILETUS. *Aerial View.* 532-537 and 558-562. (Photo Museum of St Sophia, Istanbul)

98. Constantinople, St Sophia. ANTHEMIOS OF TRALLES AND ISIDOROS OF MILETUS. *View of the West Façade.* 532-537 and 558-562. (Photo Lucien Hervé)

99. Constantinople, St Sophia. ANTHEMIOS OF TRALLES AND ISIDOROS OF MILETUS. *View of the Interior, detail.* 532-537 and 558-562. (Photo A. Perissinotto, Padua)

100. Constantinople, St Sophia. ANTHEMIOS OF TRALLES AND ISIDOROS OF MILETUS. *View of the Interior looking towards the Apse.* 532-537 and 558-562. (Photo Thomas Whittemore)

101. Constantinople, St Sophia. ANTHEMIOS OF TRALLES AND ISIDOROS OF MILETUS. *Central Dome, exterior.* 532-537 and 558-562. (Photo Boudot-Lamotte)

102. Constantinople, St Sophia. ANTHEMIOS OF TRALLES AND ISIDOROS OF MILETUS. *Central Dome and Semi-domes, interior.* 532-537 and 558-562. (Photo Boudot-Lamotte)

103. Constantinople, St Sophia. ANTHE-MIOS OF TRALLES AND ISIDOROS OF MILETUS. *Semidome, exterior.* 532-537 and 558-562. (Photo Boudot-Lamotte)

104. Ravenna, San Vitale, Choir, south-west wall. *The Empress Theodora and her Retinue, detail: Women in her Retinue.* Mosaic. Church begun in 532 and consecrated in 547. In situ. (Photo Scala)

105. Constantinople, Great Palace of the Emperors. *Water Mill.* Detail of the Mosaic Pavement. Mid 5th-early 6th century. In situ. (Photo Halük Doganbey)

106. Constantinople, Great Palace of the Emperors. *Eagle and Snake.* Detail of the Mosaic Pavement. Mid 5th-early 6th century. In situ. (Photo Held)

107. Constantinople, Great Palace of the Emperors. *Frieze: Human Head and Acanthus Scroll.* Detail of the Mosaic Pavement. Mid 5th-early 6th century. In situ. (Photo J. Powell)

108. Constantinople, Great Palace of the Emperors. *Two Children riding a Camel.* Detail of the Mosaic Pavement. Mid 5th-early 6th century. In situ. Height 55 inches. (Photo Held)

109. Antioch. *The Megalopsychia Hunt, detail: Personification of Magnanimity in a Medallion.* Mosaic Pavement. 5th century. Museum of Antiquities, Antioch. (Museum Photo)

110. Antioch. *The Megalopsychia Hunt, detail of the frieze: Street Scene in Antioch with the name of each building inscribed above it.* Mosaic Pavement. 5th century. Museum of Antiquities, Antioch. (Museum Photo)

111. Antioch. *The Megalopsychia Hunt, detail: The Lion Hunt.* Mosaic Pavement. 5th century. Museum of Antiquities, Antioch. (Museum Photo)

112. Antioch. *The Megalopsychia Hunt, detail of the frieze: View of Antioch with its Main Buildings.* Mosaic Pavement. 5th century. Cf. No. 110. (Museum Photo)

113. Antioch. House of the Phoenix. *Frieze, detail: Ibexes.* Mosaic Pavement. 5th century. Louvre, Paris. (Photo U.D.F.-La Photothèque)

114. Antioch. *The Megalopsychia Hunt, detail of the frieze: View of Antioch with its Main Buildings.* Mosaic Pavement. 5th century. Cf. No. 110. (Museum Photo)

115. Antioch, House of the Phoenix. *Nimbused Phoenix against a Flower-patterned Background, detail.* Mosaic Pavement. 5th century. Louvre, Paris. (Photo U.D.F.-La Photothèque)

116. Kabr Hiram (Phoenicia), Church of St Christopher. *Mosaic of the Months, Seasons and Winds, detail: Medallion with a Bust.* Mosaic Pavement. Louvre, Paris. (Photo U.D.F.- La Photothèque)

117. Madaba (Transjordan). *Map of the Holy Land, detail: Plan of Jerusalem with its Principal Monuments.* Mosaic Pavement. 6th century. In situ. (Photo Maurilio Sacchi)

118. Aquileia (Italy), 'Fondo Tullio' Church. *Lamb lying in the Shade of a Vine.* Mosaic. Late 5th century. In situ, in the ruins of the church, now converted into a museum of Early Christian art. (Photo Chevalier)

119. Jerusalem, Funerary Oratory. *A Christian Orpheus among the Animals.* Mosaic Pavement. 5th century. Archaeological Museum, Istanbul. (Photo Halük Doganbey)

120. Madaba (Transjordan), Private House. *Tamed Animals in Paradise, detail.* Mosaic Pavement. 6th century. In situ. (Photo Maurilio Sacchi)

121. El Tabgha (Palestine), Church of the Multiplication of the Loaves and Fishes. *Loaves and Fishes.* Mosaic Pavement behind the Altar. Mid 5th century. In situ. (Photo Israeli National Tourist Office)

122. Beit Alpha (Palestine), Synagogue. *Hen with Chicks.* Mosaic Pavement. 6th century. In situ. (Photographic Department, Press Service, Tel-Aviv)

123. Ravenna, San Vitale. *Nimbused Lamb upheld by Four Angels.* Vault Mosaic in the Choir. Church begun in 532 and consecrated in 547. (Photo Scala)

124. Ravenna, Mausoleum of Galla Placidia. *Decorative Strip with Geometric Designs, detail.* Mosaic. 5th century. In situ. (Photo A. Perissinotto, Padua)

125. Ravenna, Mausoleum of Galla Placidia. *Stag drinking at the Fountain of Life, detail.* Lunette Mosaic. 5th century. (Photo Scala)

126. Rome, San Giovanni in Laterano, Baptistery, Chapel of St John the Evangelist. *Nimbused Lamb.* Vault Mosaic, detail. 5th century. In situ. (After J. Wilpert, *Die Römischen*

*Mosaiken und Malereien der Kirchlichen Bauten vom IV. bis XIII. Jahrhundert*, Freiburg im Breisgau, 1917, Vol. III, pl. 87)

127. San Prisco (near Capua), Oratory of Santa Matrona. *Vase with Vine Shoots and Birds.* Vault Mosaic, detail. 5th century. In situ. (Photo E.P.T. di Caserta)

128. Milan, Sant'Ambrogio, Chapel of San Vittore in Ciel d'Oro. *Bust of St Victor enclosed in a Wreath.* Dome Mosaic, detail. 5th century (c. 470). In situ. (Photo Scala)

129. Naples, Baptistery of San Giovanni in Fonte. *Martyr standing beside a Cippus.* Mosaic in the Drum of the Dome, detail. Mid 5th century. In situ. (Photo Soprintendenza ai Monumenti, Naples)

130. Naples, Baptistery of San Giovanni in Fonte. *The Wedding at Cana.* Dome Mosaic, detail. Mid 5th century. In situ. (Photo Soprintendenza ai Monumenti, Naples)

131. Ravenna, Orthodox Baptistery (also called Cathedral Baptistery or Baptistery of Neon). *Jude the Apostle.* Dome Mosaic, detail. 5th century. In situ. (Photo Draeger-Galerie de la Pléiade)

132. Ravenna, Orthodox Baptistery (also called Cathedral Baptistery or Baptistery of Neon). *The Baptism of Christ in a Medallion surrounded by Apostles.* Dome Mosaic. 5th century. In situ. (Photo Scala)

133. Ravenna, Mausoleum of Galla Placidia. *Starry Sky.* Vault Mosaic, detail. 5th century. In situ. (Photo Scala)

134. Ravenna, Mausoleum of Galla Placidia. *The Good Shepherd, detail.* Lunette Mosaic above the entrance. 5th century. In situ. (Photo Scala)

135. Ravenna, Mausoleum of Galla Placidia. *An Apostle.* Lunette Mosaic, detail. 5th century. In situ. (Photo Villani & Figli, Bologna)

136. Ravenna, Mausoleum of Galla Placidia. *View of the Mosaics.* 5th century. (Photo Held)

137. Salonica, Church of St George. *Young Martyr in front of an Aedicule, detail.* Dome Mosaic. 5th century. Our plate reproduces a copy by Father Lefakis in the Salonica Museum. (Photo Hassia)

138. Salonica, Church of St George. *Martyr in front of an Aedicule, detail.* Dome Mosaic. 5th century. Our plate reproduces a copy by Father Lefakis in the Salonica Museum. (Photo Hassia)

139. Salonica, Church of St George. *Elderly Martyr in front of an Aedicule, detail.* Dome Mosaic. 5th century. Our plate reproduces a copy by Father Lefakis in the Salonica Museum. (Photo Hassia)

140. Salonica, Oratory of Christ Latomos. *The Vision of Ezekiel and Habakkuk, detail: The Prophet Ezekiel.* Apse Mosaic. 5th century. In situ. (Photo Hassia)

141. Salonica, Oratory of Christ Latomos. *The Vision of Ezekiel and Habakkuk, detail: The Four Rivers of Paradise at the feet of the Young Christ.* Apse Mosaic. 5th century. In situ. (Photo Hassia)

142. Mount Sinai, Church of the Monastery of St Catherine. *The Transfiguration, with Busts of the Apostles and Founders in Medallions.* Apse Mosaic. About 600. In situ. (Photo Hassia)

143. Salonica, Church of St Demetrios. *St Demetrios between a Bishop and a High Dignitary.* Mosaic on a pillar in the nave at the entrance of the choir. Early 7th century. In situ. (Photo Held)

144. Kiti (Cyprus), Church of the Mother of God, called Angeloktistos. *Apse Mosaic, detail.* 6th-7th century. In situ. (Photo Costas Savvides)

145. Rome, Santa Pudenziana. *Christ surrounded by the Apostles and Perso-nifications of the Two Churches. In the background, Golgotha and Jerusa-lem.* Apse Mosaic. 4th century, pontificate of Pope Siricius (384-399). In situ. Cut down in the 16th century. (Gabinetto Fotografico Nazionale, Rome)

146. Rome, Santi Cosma e Damiano. *Christ surrounded by Saints.* Apse Mosaic. 526-530. In situ. (Photo Anderson)

147. Ravenna, San Vitale. *Christ between Two Archangels handing the Crown of Martyrdom to St Vitalis and receiv-ing the Model of the Church from its Founder Bishop Ecclesius.* Apse Mosaic. Church begun in 532 and consecrated in 547. In situ. (Photo Anderson)

148. Ravenna, Sant'Apollinare in Classe. *The Transfiguration (above) and St Apollinaris as an Orant (below).* Apse Mosaic. Church consecrated in 549. In situ. (Photo Villani & Figli, Bologna)

149. Rome, Santi Cosma e Damiano. *Christ walking on the Clouds.* Apse Mosaic, detail. 526-530. In situ. Cf. No. 146. (Photo Scala)

150. Ravenna, San Vitale. *Apse Mosaic, detail.* Church begun in 532 and consecrated in 547. In situ. Cf. No. 147. (Photo Scala)

151. Ravenna, Sant'Apollinare in Classe. *Apse Mosaic, detail.* Church conse-crated in 549. Cf. No. 148. (Photo Scala)

152. Ravenna, Sant'Apollinare in Classe. *Bishop Ursicinus.* Mosaic on the wall of the Apse. Church consecrated in 549. In situ. (Photo Scala)

153. Ravenna, Sant'Apollinare in Classe. *The Transfiguration, detail.* Apse Mosaic. Church consecrated in 549. In situ. Cf. No. 148. (Photo Scala)

154. Ravenna, Sant'Apollinare in Classe. *The Prophet Elijah.* Apse Mosaic, detail. Church consecrated in 549. In situ. Cf. No. 148. (Photo Scala)

155. Rome, Santa Maria Maggiore. *Mel-chizedek offering Bread and Wine to Abraham.* Mosaic in the Nave, detail. Pontificate of Sixtus III (432-440). In situ. (Photo De Antonis)

156. Rome, Santa Maria Maggiore. *The Parting of Abraham and Lot.* Mosaic in the Nave, detail. Pontificate of Sixtus III (432-440). In situ. (Photo De Antonis)

157. Rome, Santa Maria Maggiore. *Abra-ham entertaining the Three Angels.* Mosaic in the Nave, detail. Pontificate of Sixtus III (432-440). In situ. (Photo De Antonis)

158. Rome, Santa Maria Maggiore. *The Crossing of the Red Sea.* Mosaic in the Nave, detail. Pontificate of Sixtus III (432-440). In situ. (Photo De Antonis)

159. Rome, Santa Maria Maggiore. *Moses and his Companions stoned by the People but protected by the Lord.* Mosaic in the Nave, detail. Pontificate of Sixtus III (432-440). In situ. (Photo De Antonis)

160. Rome, Santa Maria Maggiore. *The Priests bearing the Ark of the Covenant (below) and the Walls of Jericho falling down (above).* Mosaic in the Nave, detail. Pontificate of Sixtus III

(432-440). In situ. (Photo De Anto-nis)

161. Rome, Santa Maria Maggiore. *Scenes from the Life of Christ and the Virgin: The Annunciation, detail.* Mosaic on the Triumphal Arch, upper register. Pontificate of Sixtus III (432-440). In situ. (Photo De Antonis)

162. Rome, Santa Maria Maggiore. *Scenes from the Life of Christ and the Virgin, detail.* Mosaic on the Triumphal Arch, right side. Pontificate of Six-tus III (432-440). In situ. (Photo De Antonis)

163. Ravenna, Sant'Apollinare Nuovo. *The Parable of the Pharisee and the Publican.* Mosaic in the Nave, upper register. First quarter of the 6th cen-tury. In situ. (Photo Scala)

164. Ravenna, Sant'Apollinare Nuovo. *The Holy Women at the Tomb.* Mosaic in the Nave, upper register. First quarter of the 6th century. In situ. (Photo Scala)

165. Ravenna, Sant'Apollinare Nuovo. *The Judgment of the Nations.* Mosaic in the Nave, upper register. First quarter of the 6th century. In situ. (Photo Scala).

166. Ravenna, Sant'Apollinare Nuovo. *Procession of Virgins, detail.* Mosaic in the Nave, lower register. After 527. In situ. (Photo Scala)

167. Ravenna, Sant'Apollinare Nuovo. *Procession of Martyrs, detail.* Mosaic in the Nave, lower register. After 527. In situ. (Photo Scala)

168. Ravenna, San Vitale. *The Sacrifices of Abel and Melchizedek, detail.* Lunette Mosaic in the Choir above the lower arcades. Church begun in 532, consecrated in 547. In situ. (Photo Scala)

169. Ravenna, San Vitale. *Abraham entertaining the Three Angels in the Plain of Mamre, detail.* Mosaic on the Side Wall of the Choir. Church begun in 532, consecrated in 547. In situ. (Photo Scala)

170. Ravenna, San Vitale. *The Emperor Justinian and his Retinue, detail: Head of Justinian.* Mosaic on the North Wall of the Choir. Church begun in 532, consecrated in 547. In situ. (Photo Scala)

171. Ravenna, San Vitale. *The Emperor Justinian and his Retinue.* Mosaic on the North Wall of the Choir. Church begun in 532, consecrated in 547. In situ. (Photo Scala)

172. Ravenna, San Vitale. *The Empress Theodora and her Retinue.* Mosaic on the South Wall of the Choir. Church begun in 532, consecrated in 547. In situ. (Photo Scala)

173. Ravenna, San Vitale. *The Empress Theodora and her Retinue, detail: Head of Theodora.* Mosaic on the South Wall of the Choir. Church begun in 532, consecrated in 547. In situ. (Photo Scala)

174. Milan, San Lorenzo, Chapel of Sant'Aquilino. *Chariot of Christ and Shepherd in a Rocky Landscape.* Apse Mosaic. 5th century. In situ. (Photo Scala)

175. Milan, Sant'Ambrogio, Chapel of San Vittore in Ciel d'Oro. *St Ambrose, detail.* Mosaic. Late 5th century (470). In situ. (Photo Scala)

176. Rome, Catacomb of Commodilla. *Virgin and Child enthroned between St Felix and St Adauctus, with the Donatrix Turtura.* Fresco Icon. 6th century (528). In situ. (Photo Held)

177. Rome, Catacomb of Commodilla. *St Luke.* Fresco Icon. 7th century. In situ. (Photo Held)

178. Rome, Santa Maria Antiqua, on a pillar in front of the apse. *St Demetrios of Salonica.* Fresco. 7th century. In situ. 65 by 27 $^1/_2$ inches. (Photo De Antonis)

179. Rome, Santa Maria Antiqua, in a niche in the atrium. *St Abbacyr the Physician.* Fresco. 7th century. In situ. (Photo Held)

180. Rome, Santa Maria Antiqua, in a small niche in the right aisle. *The Three Holy Mothers: The Virgin between St Elizabeth and St Anne.* Fresco Icon. 7th century. In situ. 50 $^3/_4$ by 44 inches. (Photo Gabinetto Fotografico, Rome)

181. Rome, Santa Maria Antiqua, near the apse. *Fragment of an Annunciation: The Archangel Gabriel.* Fresco. 6th-7th century. In situ. (Photo De Antonis)

182. Rome, Santa Maria Antiqua, in a small niche in the nave. *Virgin and Child.* Fresco Icon. 6th-7th century. In situ. 17 $^3/_4$ by 18 $^3/_4$ inches. (Photo Held)

183. Carthage, Underground Baptistery, Room II, north-west wall. *Bust of a Young Saint.* Fresco. 5th-6th century. In situ. Size of the plaster panel on which the figure is painted: 31 $^1/_2$ by

55 inches. (After N. Duval, *Nécropole chrétienne et baptistère souterrain à Carthage,* in *Cahiers Archéologiques,* X, 1959, fig. 39, p. 120)

184. Coptic Art. Bawit (Egypt), Monastery of St Apollo, Chapel XVIII, west wall. *Decorative Frieze: Medallion with the Head of a Woman.* Fresco. 6th-7th century. Painting left in situ and probably no longer extant. (Photo École des Hautes Études, Paris)

185. Coptic Art. Antinoe (Egypt). *Theodosia between St Colluthus and St Mary.* Fresco. 6th-7th century. Painting left in situ and probably no longer extant. (Missi-Photo-Montgolfier, Paris)

186. Coptic Art. Bawit (Egypt), Monastery of St Apollo, Chapel VI, niche in the form of an apse. *Christ in Majesty (above) and The Virgin and Child enthroned with the Apostles and Two Evangelists (below).* Fresco. 6th-7th century. Coptic Museum, Old Cairo. (Photo Held)

187. Coptic Art. Bawit (Egypt), Monastery of St Apollo, Chapel VI, niche in the form of an apse. *The Virgin and Child enthroned with the Apostles and Two Evangelists, detail: Five Apostles.* Fresco. 6th-7th century. Coptic Museum, Old Cairo. (Photo Held)

188. Sakkara (Egypt), Monastery of St Jeremiah, Chapel B, in the apse. *Medallion with the Head of the Virgin.* Fresco. 6th-7th century. Painting left in situ and probably no longer extant. (After J.E. Quibell, *Excavations at Saqqara, 1906-1907,* II, Cairo, 1908, pl. XLIX)

189. Bawit (Egypt), Monastery of St Apollo, Chapel XVII, apse. *Lower Register: Orant Virgin with the Apostles, detail.* Fresco. 6th-7th century. Painting left in situ and probably no longer extant. Dimensions of the lower register: 78 $^3/_4$ by 59 inches. (Photo École des Hautes Études, Paris)

190. Coptic Art. Karanis (Egypt). *Isis suckling Harpocrates.* Fresco. 3rd-4th century. (Photo by Courtesy of the University of Michigan, Kelsey Museum of Archaeology) The theme of the Virgin suckling the Child may have been inspired by imagery of this type.

191. Coptic Art. Sakkara (Egypt), Monastery of St Jeremiah, Cell A, north wall. *Holy Monks with Kneeling Donor.* Fresco. 6th-7th century. Coptic Museum, Old Cairo. Height of the tallest figure: 45 inches. (Photo Costa, Cairo). One of the monks is St Apollo, patron saint of the Bawit monastery.

192. Coptic Art. Bawit (Egypt), Monastery of St Apollo, Chapel XVII, west wall. *St Sisinnios on Horseback piercing the Right Breast of a Female Demon with his Spear.* Fresco. 6th-7th century. Painting left in situ and probably no longer extant. (Photo École des Hautes Études, Paris)

193. Coptic Art. Bawit (Egypt), Monastery of St Apollo, Chapel XVIII, east wall. *Virgin enthroned between Two Angels, presenting the Christ Child in a Medallion.* Fresco. 6th-7th century. Painting left in situ and probably no longer extant. (Photo École des Hautes Études, Paris)

194. Coptic Art. Sakkara (Egypt), Monastery of St Jeremiah, Cell 1725. *The Virgin suckling the Child, with Personifications of the Virtues in Medallions above her.* Fresco. 6th-7th century. Coptic Museum, Old Cairo. (Photo Costa, Cairo)

195. Perushtitsa (Bulgaria), Red Church, vault of a passage between the outer tribune and the room on the north side. *Angel Caryatid holding up the Mystic Lamb.* Fresco. 7th century (before 692). In situ (?). Reproduced from a copy in the National Museum of Archaeology, Sofia. (After A. Frolow, *L'Eglise Rouge de Pérouchtitza,* in *The Bulletin of the Byzantine Institute of America,* I, Paris, 1946, p. IX)

196. Perushtitsa (Bulgaria), Red Church, west arch between the church and the ambulatory around the north apse. *Moses receiving the Tables of the Law, in a Beaded Medallion.* Fresco. 7th century (before 692). In situ. Reproduced from a copy in the National Museum of Archaeology, Sofia. (After A. Frolow, *L'Eglise Rouge de Pérouchtitza,* in *The Bulletin of the Byzantine Institute of America,* I, Paris, 1946, pl. XIV, 2)

197. Stobi (Yugoslavia), Cathedral Church, narthex. *Fragment of a Head.* Fresco. 6th century. National Museum of Archaeology, Belgrade. (Museum Photo)

198. Salonica, Church of St Demetrios, right aisle. *Emperor at the Head of his Army entering Salonica.* Fresco. 6th century. In situ. Discovered shortly before the fire of 1917. (Photo Emile Séraf, Athens)

199. Coptic Art. Bawit (Egypt). *Icon of Bishop Abraham.* 6th-7th century. Staatliche Museen, Berlin. Tempera Painting. 14 $^1/_2$ by 10 $^1/_2$ inches. (Museum Photo)

200. Sinai (Egypt), Monastery of St Catherine, church. *The Sacrifice of Abraham, detail.* 6th-7th century. Encaustic painting on a wall, brought to light by Kurt Weitzmann in 1958. In situ. (Photo Kurt Weitzmann)

201. Sinai (Egypt), Monastery of St Catherine. *Double Icon of St Sergius and St Bacchus, with the Head of Christ in a Small Medallion.* 6th-7th century. Kiev Museum. Encaustic Painting. 16 ¹/₂ by 11 inches. (Photo Musée du Louvre, Antiquités chrétiennes)

202. Sinai (Egypt), Monastery of St Catherine. *Icon of St Peter, detail.* 6th century. Encaustic Painting. In situ. (Photo Hassia)

203. Sinai (Egypt), Monastery of St Catherine. *Icon of the Virgin and Child enthroned between Saints and Angels, detail.* 6th century. Encaustic Painting. In situ. (Photo Hassia)

204. Coptic Art. Bawit (Egypt). *Icon representing Christ and the Abbot Menas, with Inscriptions.* 6th-7th century. Tempera painting on wood. Louvre, Paris. Height 22 ¹/₂ inches, width 22 ¹/₂ inches, thickness of the panel 3/4 of an inch. (Photo U.D.F.-Draeger)

205. *Icon with Gospel Scenes.* Originally the lid of a reliquary casket. 6th century. Museo Sacro, Vatican City. (Photo Biblioteca apostolica vaticana)

206. Place of origin unknown. *Icon of the Virgin and Child, detail.* 6th century. Rome, Santa Maria Nuova, sacristy. Encaustic Painting. (Photo Scala)

207. *Ashburnham Pentateuch: The Story of Jacob and Esau.* Late 6th-early 7th century. Paris, Bibliothèque Nationale, Nouv. acq. lat. 2334, folio 25. Miniature painting on vellum. 14 ¹/₂ by 13 inches. (Photo Bibliothèque Nationale)

208. *Fragment of a Greek Manuscript with Various Figures.* 1st-2nd century A.D. Paris, Bibliothèque Nationale, Suppl. grec 1294. Papyrus. 7¹/₂ by 15³/₄ inches. (Photo Bibliothèque Nationale)

209. *Fragment of the Alexandrine Chronicle. Marginal Figure: The Patriarch Theophilus.* 5th century. Pushkin Museum of Fine Arts, Moscow (Golenischev Collection). Papyrus. (Museum Photo)

210. Rome. *Codex Vergilius Vaticanus: The Death of Dido (Aeneid, Book IV).* Late 4th century. Vatican Library, Vat. lat. 3225, folio 41 recto. Miniature painting on vellum. 4 ⁵/₈ by 6 ¹/₈ inches. (Photo Vatican Library)

211. Rome. *Codex Vergilius Vaticanus: The Construction of a City (Aeneid, Book I).* Late 4th century. Vatican Library, Vat. lat. 3225, folio 13 recto. Miniature painting on vellum. 6¹/₄ by 6¹/₂ inches. (Photo Vatican Library)

212. Rome. *Codex Vergilius Romanus: Shepherds tending their Flocks (Georgics, Book III).* Late 4th century. Vatican Library, Vat. lat. 3867, folio 44 recto. Miniature painting on vellum. 8⁵/₈ by 8³/₄ inches. (Photo Vatican Library)

213. Greek Artist. *Homer's Iliad: Battle Scenes.* About 500. Biblioteca Ambrosiana, Milan. (Photo Biblioteca Ambrosiana)

214. Constantinople. *Manuscript of Dioscorides, De Materia Medica: Juliana Anicia escorted by Magnanimity and Reflection, with Winged Genii.* Early 6th century. Vienna, Nationalbibliothek, Vindob. med. gr. 1. Miniature painting. Size of the page 14¹/₂ by 11³/₄ inches. Diameter of the circle 9 inches. Manuscript illustrated for Princess Juliana Anicia, grand-daughter of Valentinian III and wife of the Consul Areobindus. (Photo Nationalbibliothek)

215. Constantinople. *Manuscript of Dioscorides, De Materia Medica: Dioscorides receiving the Mandrake Root from Euresis, with a Dog in Convulsions at his Feet.* Early 6th century. Vienna, Nationalbibliothek, Vindob. med. gr. 1, folio 4 recto. Miniature painting. 14¹/₂ by 11³/₄ inches. (Photo Nationalbibliothek)

216. *Book of Genesis, known as the Vienna Genesis. Eliezer and Rebecca at the Well, detail: Personification of the Well.* Early 6th century. Vienna, Nationalbibliothek, Vindob. theol. gr. 31, folio 7, page 13. Miniature painting on purple vellum. 12 ¹/₄ by 9 ³/₄ inches. (Photo U.D.F.-Draeger) Cf. fig. 223.

217. *Book of Genesis, known as the Vienna Genesis. Eliezer and Rebecca at the Well, detail: Rebecca giving Eliezer Water to Drink.* Early 6th century. Vienna, Nationalbibliothek, Vindob. theol. gr. 31, folio 7, page 13. Miniature painting on purple vellum. 12¹/₄ by 9³/₄ inches. (Photo U.D.F.-Draeger). Cf. fig. 223.

218. *Book of Genesis, known as the Vienna Genesis. Eliezer and Rebecca's Parents.* Early 6th century. Vienna, Nationalbibliothek, Vindob. theol. gr. 31, folio 7, page 14. Miniature painting on purple vellum. 12 ¹/₄ by 9 ³/₄ inches. (Photo U.D.F-Draeger)

219. *Book of Genesis, known as the Vienna Genesis. Eliezer and Rebecca at the Well, detail: The City of Nahor.* Early 6th century. Vienna, Nationalbibliothek, Vindob. theol. gr. 31, folio 7, page 13. Miniature painting on purple vellum. 12 ¹/₄ by 9 ³/₄ inches. (Photo U.D.F.- Draeger) Cf. fig. 223.

220. *Book of Genesis, known as the Vienna Genesis. The Death of Deborah.* Early 6th century. Vienna, Nationalbibliothek, Vindob. theol. gr. 31, folio 13, page 26. Miniature painting on purple vellum. 12 ¹/₄ by 9 ³/₄ inches. (Photo Nationalbibliothek)

221. *Book of Genesis, known as the Vienna Genesis. The Death and Burial of Jacob.* Early 6th century. Vienna, Nationalbibliothek, Vindob. theol. gr. 31, folio 24, page 48. Miniature painting on purple vellum. 12 ¹/₄ by 9 ³/₄ inches. (Photo Nationalbibliothek)

222. *Book of Genesis, known as the Vienna Genesis. The Episode of Potiphar's Wife.* Early 6th century. Vienna, Nationalbibliothek, Vindob. theol. gr. 31, folio 16, page 32. Miniature painting on purple vellum. 12 ¹/₄ by 9 ³/₄ inches. (Photo U.D.F.-Draeger)

223. *Book of Genesis, known as the Vienna Genesis. Eliezer and Rebecca at the Well.* Early 6th century. Vienna, Nationalbibliothek, Vindob. theol. gr. 31, folio 7, page 13. Miniature painting on purple vellum. 12 ¹/₄ by 9 ³/₄ inches. (Photo U.D.F.-Draeger)

224. *Cottonian Genesis. The Third Day of Creation: The Lord with Three Angels, detail.* Date of the original manuscript (British Museum): 6th century. Reproduced from the early 17th century copy of Peiresc in the Bibliothèque Nationale, Paris (MS fr. 9530). Miniature Painting. (Photo Bibliothèque Nationale)
The original manuscript in the Cottonian library was badly damaged in a fire at Ashburnham House, Westminster, in 1731; only charred fragments remain (in the British Museum). Two copies however were made before the fire on the initiative of Nicolas Peiresc.

225. Sinope (Asia Minor). *Codex Sinopensis. The Multiplication of the Loaves and Fishes, detail.* 6th century. Paris, Bibliothèque Nationale, Suppl. gr. 1286, folio 11. Purple vellum with golden uncials. Miniature at the bottom of the page. Size of the page 11³/₄ by 9³/₄ inches. (Photo Bibliothèque Nationale)

226. Sinope (Asia Minor). *Codex Sinopensis. Christ healing the Two Blind Men of Jericho.* 6th century. Paris, Bibliothèque Nationale, Suppl. gr. 1286, folio 29. Purple vellum with golden uncials. Miniature at the bottom of the page. Size of the page 11 ³/₄ by 9 ³/₄ inches. (Photo Bibliothèque Nationale)

227. Sinope (Asia Minor). *Codex Sinopensis. Herod's Feast, with Salome receiving John the Baptist's Head in a Charger.* 6th century. Paris, Bibliothèque Nationale, Suppl. gr. 1286, folio 10 verso. Purple vellum with golden uncials. Miniature at the bottom of the page. Size of the page 11 ³/₄ by 9 ³/₄ inches. (Photo Bibliothèque Nationale)

228. *Rossano Gospel Book (Codex Purpureus). Entry of Christ into Jerusalem.* 6th century. Rossano (Calabria), Palazzo Arcivescovile, Museo Diocesano, folio 11. Miniature painting on purple vellum, with text written in silver letters. (Hirmer Fotoarchiv, Munich)

229. *Rossano Gospel Book (Codex Purpureus). The Communion of the Apostles, detail.* 6th century. Rossano (Calabria), Palazzo Arcivescovile, Museo Diocesano, folio 61. Miniature painting on purple vellum, with text written in silver letters. (Hirmer Fotoarchiv, Munich)

230. *Rossano Gospel Book (Codex Purpureus). The Last Supper.* 6th century. Rossano (Calabria), Palazzo Arcivescovile, Museo Diocesano, folio 3. Miniature painting on purple vellum, with text written in silver letters. (Hirmer Fotoarchiv, Munich)

231. *Rossano Gospel Book (Codex Purpureus). Parable of the Wise and Foolish Virgins.* 6th century. Rossano (Calabria), Palazzo Arcivescovile, Museo Diocesano, folio 4. Miniature painting on purple vellum, with text written in silver letters. (Hirmer Fotoarchiv, Munich)

232. *Rossano Gospel Book (Codex Purpureus). Pilate bidding the Jews choose between Christ and Barabbas.* 6th century. Rossano (Calabria), Palazzo Arcivescovile, Museo Diocesano, folio 16. Miniature painting on purple vellum, with text written in silver letters. (Hirmer Fotoarchiv, Munich)

233. *Rabula Gospels. Pentecost.* 6th century. Text written in 586. Florence, Biblioteca Laurenziana, Plut. I, Cod. 56, folio 14b. Miniature painting on vellum. Manuscript written by the monk Rabula at the Monastery of

Zagba (Mesopotamia) on the Euphrates. (Photo Guido Sansoni)

234. *Rabula Gospels.* Canon Tables. 6th century. Text written in 586. Florence, Biblioteca Laurenziana, Plut. I, Cod. 56, folio 10. Miniature painting on vellum. Cf. fig. 233. (Photo Guido Sansoni)

235. *Rabula Gospels. Canon Tables and Marginal Decoration, detail.* 6th century. Text written in 586. Florence, Biblioteca Laurenziana, Plut. I, Cod. 56, folio 11a. Miniature painting on vellum. Cf. fig. 233. (Photo Guido Sansoni)

236. *Rabula Gospels. An Evangelist* (?). 6th century. Text written in 586. Florence, Biblioteca Laurenziana, Plut. I, Cod. 56, folio 14a. Miniature painting on vellum. Cf. fig. 233. (Photo Guido Sansoni)

237. *Rabula Gospels. The Ascension, detail: Christ ascending into Heaven.* 6th century. Text written in 586. Florence, Biblioteca Laurenziana, Plut. I, Cod. 56, folio 13b. Miniature painting on vellum. Cf. fig. 233. (Photo Guido Sansoni)

238. Italy. *Eusebian Canon Tables.* 6th century. Vatican Library, Vat. lat. 3806, folio 11 verso. Miniature painting on vellum, 13 ³/₈ by 10 ³/₄ inches. (Photo Vatican Library)

239. Italy. *So-called Gospel Book of St Augustine. St Luke enthroned in a Tabernacle flanked by Twin Columns enclosing superimposed Scenes from the Life of Christ.* Late 6th century. Cambridge, Corpus Christi College Library, MS 286, folio 129 verso. Miniature painting on vellum, 7 ⁷/₈ by 6 inches. (Photo Stearn & Sons)

240. Italy. *So-called Gospel Book of St Augustine. Detail of the Scenes from the Life of Christ on folio 129 verso.* Late 6th century. Cambridge, Corpus Christi College Library, MS 286. Cf. No. 239. (Photo Stearn & Sons)

241. Italy. *So-called Gospel Book of St Augustine. Detail of the Scenes from the Life of Christ on folio 129 verso.* Late 6th century. Cambridge, Corpus Christi College Library, MS 286. Cf. No. 239. (Photo Stearn & Sons)

242. Place of origin unknown. *Ashburnham Pentateuch. The Story of Adam.* Late 6th-early 7th century. Paris, Bibliothèque Nationale, Nouv. acq. lat. 2334, folio 6. Miniature painting on vellum, 14 ¹/₂ by 13 inches. (Photo Bibliothèque Nationale)

243. Place of origin unknown. *Ashburnham Pentateuch. The Flood.* Late 6th-early 7th century. Paris, Bibliothèque Nationale, Nouv. acq. lat. 2334, folio 9. Miniature painting on vellum, 14 ¹/₂ by 13 inches. (Photo Bibliothèque Nationale)

244. Place of origin unknown. *Head of a Man: Eutropios, Citizen of Ephesus.* 5th century. Vienna, Kunsthistorisches Museum, Antikensammlung. Pentelic marble. Height 12 ¹/₂ inches. (Museum Photo)

245. Constantinople, Spina of the Hippodrome. *Base of the Obelisk of Theodosius I: The Emperor Theodosius in the Circus with his Court.* About 390-395. In situ. Marble. Height 19 ¹/₂ ft. (Photo Roger Viollet)

246. Constantinople, Spina of the Hippodrome. *Base of the Obelisk of Theodosius I: The Emperor Theodosius with his Court, his Guards, and Spectators. On the pedestal, Inscriptions.* About 390-395. In situ. Marble. Height 19 ¹/₂ ft. (Photo A. Perissinotto, Padua)

247. *Colossal Statue of the Emperor Valentinian I ( ? ) in Military Costume.* 4th century. Bronze. Barletta (Apulia, Italy), beside the Church of San Sepolcro. Height 16 ft 9 inches. (Hirmer Fotoarchiv, Munich)

248. *Headless Statue of a Figure wearing a Chlamys.* 5th century. Corinth Museum. Marble. (Photo Hassia)

249. Constantinople. *Headless Statue of a Figure wearing a Toga.* 5th century. Istanbul, Archaeological Museum. Marble and alabaster. Height 50 ³/₄ inches. Found in the Labli Jami district. (Photo Halük Doganbey)

250. *Torso of an Emperor wearing a Chlamys.* 5th century. Berlin, Staatliche Museen. Porphyry. Height 37 ¹/₄ inches. (Museum Photo)

251. *Torso of an Emperor wearing a Chlamys.* 5th century. Ravenna, Museo Arcivescovile. Porphyry. (Photo Villani & Figli, Bologna)

252. Aphrodisias (Asia Minor). *Dignitary wearing a Chlamys.* 5th century. Istanbul, Archaeological Museum. (Photo Halük Doganbey)

253. *Head of the Empress Ariadne ( ? ).* 6th century. Paris, Louvre (Isaac de Camondo Bequest). Marble (nose restored). 11 by 8 ¹/₄ inches. (Photo U.D.F.-La Photothèque)

254. Aphrodisias (Asia Minor). *Dignitary wearing a Chlamys, detail.* 5th century. Istanbul, Archaeological Museum. Cf. No. 252. (Photo A. Perissinotto, Padua)

255. Constantinople. *Sarcophagus of a Child, detail of the long side: Winged Angels holding the Monogram of Christ.* About 400. Istanbul, Archaeological Museum. White marble. Length 59 inches, width 24 ³/₄ inches. Found in the suburb of Sariguzel. (Photo A. Perissinotto, Padua)

256. Constantinople. *Sarcophagus of a Child, detail of the short side: Head of an Apostle.* About 400. Istanbul, Archaeological Museum. Cf. No. 255. (Photo A. Perissinotto, Padua)

257. Constantinople. *Sarcophagus of a Child, short side: Two Apostles venerating the Cross.* About 400. Istanbul, Archaeological Museum. Cf. No. 255. (Photo A. Perissinotto)

258. Constantinople. *Fragment of a Sarcophagus: The so-called Psamatia Christ.* About 400. Berlin, Staatliche Museen. Marble. 56 by 49 inches. (Museum Photo)

259. Constantinople, Church of St John of Studion. *Fragment of a Sarcophagus, detail: Five Apostles under a Mitre Arch.* 5th century. Istanbul, Archaeological Museum. Limestone. 52 by 23 ¹/₂ inches. (Photo A. Perissinotto, Padua)

260. Constantinople. *Medallion with the Bust of an Evangelist.* 5th century. Istanbul, Archaeological Museum. (Photo A. Perissinotto, Padua)

261. Constantinople. *Fragment of a Sarcophagus, detail: Christ enthroned and St Peter under an Ornamental Band.* 5th-6th century. Istanbul, Archaeological Museum. Stone. (Museum Photo)

262. Constantinople. *Column Drum, detail: The Baptism of Christ.* 5th century. Istanbul, Archaeological Museum. Marble. Height 25 ¹/₂ inches. (Photo A. Perissinotto, Padua)

263. Salonica, Church of St George. *Ambo, detail: One of the Magi in a Niche.* 5th century. Istanbul, Archaeological Museum. Stone. 70 ¹/₂ by 32 ¹/₄ inches. (Photo A. Perissinotto, Padua)

264. Salonica, Church of St George. *Ambo, detail: Virgin and Child in a Niche.* 5th century. Istanbul, Archaeological Museum. Cf. No. 263. (Photo A. Perissinotto, Padua)

265. Salonica, Church of St George. *Ambo, detail of the side: Virgin and Child surrounded by Angels, in a Conch-shaped Niche surmounted by a Carved Entablature.* 5th century. Istanbul, Archaeological Museum. Cf. No. 263. (Photo A. Perissinotto, Padua)

266. Antioch, Martyrium of Antioch-Seleucia. *Fragment of a Piece of Church Furniture: Daniel.* 5th-6th century. Princeton University. White marble streaked with grey. Height 15 inches, thickness 2 ¹/₄ inches. (University Photo by courtesy of the committee in charge of the Antioch excavations)

267. Antioch, Martyrium of Antioch-Seleucia. *Fragment of a Piece of Church Furniture: Joseph in Prison.* 5th-6th century. Princeton University. Greyish marble with incised reliefs. Height 10 ¹/₂ inches, thickness 1 inch. (University Photo by courtesy of the committee in charge of the Antioch excavations)

268. Antioch, Martyrium of Antioch-Seleucia. *Fragment of a Piece of Church Furniture: Goliath.* 5th-6th century. Princeton University. Marble. Height 12 ¹/₂ inches, thickness 7/8 of an inch. (University Photo by courtesy of the committee in charge of the Antioch excavations)

269. Coptic Art. Ahnas el-Medineh (Egypt). *Fragment of an Acanthus Frieze with a Bust of Hercules.* 5th century. Old Cairo, Coptic Museum. Limestone. 14 ¹/₂ by 15 ³/₄ inches. (Photo École des Hautes Études, Paris)

270. Coptic Art. Ahnas el-Medineh (Egypt). *Niche with a Pediment, detail: Nereid on a Sea Lion.* 5th century. Old Cairo, Coptic Museum. Limestone. Overall size (with acroteria) 40 ¹/₈ by 21 inches. (Photo Costa, Cairo)

271. Coptic Art. Ahnas el-Medineh (Egypt). *Niche with a Pediment, detail: Pan Pursuing a Bacchante.* 5th century. Old Cairo, Coptic Museum. Limestone. Overall size 45 ¹/₄ by 15 ³/₄ inches. (Photo Costa, Cairo)

272. Coptic Art. Ahnas el-Medineh (Egypt). *Fragment of a Pilaster, detail: Bust of a Bearded Man with Two Figurines on his Shoulders.* 5th century. Old Cairo, Coptic Museum. Limestone. (Photo École des Hautes Études, Paris)

273. Coptic Art. Ahnas el-Medineh (Egypt). *Nereid dancing and Cupid on a Dolphin.* 5th century. Trieste, Civico Museo di Storia ed Arte. Limestone. 23 ¹/₂ by 20 ¹/₂ inches. (Photo U.D.F.-Draeger)

274. Coptic Art. Sohag (Egypt). *Fragment of a Niche: Flying Angel carrying the Monogram of Christ in a Wreath.* 5th-6th century. Old Cairo, Coptic Museum. Limestone. (Photo École des Hautes Études, Paris)

275. Coptic Art. Sohag (Egypt). *Fragment of a Pediment, detail: Flying Angel carrying the Monogram of Christ in a Wreath.* 5th-6th century. Old Cairo, Coptic Museum. Limestone. Overall size 15 ¹/₄ by 63 inches. (Photo Costa, Cairo)

276. Coptic Art. Ahnas el-Medineh (Egypt). *Niche, detail: Venus crouching in a Shell.* 5th century. Old Cairo, Coptic Museum. Limestone. Overall width 30 ³/₄ inches. (Photo Costa, Cairo)

277. Coptic Art. Ahnas el-Medineh (Egypt). *Pilaster Capital: Two Flying Genii holding forth a Mask.* 5th century. Old Cairo, Coptic Museum. Limestone. Width 30 inches. (Photo Costa, Cairo)

278. Coptic Art. Bawit (Egypt). *Lintel, detail: Two Flying Angels holding an Image of Christ in Majesty.* 6th century. Old Cairo, Coptic Museum. Limestone. Overall size 47 ¹/₄ by 35 ¹/₂ inches. (Photo Costa, Cairo)

279. Coptic Art. Egypt. *Pediment, detail: Dionysos driving a Chariot drawn by Bulls.* Mid 5th century. Washington, Dumbarton Oaks Collections. Limestone. Height 17 ¹/₂ inches, width at the top 45 inches, width at the bottom 44 ⁷/₈ inches. (Collection Photo)

280. Coptic Art. Egypt. *Funerary Stele: Orant under a Mitre Arch.* 5th-6th century. Old Cairo, Coptic Museum. Limestone. 28 by 23 ⁵/₈ inches. (Photo Costa, Cairo)

281. Coptic Art. Egypt. *Funerary Stele: Orant under a Mitre Arch flanked by two Crosses.* 5th-6th century. Old Cairo, Coptic Museum. Limestone. 28 ³/₈ by 17 ³/₄ inches. (Photo Costa, Cairo)

282. Ravenna, Orthodox Baptistery (also called Cathedral Baptistery or Baptistery of Neon). *View of the Interior, detail: Prophets in a Simulated 'Tabernacle.'* Stucco. First quarter of the 5th century. (Photo A. Perissinotto, Padua)

283. Tralles (Asia Minor). *Baluster of an Ambo, detail: The Good Shepherd and his Dog.* 5th century. Istanbul, Archaeological Museum. (Photo A. Perissinotto, Padua)

284. Ravenna. *Ambo of Bishop Agnellus, detail.* 5th century. Ravenna Cathedral. Marble. Overall size about 10 by 21 ft. (Photo Villani & Figli, Bologna)

285. Constantinople. *Front of a Sarcophagus: Christ enthroned between the Four Evangelists, detail.* 6th century. Istanbul, Archaeological Museum. Limestone. Overall size: length 81 inches; height on the right (with acroterium) 49 ¹/₂ inches; height on the left (with acroterium) 47 ¹/₄ inches; thickness 7 ⁷/₈ inches; height of the columns 12 ¹/₈ to 13 ³/₈ inches; height of the capitals 4 inches. Found in the Taskasap district. (Photo A. Perissinotto, Padua)

286. Ravenna. *Sarcophagus: The Young Christ delivering the Law to St Peter.* 4th century. Ravenna, San Francesco. Proconnesos marble. (Photo Alinari)

287. Constantinople. *Front of a Sarcophagus: Christ enthroned between the Four Evangelists (?). Busts in the Acroteria.* 6th century. Istanbul, Archaeological Museum. Cf. No. 285. (Photo A. Perissinotto, Padua)

288. Ravenna. *So-called Sarcophagus of the Twelve Apostles: Christ enthroned delivering the Law to St Peter.* 5th century. Ravenna, Sant'Apollinare in Classe. Proconnesos marble. (Photo Alinari)

289. *Figure of an Orant on a Sarcophagus.* 5th century. Tarragona, Palaeochristian Museum. White marble with very low reliefs. Sarcophagus found in the Christian cemetery at Tarragona (Spain). (Photo Mas, Barcelona)

290. Ravenna. *So-called Rinaldo Sarcophagus: Christ enthroned receiving Crowns from Two Apostles.* 5th century. Ravenna Cathedral. Proconnesos marble. (Photo Villani & Figli, Bologna)

291. Ravenna. *So-called Sarcophagus of Constantius, detail: Lamb and Sheep.* 5th century. Ravenna, Mausoleum of Galla Placidia. Proconnesos marble. (Photo Villani & Figli, Bologna)

292. *So-called Sarcophagus of St Sidonius.* 5th century. Saint-Maximin-la-Sainte-Baume (Var), Basilica of the Madeleine. (Photo U.D.F.-La Photothèque)

293. Ravenna. *Sarcophagus: Christ on a Mound delivering the Law and giving Benediction.* 5th century. Ravenna, Museo Nazionale. Proconnesos marble. (Photo Alinari)

294. *So-called Sarcophagus of St Sidonius, detail: Tabitha raised from the Dead by St Peter.* 5th century. Saint-Maximin-la-Sainte-Baume (Var), Basilica of the Madeleine. Cf. No. 292. (Photo U.D.F.-La Photothèque)

295. South-western France. *Sarcophagus: Christ with the Twelve Apostles in an Architectural Setting. On the lid, Daniel in the Lions' Den.* 6th-7th century. Saint-Guilhem-le-Désert (Hérault), Church. Marble. (Photo R. Dunoyer, Clermont-l'Hérault)

296. *So-called Sarcophagus of Archbishop Theodore: Confronted Peacocks flanking the Monogram of Christ. On the lid, Christological Symbols.* 5th-6th century. Re-employed in the 7th century for the body of Theodore. Ravenna, Sant'Apollinare in Classe. Proconnesos marble. (Photo Villani & Figli, Bologna)

297. South-western France. *Sarcophagus, detail of the lid: Daniel in the Lions' Den.* 6th-7th century. Saint-Guilhem-le-Désert (Hérault), Church. Cf. No. 295. (Photo R. Dunoyer, Clermont-l'Hérault)

298. *Sarcophagus of St Drausius, Bishop of Soissons, detail: Scrollwork.* 7th century. Paris, Louvre. Marble. (Photo U.D.F.-La Photothèque)

299. Rome. *Scenes from the Old and New Testaments, detail: The Crucifixion.* Wood carvings on the door of Santa Sabina, Rome. 5th century. Cypress wood. (Photo Alinari)

300. Rome. *Scenes from the Old and New Testaments, detail: The Ascension of Elijah.* Wood carvings on the door of Santa Sabina, Rome. 5th century. Cypress wood. (Photo Alinari)

301. Antioch. *Frieze with Floral Reliefs.* 5th century. Present whereabouts unknown. Marble. Length at the top 49 ¹/₂ inches; height 17 ³/₈ inches; thickness 5 ¹/₂ inches. (Photo Fadihl Saba)

302. Antioch. *Fragment of the Revetment from the Edge of a Fountain.* 5th century. The Baltimore Museum of Art. White marble. Height 25 ³/₄ inches; width 27 ¹/₂ inches; thickness 3 ¹/₂ inches. (Museum Photo)

303. Coptic Art. Bawit (Egypt). *Circular Relief between Two Columns.* 6th century. Berlin, Staatliche Museen. Limestone. 24 by 33 ¹/₂ inches. (Museum Photo)

304. Coptic Art. Sakkara (Egypt). *Capital with Vine Tendrils and Bunches of Grapes.* 6th century. Old Cairo, Coptic Museum. Limestone. 15 by 12 ¹/₂ inches. (Photo U.D.F.-Draeger)

305. Coptic Art. Sohag (Egypt), Red Monastery (Deir el-Ahmar). *Carved Frame of the South Door.* 5th-6th century. In situ. (After G. Duthuit, *La sculpture copte*, Paris, 1941, pl. LI)

306. Coptic Art. Egypt. *Frieze: Circles with Crosses and Fruit forming Scrollwork.* 6th century. Old Cairo, Coptic Museum. Limestone. 45 ³/₄ by 15 inches. (Photo Costa, Cairo)

307. Coptic Art. Alexandria. *Basket-shaped Capital with a Floral Motif in the Centre.* 6th century. Old Cairo, Coptic Museum. Marble. Height 32 ¹/₂ inches. (Photo Costa, Cairo)

308. Salonica, Basilica of the Virgin Acheiropoietos. *Capital with 'Windblown' Acanthus Leaves.* 5th century. In situ. (Photo Hassia)

309. Coptic Art. Sakkara (Egypt). *Column Shaft.* 5th-6th century. Old Cairo, Coptic Museum. Limestone. (Photo Costa, Cairo)

310. Constantinople. *Pedestal carved on Three Sides, detail.* About 500. Istanbul, Archaeological Museum. Marble. Height 59 ³/₄ inches. Found near the Hippodrome, Istanbul. (Photo A. Perissinotto, Padua)

311. Philippi (Greece), Church A. *Corinthian Capital.* Late 5th century. In situ. (Photo Émile Séraf, Athens)

312. Constantinople, St Sophia. *Openwork Capitals.* 6th century. In situ. Marble. (Photo A. Perissinotto, Padua)

313. Philippi (Greece), Church B. *Capital.* Second half of the 6th century. In situ. (Photo Émile Séraf, Athens)

314. Constantinople, St Sophia. *Openwork Capital.* 6th century. In situ. Marble. (Photo A. Perissinotto, Padua)

315. Ravenna. *Closure Slab of the Chancel Screen.* 6th century. Ravenna, San Vitale. Marble. (Photo Alinari)

316. Ravenna. *Closure Slab of the Chancel Screen.* 6th century. Ravenna, Sant' Apollinare Nuovo. Marble. (Photo Villani & Figli, Bologna)

317. Ravenna. *Closure Slab of the Chancel Screen.* 6th century. Ravenna, Sant' Apollinare Nuovo. Marble. (Photo Villani & Figli, Bologna)

318. Constantinople (?). *Leaf of a Diptych, detail: The Empress Ariadne.* 6th century (c. 500). Florence, Museo Nazionale (Bargello). Ivory. Overall size: height 14 3/8 inches; width 5 3/8 inches; thickness 7/8 of an inch. (Photo Alinari)

319. Constantinople (?). *Leaf of the Diptych known as the Barberini Ivory.* Late 5th or 6th century. Paris, Louvre. Ivory. Overall size 13 3/8 by 10 3/8 inches. Size of the central panel 7 7/8 inches by 5 1/4 inches. Inscriptions on the back record the presence of this diptych at Trier in the early Middle Ages and at Aix-en-Provence in the 17th century. (Photo U.D.F.-La Photothèque)

320. Constantinople. *Leaf of the Diptych of the Consul Areobindus: Consul, Spectators, Circus.* About 506. Zurich, Schweizerisches Landesmuseum. Ivory. 14 1/8 by 5 1/8 inches. (Museum Photo)

321. Constantinople. *Leaf of a Diptych: The Archangel Michael.* Early 6th century. London, British Museum. Ivory. 17 by 5 5/8 inches. (Museum Photo)

322. Constantinople (?). *Leaf of the Diptych known as the Barberini Ivory, detail: Triumph of an Emperor.* Late 5th or 6th century. Paris, Louvre. Cf. No. 319. (Photo U.D.F.-La Photothèque)

323. Gaul (?). *Leaf of a Diptych: Muses and Poets.* 5th-6th century. Paris, Louvre. Ivory. (Museum Photo, M. Chuzeville)

324. *Apollo and Daphne.* 5th-6th century. Ravenna, Museo Nazionale. Ivory. 4 7/8 by 3 3/8 inches. (Photo Villani & Figli, Bologna)

325. Constantinople. *Leaf of the Diptych of the Consul Areobindus, detail: Games in the Circus.* About 506. Zurich, Schweizerisches Landesmuseum. Cf. No. 320. (Museum Photo)

326. Constantinople. *Leaf of the Diptych of the Consul Magnus: The Consul seated between two Figures personifying Rome and Constantinople.* 518. Paris, Bibliothèque Nationale, Cabinet des Médailles. Ivory. 10 1/4 (originally 15 1/8) by 5 1/8 inches. (Photo Bibliothèque Nationale)

327. Rome. *Apotheosis of an Emperor.* 5th century. London, British Museum. Ivory. (Museum Photo)

328. Rome. *Apotheosis of an Emperor, detail: The Emperor borne by the Winds.* 5th century. London, British Museum. Cf. No. 327. (Museum Photo)

329. Rome. *Diptych of the Consul Probus Anicius. On one leaf, the Consul. On the other, the Emperor Honorius dressed as a Roman General and holding a Sceptre.* 406. Aosta, Cathedral Treasury. Ivory. 11 3/4 by 5 1/8 inches. (Photo Alinari)

330. Constantinople. *Leaf of the Diptych of the Consul Flavius Anastasius, detail: Amazons and Tragic Actors.* 517. Paris, Bibliothèque Nationale, Cabinet des Médailles. Ivory. Overall size 14 1/8 by 5 1/8 inches. (Photo Bibliothèque Nationale)

331. Milan (?). *The Holy Women at the Tomb and Soldiers asleep beside the Holy Sepulchre.* 5th century. Milan, Castello Sforzesco, Museo d'arte antica. Ivory. 12 by 5 1/4 inches. (Museum Photo)

332. Milan (?). *Leaf of the so-called Ascension Diptych: The Ascension and the Holy Women at the Tomb.* 5th century. Munich, Bayerisches Nationalmuseum. Ivory. 7 3/8 by 4 1/2 inches. (Museum Photo)

333. *Cover of a Binding: Scenes from the Life of Christ.* 5th century. Milan, Cathedral Treasury. Ivory, with cross of precious stones. 14 3/4 by 11 inches. (Photo Scala)

334. *Throne of Bishop Maximian.* Between 546 and 556. Ravenna, Museo Arcivescovile. Ivory. (Photo Anderson)

335. *Throne of Bishop Maximian, detail: Two Evangelists.* Between 546 and 556. Ravenna, Museo Arcivescovile. Cf. No. 334. (Photo Anderson)

336. *Throne of Bishop Maximian, detail: Joseph commanding his Brothers' Sacks to be filled with Corn.* Between 546 and 556. Ravenna, Museo Arcivescovile. Cf. No. 334. (Photo Anderson)

337. *Throne of Bishop Maximian, detail: The Meeting of Joseph and Jacob at Goshen.* Between 546 and 556. Ravenna, Museo Arcivescovile. Cf. No. 334. (Photo Anderson)

338. Constantinople. *The Saint-Lupicin Diptych. Above, Two Flying Angels holding a Medallion enclosing the Cross. In the centre, Christ enthroned between St Peter and St Paul. On either side and below, Miracles of Christ.* 6th century. Paris, Bibliothèque Nationale, Cabinet des Médailles (MS lat. 9384). Ivory. This diptych was used as the cover of a binding. (Photo Bibliothèque Nationale)

339. Constantinople. *The Saint-Lupicin Diptych, detail: Christ enthroned between St Peter and St Paul.* 6th century. Paris, Bibliothèque Nationale, Cabinet des Médailles. Cf. No. 338. (Photo Bibliothèque Nationale)

340. *The Baptism of Christ.* 6th century. Lyons, Musée des Beaux-Arts. Ivory. Height 7 1/2 inches. (Photo J. Camponogara)

341. Constantinople. *The Saint-Lupicin Diptych, detail: Christ healing a Blind Man.* 6th century. Paris, Bibliothèque Nationale, Cabinet des Médailles. Cf. No. 338. (Photo Bibliothèque Nationale)

342. *Pyxis, detail: The Martyrdom of St Menas.* 6th century. London, British Museum. Ivory. (Museum Photo)

343. Constantinople (?). *Plate with Silenus and a Maenad, marked on the back with five official stamps, including the monogram and bust of an emperor.* Between 610 and 629. Leningrad, Hermitage. Silver, partly gilt (the bottom). Diameter 10 inches. (Museum Photo)

344. Rome. *Bridal Casket inscribed with the names of Secundus and Projecta.* Early 5th century. London, British Museum. Silver, gilt in places. Found in Rome, on the Esquiline, in 1793. (Museum Photo)

345. Rome. *Bridal Casket of Secundus and Projecta, detail of the lid: Portraits of the Bride and Bridegroom.* Early 5th century. London, British Museum. Cf. No. 344. (Museum Photo)

346. *Plate with Venus and Adonis.* 6th century. Paris, Bibliothèque Nationale, Cabinet des Médailles. Silver. Diameter 11 3/8 inches. (Photo Bibliothèque Nationale)

347. Constantinople. *Plate with Equestrian Portrait of Constantius II.* About 350. Leningrad, Hermitage. Silver, partly gilt (figure and horse). (Museum Photo)

348. Constantinople (?). *Missorium of Theodosius I. The Emperor conferring the Investiture on a High Dignitary in the presence of his Sons, detail: The Emperor Theodosius.* 379-395. Madrid, Academia de la Historia. Silver, with traces of gilding in the inscription. Diameter 29 inches. Discovered in 1847 at Almendralejo (province of Badajoz), Spain. (Photo David Manso Martin)

349. Constantinople (?). *Missorium of Theodosius I, detail: One of the Emperor's Sons.* 379-395. Madrid, Academia de la Historia. Cf. No. 348. (Photo David Manso Martin)

350. Constantinople (?). *Missorium of Theodosius I, detail: Figure personifying Abundance.* 379-395. Madrid, Academia de la Historia. Cf. No. 348. (Photo David Manso Martin)

351. Constantinople (?). *Missorium of Theodosius I, entire.* 379-395. Madrid, Academia de la Historia. Cf. No. 348. (Photo David Manso Martin)

352. Constantinople. *Plate: The Marriage of David in the presence of Saul, detail.* Between 613 and 629-630 (reign of the Emperor Heraclius). Nicosia, Museum of Antiquities. Silver gilt. Diameter 10 ¹/₂ inches. From the treasure discovered in 1902 at Lampoussa, near Kerinia (Cyprus). (Photo Costas Savvides)

353. Constantinople. *Plate: David receiving the Messenger from Samuel.* Between 613 and 629-630 (reign of the Emperor Heraclius). Nicosia, Museum of Antiquities. Silver. Diameter 5 ¹/₂ inches. From the treasure discovered in 1902 at Lampoussa, near Kerinia (Cyprus). (Museum Photo)

354. Constantinople. *Plate: David killing a Bear.* Between 613 and 629-630 (reign of the Emperor Heraclius). Nicosia, Museum of Antiquities. Silver. Diameter 5 ¹/₂ inches. From the treasure discovered in 1902 at Lampoussa, near Kerinia (Cyprus). (Museum Photo)

355. Constantinople. *Plate: The Marriage of David.* Between 613 and 629-630 (reign of the Emperor Heraclius). Nicosia, Museum of Antiquities. Cf. No. 352. (Photo Costas Savvides)

356. *Oval Reliquary with Busts of Saints in Medallions. On the lid, the Cross adored by Angels.* 6th century. Vatican City, Museo Sacro. Silver. (Photo Vatican Library)

357. North Africa. *Lid of the Reliquary known as the Capsella Africana:* Christ crowned, standing on the Four Rivers of Paradise. 5th-6th century. Vatican City, Museo Sacro. Silver. (Photo Vatican Library)

358. *Lid of a Reliquary: The Virgin enthroned.* 6th century. Grado (Venetia), Cathedral Treasury. Silver. (Photo O. Böhm, Venice)

359. Constantinople. *Cross of Justin II, with Scrollwork and Figures in Medallions. The other side is encrusted with precious stones.* 565-578. Vatican City, Treasure of St Peter's. Silver gilt. Height 15 ³/₄ inches; width of the arm 12 ¹/₄ inches. (Photo De Antonis)

360. Syria (?). *The Antioch Chalice: Christ and the Evangelists amid Vine Shoots.* 5th-6th century. New York, The Metropolitan Museum of Art, The Cloisters (formerly Kouchakji Collection). Silver gilt. Height 7 ¹/₂ inches; diameter at the rim 7 inches. (Photo Taylor and Dull, New York)

361. Milan. *Reliquary with Scenes from the Old and New Testaments.* 4th century. Milan, San Nazzaro Maggiore. Silver. (Photo Scala)

362. Syria (?). *The Riha Paten: The Communion of the Apostles. On the back, five official stamps.* 565-578. Washington, Dumbarton Oaks Collections. Silver, partly gilt. Diameter 13 ⁸/₄ inches. Found at Riha, Syria. (Collection Photo)

363. Palestine. *Ampulla, back: The Ascension.* About 600. Monza (North Italy), Cathedral Treasury (Ampulla No. 11). Silver. (Photo Farina)

364. Palestine. *Ampulla, back: The Resurrection.* About 600. Monza (North Italy), Cathedral Treasury (Ampulla No. 3). Silver. (Photo Farina)

365. Syria. *The Stuma Paten: The Communion of the Apostles. On the back, five official stamps.* 565-578. Istanbul, Archaeological Museum. Silver, partly gilt. Diameter 14 ⁵/₄ inches. Found in 1908 at Stuma, Syria. (Photo Halük Doganbey)

366. Syria. *The Homs Vase, detail of the ornamental band with medallions: Christ in a Medallion.* Early 6th century. Paris, Louvre. Silver. Height 17 ¹/₄ inches. Found at Homs, Syria. (Photo U.D.F.-La Photothèque)

367. Syria. *The Homs Vase.* Early 6th century. Paris, Louvre. Cf. No. 366. (Photo U.D.F.-La Photothèque)

368. *Medallion of Licinia Eudoxia.* 5th century. Paris, Bibliothèque Nationale, Cabinet des Médailles. Gold. (Photo Bibliothèque Nationale)

369. Constantinople. *Medallion from a Pectoral Cross: Virgin and Child, Nativity, and Adoration of the Magi.* About 600. Washington, Dumbarton Oaks Collections. Gold. Diameter 25 ¹/₄ inches. (Collection Photo)

370. Constantinople. *Medallion from a Pectoral Cross, obverse: The Baptism of Christ.* About 600. Washington, Dumbarton Oaks Collections. Cf. No. 369. (Collection Photo)

371. *Bracelet with Floral Designs and Encrusted Stones.* 5th-6th century. Berlin, Staatliche Museen. Gold. (Museum Photo)

372. *Bracelet with Bust of an Orant in a Medallion.* London, British Museum. Gold. (Museum Photo)

373. *Bracelet with Plant Motifs.* 6th century. New York, The Metropolitan Museum of Art, Pierpont Morgan Donation. Gold. (Museum Photo)

374. *Cross adorned with Reliefs: Christ surrounded by Four Medallions.* 6th-7th century. Washington, Dumbarton Oaks Collections. Gold. (Collection Photo)

375. *Necklet with Medallion representing the Annunciation.* 5th-6th century. Berlin, Staatliche Museen. (Museum Photo, Jutta Tietz-Glagow)

376. *Pail with Dionysian Scenes.* 5th century. Venice, Treasure of St Mark's. Tinted glass. (Photo O. Böhm, Venice)

377. *Pail with Dionysian Scenes, detail: A Maenad.* 5th century. Venice, Treasure of St Mark's. Cf. No. 376. (Photo O. Böhm, Venice)

378. *Pail with Hunting Scenes.* 4th century. Venice, Treasure of St Mark's. Tinted Glass. (Photo O. Böhm, Venice)

379. Tunisia. *Lamp in the form of a Church with projecting Apse.* 5th century. Leningrad, Hermitage. Bronze. (Museum Photo)

380. Egypt. *Personification of Earth: The Goddess Gaea.* 3rd century. Leningrad, Hermitage. Woollen tapestry on linen. Diameter of medallion 10 inches. (Museum Photo)

381. Egypt. *Fragment of a Tunic.* 5th century. The Museum of Fine Arts, Boston, Charles Potter Kling Fund. Tapestry of wool, silk and gold. (Museum Photo)

382. Egypt. *Chosroes I watching a Battle between Mounted Archers and Abyssinians of the Kingdom of Axum ( ?).* 6th century. Lyons, Musée Historique des Tissus. Woollen Tapestry. 29 ¹/₂ by 19 ⁵/₈ inches. Found at Antinoe, Egypt. (Photo René Basset)

383. Egypt. *Tapestry Hanging: Two Naiads.* 5th century. Washington, Dumbarton Oaks Collections. Woollen Tapestry. (Collection Photo)

384. Egypt. *Tapestry Hanging, detail: Naiad looking at her Reflection in a Shell.* 5th century. Washington, Dumbarton Oaks Collections. Cf. No. 383. (Collection Photo)

385. Egypt. *Tapestry Hanging: Flying Genii with Bird and Flower Designs.* 5th-6th century. New York, The Metropolitan Museum of Art, Rogers Fund. Tapestry. 59 by 35 ¹/₂ inches. (Museum Photo)

386. Egypt. *Tapestry Hanging with an Orant.* 6th-7th century. The Detroit Institute of Arts. Woollen tapestry on linen. 27 ¹/₂ by 25 ¹/₂ inches. Found in the necropolis of Sheikh Sayed, near Akhmin (Egypt). (Photo U.D.F.-Draeger)

387. Egypt. *Tapestry Hanging: Busts in Medallions, Horsemen under Arches, and Other Motifs.* 5th century. New York, The Metropolitan Museum of Art, George F. Baker Donation. Tapestry of wool and linen. 47 ¹/₄ by 23 ¹/₄ inches. (Museum Photo)

388. Egypt. *Fragment of a Garment: Hare nibbling a Vine Branch.* 6th century. Private Collection. Woollen tapestry on linen. 8 ¹/₂ by 8 inches. Found at Sheikh Anadeh (Antinoe), Egypt. (Photo U.D.F.-Draeger)

389. Egypt. *Tapestry Hanging known as the Antinoe Shawl, detail: Bacchic Thiasos.* 4th century. Paris, Louvre. Muslin with stencilled designs. Overall size 4 by 11 ft. This hanging was found in an Egyptian tomb: used as padding, it had been twisted round the arms and neck of a shabbily dressed woman. (Archives photographiques des Monuments historiques)

390. Egypt. *Fragment of a Tapestry Hanging with Fish Designs.* 2nd-3rd century. Paris, Louvre. Wool and linen. 13 by 17 ¹/₄ inches. (Photo U.D.F.-La Photothèque)

391. Egypt. *Tapestry Hanging: The Nativity in an Ornamental Medallion.* 6th century. Vatican City, Museo Sacro, Treasure of the Sancta Sanctorum. Silk. (Photo Vatican Library)

392. Egypt. *Tapestry Hanging: The Annunciation in an Ornamental Medallion.* First half of the 6th century. Vatican City, Museo Sacro, Treasure of the Sancta Sanctorum. Silk. (Photo Vatican Library)

393. *Plan of Rome.*

394. *Plan of Constantinople.*

395. *Plan of Ravenna.*

396. *Plan of Salonica.*

397. Milan, Church of San Lorenzo with the Chapels of Sant'Aquilino, San Sisto and Sant'Ippolito. *Plan.* 5th century. (After Paolo Verzone, *L'architettura religiosa dell'alto medio evo nell'Italia settentrionale*, Milan, 1942, fig. 37, p. 80)

398. Portbail (Manche), Baptistery. *Plan.* Between the 4th and 6th century. (After M. de Boüard, *Le Baptistère de Port-Bail (Manche)*, in *Cahiers archéologiques*, IX, 1957, fig. 2, p. 4)

399. Parenzo (now Porec, Yugoslavia), Basilica and Baptistery. *Plan.* About 540. (After Bruno Molajoli, *La basilica eufrasiana di Parenzo*, Padua, 2nd edition, 1943, fig. 3, p. 10)

400. Ravenna, Church of San Vitale. *Plan.* Begun in 532, consecrated in 547. (After Paolo Verzone, *L'architettura religiosa dell'alto medio evo nell'Italia settentrionale*, Milan, 1942, fig. 41)

401. Milan, Church of Santi Apostoli, now San Nazzaro. *Plan.* 382. (After Gino Traversi, *Architettura paleocristiana milanese*, Milan, 1964, fig. 7, p. 96)

402. Carthage, Basilica of Dermesh. *Plan.* 6th century. (After Ugo Monneret de Villard, *Le chiese della Mesopotamia*, Rome, 1940, fig. 36)

403. Henshir Goussa (Tunisia), Basilica. *Plan.* (After Paul Gauckler, *Les Basiliques chrétiennes de Tunisie*, Paris, 1913, pl. XXVI top)

404. Feriana (Tunisia), Basilica. *Plan.* 5th-6th century. (After Paul Gauckler, *Les Basiliques chrétiennes de Tunisie*, Paris, 1913, pl. XXIV)

405. Tipasa (Algeria), Basilica of St Salsa and Martyrium. *Plan.* 5th-6th century. (After Stéphane Gsell, *Les Monuments antiques de l'Algérie*, II, Paris, 1901, fig. 150)

406. Tabarka (Tunisia), Basilica and detail of the Octagonal Baptistery. *Plan.* 5th century. (After Paul Gauckler, *Les Basiliques chrétiennes de Tunisie*, Paris, 1913, pl. XVI)

407. Mididi (Tunisia), Basilica. *Plan and Longitudinal Section.* 5th-6th century. (After Paul Gauckler, *Les Basiliques chrétiennes de Tunisie*, Paris, 1913, pl. XXVIII)

408. Henshir Rhiria (Tunisia), Basilica and Baptistery. *Plan.* 5th century. (After Paul Gauckler, *Les Basiliques chrétiennes de Tunisie*, Paris, 1913, pl. XV)

409. Ain Tamda (Algeria), Church and Cloister. *Plan.* (After William Seston, *Le Monastère d'Aïn-Tamda et les origines de l'architecture monastique en Afrique du Nord*, in *Mélanges d'archéologie et d'histoire*, LI, Paris, 1934, fig. 2, p. 11)

410. Tebessa (Algeria), Group of Early Christian Buildings. *Plan.* 5th-6th century. (After Stéphane Gsell, *Les Monuments antiques de l'Algérie*, II, Paris, 1901, fig. 134, p. 267)

411. St Menas (Egypt). *Overall Plan of the Sanctuary.* 5th century. (After *Papers of the British School at Rome*, XVII, New Series IV, London, 1949, pl. XI)

412. Dendera (Egypt), Room in the Temple of Hathor converted into a Church. *Plan.* 6th century. (After Ugo Monneret de Villard, *Les Couvents près de Sohag*, I, Milan, 1925, fig. 52)

413. Sohag (Egypt), White Monastery (Deir el-Abiad), Church. *Plan.* Early 5th century. (After Ugo Monneret de Villard, *Les Couvents près de Sohag*, I, Milan, 1925, fig. 3)

414. Sakkara (Egypt), Monastery of St Jeremiah. *Overall Plan of the Excavations.* 5th century. (After J.E. Quibell, *Explorations at Saqqara. The Monastery of Apa Jeremias, 1908-1910*, Cairo, 1912, pl. I)

415. El Hosn (Syria), Church I. *Plan.* 5th century. (After F. Cabrol and H. Leclerc, *Dictionnaire d'archéologie chrétienne et de liturgie*, XV, part two, Paris, 1953, fig. 11015, p. 1885)

416. Dar Kita (Syria). *Overall Plan.* 5th century. (After H.C. Butler, *Early Churches in Syria, Fourth to Seventh Centuries*, Princeton, 1929, fig. 48, p. 51)

417. Ir-Ruhaiyeh (Syria). *Overall Plan of the Three Churches.* 529-530, 556-557, 564-565. (After H.C. Butler, *Early Churches in Syria, Fourth to Seventh Centuries*, Princeton, 1929, fig. 113, p. 111)

418. Deir Seman (Syria), West Monastery. *Plan.* 6th century. (After H.C. Butler, *Early Churches in Syria, Fourth to Seventh Centuries*, Princeton, 1929, fig. 105, p. 104)

419. Ed Deir (Syria), Church and Atrium. *Plan.* 6th century. (After H.C. Butler, *Early Churches in Syria, Fourth to Seventh Centuries*, Princeton, 1929, fig. 91, p. 88)

420. El Anderin (Syria), South Church and Peribole. *Plan.* 6th century. (After H.C. Butler, *Early Churches in Syria, Fourth to Seventh Centuries*, Princeton, 1929, fig. 209, p. 209)

421. Ruweiha (Syria), Church of Bizzos and Mausolea. *Plan.* 5th-6th century. (After H.C. Butler, *Early Churches in Syria, Fourth to Seventh Centuries*, Princeton, 1929, fig. 208, p. 208)

422. Kasr Ibn Wardan (Syria), Church. *Longitudinal Section.* 6th century. (After H.C. Butler, *Early Churches in Syria, Fourth to Seventh Centuries*, Princeton, 1929, fig. 178, p. 167)

423. Kalat Seman (Syria), Sanctuary of St Simeon Stylites. *Overall Plan.* About 480. (After Georges Tchalenko, *Villages antiques de la Syrie du Nord. Le massif du Bélus à l'époque romaine*, II, Paris, 1953, pl. L, 1)

424. Kalat Seman (Syria), Sanctuary of St Simeon Stylites, detail. *Plan.* About 480. (After H.C. Butler, *Early Churches in Syria, Fourth to Seventh Centuries*, Princeton, 1929, fig. 194, p. 191)

425. Resafa (Syria), Cathedral of St Sergius. *Perspective View of the Choir.* 6th century. (After F. Chabrol and H. Leclerc, *Dictionnaire d'archéologie chrétienne et de liturgie*, XV, part two, Paris, 1953, fig. 11013, p. 1881)

426. Bosra (Syria), Cathedral. *Plan.* 6th century. (After J.W. Crowfoot, *Churches at Bosra and Samaria-Sebaste*, British School of Archaeology in Jerusalem, Supplementary Paper 4, London, 1937, pl. IIa)

427. Bosra (Syria), Cathedral. *Cross-Section.* 6th century. (After H.C. Butler, *Early Churches in Syria, Fourth to Seventh Centuries*, Princeton, 1929, fig. 125, p. 126)

428. Ezra (Syria), Church of St George. *Plan.* 6th century. (After F. Cabrol and H. Leclerc, *Dictionnaire d'archéologie chrétienne et de liturgie*, XV, part two, Paris, 1953, fig. 11023)

429. Shagra (Syria), Martyrium. *Plan.* 6th century. (After F. Cabrol and H. Leclerc, *Dictionnaire d'archéologie chrétienne et de liturgie*, XV, part two, Paris, 1953, fig. 11024)

430. Jerusalem, Church of the Tomb of the Virgin. *Plan.* 5th century. (After Jean Lassus, *Sanctuaires chrétiens de Syrie*, Paris, 1947, fig. 46, p. 107)

431. Mount Garizim (Palestine), Church of the Virgin. *Plan.* 5th century. (After Jean Lassus, *Sanctuaires chrétiens de Syrie*, Paris, 1947, fig. 47, p. 108)

432. Jerusalem, Church of St John the Baptist. *Trefoil Plan.* Mid 5th century. (After H. Vincent and F.M. Abel, *Jérusalem nouvelle*, II, 3, Paris, 1922, pl. LXV)

433. Beit Alpha (Palestine), Synagogue. *Plan.* 6th-7th century. (After Erwin R. Goodenough, *Jewish Symbols in the Greco-Roman Period*, III, Bollingen Series, XXXVII, New York, 1953, fig. 631)

434. El Tabgha (Palestine), Basilica of the Multiplication of Loaves and Fishes. *Plan.* 4th-early 5th century. (After A.M. Schneider, *The Church of the Multiplying of the Loaves and Fishes at Tabgha on the Lake of Gennesareth and its Mosaics*, London, 1937, plan I)

435. Gerasa (Palestine), Church of Sts Peter and Paul. *Plan.* About 540. (After C.H. Kraeling, *Gerasa, City of the Decapolis*, New Haven, Conn., 1938, plan XXXIX)

436. El Hammeh (Palestine), Synagogue with enclosed apse. *Plan.* 6th century. (After Erwin R. Goodenough, *Jewish Symbols in the Greco-Roman Period*, III, Bollingen Series, XXXVII, New York, 1953, fig. 626)

437. Damgan (Mesopotamia), Sassanian House. *Plan.* 5th-6th century. (After Ugo Monneret de Villard, *Le chiese della Mesopotamia*, Rome, 1940, fig. 2)

438. Al Hirah (Mesopotamia), Church XI. *Plan.* Dating uncertain. (After Ugo Monneret de Villard, *Le chiese della Mesopotamia*, Rome, 1940, fig. 31)

439. Nisibis (Mesopotamia), Martyrium of St James of Nisibis. *Plan.* Founded in 359, completed later. (After Ugo Monneret de Villard, *Le chiese della Mesopotamia*, Rome, 1940, fig. 93)

440. Behnam (Syria), Church and underground room joined by an underground passage. *Plan.* Late 6th century. (After Ugo Monneret de Villard, *Le chiese della Mesopotamia*, Rome, 1940, fig. 91)

441. Hah (Mesopotamia), Church of the Virgin (al-Hadra). *Trefoil Plan.* 6th century. (After Ugo Monneret de Villard, *Le chiese della Mesopotamia*, Rome, 1940, fig. 61)

442. Kartamin (Mesopotamia), Monastery, detail. *Plan of the Church.* Founded in the late 4th century, rebuilt in 512. (After Ugo Monneret de Villard, *Le chiese della Mesopotamia*, Rome, 1940, fig. 52)

443. Kartamin (Mesopotamia), Monastery. *Overall Plan.* Founded in the late 4th century, rebuilt in 512. (After Ugo Monneret de Villard, *Le chiese della Mesopotamia*, Rome, 1940, fig. 52)

444. Korykos (Asia Minor), Church 'extra muros.' *Plan.* 5th century. (After E. Herzfeld and S. Guyer, *Meriamlik and Korykos*, in *Monumenta Asiae Minoris Antiqua*, II, The Manchester University Press, 1930, fig. 109, p. 111)

445. Korykos (Asia Minor), Martyrium Church. *Plan.* 5th century. (After E. Herzfeld and S. Guyer, *Monumenta Asiae Minoris Antiqua*, II, The Manchester University Press, 1930, fig. 130)

446. Side (Asia Minor), Baptistery. *Plan.* 5th century. (After Semavi Eyice, *Unb aptistère byzantin à Sidé, en Pamphylie*, in *Actes du Vᵉ Congrès international d'archéologie chrétienne*, *Aix, 1954*, Paris, 1957, fig. 1)

447. Meriamlik (Asia Minor), Basilica (reconstruction). *Plan.* Second half of the 5th century. (After E. Herzfeld and S. Guyer, *Monumenta Asiae Minoris Antiqua*, II, The Manchester University Press, 1930, fig. 46, p. 47)

448. Perga (Asia Minor), Church. *Plan.* 5th-6th century. (After Hans Roth, *Kleinasiatische Denkmäler*, Leipzig, 1908, fig. 19, p. 47)

449. Bin Bir Kilisseh (Asia Minor), Church I (after J. Strzygowski). *Plan.* 4th-6th century. (After J.W. Crowfoot, in J. Strzygowski, *Kleinasien, Ein Neuland der Kunstgeschichte*, Leipzig, 1903, fig. 5, p. 10)

450. Bin Bir Kilisseh (Asia Minor), Church III (after J. Strzygowski). *Plan.* 4th-6th century. (After J.W. Crowfoot, in J. Strzygowski, *Kleinasien, Ein Neuland der Kunstgeschichte*, Leipzig, 1903, fig. 9, p. 14)

Plans and Maps drawn by Jacques Rochette.

# Maps

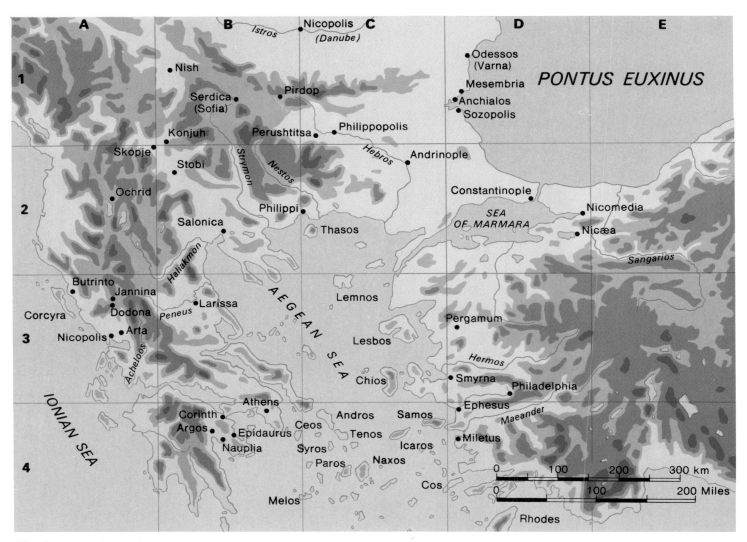

A  B  Istros  Nicopolis  C  D  E
(Danube)

1  ● Nish  Odessos
(Varna)

● Serdica  ● Pirdop  Mesembria
(Sofia)  ● Anchialos
Konjuh  Perushtitsa  ● Philippopolis  Sozopolis

● Skopje  Strymon  Nestos  Hebros  Andrinople

● Stobi

2  ● Ochrid  Constantinople  SEA  Nicomedia
OF MARMARA
Salonica  Philippi  Nicæa
Thasos  Sangarios

PONTUS EUXINUS

Haliakmon  AEGEAN SEA
Butrinto  Lemnos
Jannina  Larissa  Pergamum
Corcyra  Dodona  Peneus
3  Nicopolis  Arta  Lesbos  Hermos
Acheloos  Chios  Smyrna  Philadelphia
Ephesus
Athens  Andros  Samos  Maeander
Corinth  Ceos  Tenos
Argos  Epidaurus  Syros  Icaros  Miletus
Nauplia  Paros  Naxos
4  IONIAN SEA  Cos  0  100  200  300 km
0  100  200 Miles
Melos  Rhodes

470. *Constantinople and the Aegean Region.*

# Constantinople and the Aegean Region

# The Mediterranean World

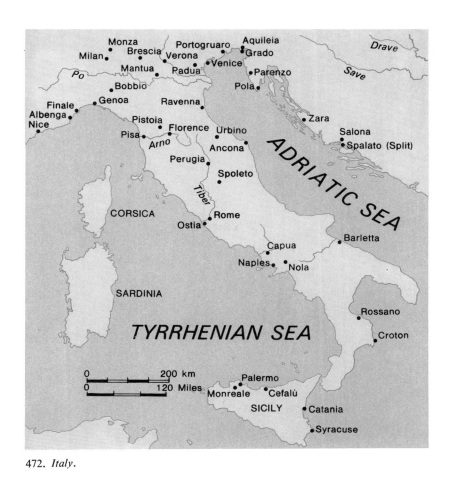

472. *Italy.*

Monza
Milan
Brescia
Verona
Portogruaro
Aquileia
Grado
Mantua
Padua
Venice
Parenzo
Po
Bobbio
Pola
Genoa
Ravenna
Finale
Albenga
Nice
Pistoia
Zara
Florence
Urbino
Salona
Spalato (Split)
Pisa
Arno
Ancona
Perugia
Spoleto
Tiber
ADRIATIC SEA
CORSICA
Rome
Ostia
Barletta
Capua
Naples
Nola
SARDINIA
Rossano
TYRRHENIAN SEA
Croton
0   200 km
0   120 Miles
Palermo
Monreale
Cefalù
SICILY
Catania
Syracuse

473. *Palestine.*

Se
Qishon
Caesarea
Mt Garizi
Emmaus
Jerusalem
Ascalon
Bethlehem
Gaza
0   50 km
0   30 Mile

MEDITERRANEAN SEA

Cape Bon
Icosium
(Algiers)
Busguniae
Tipasa
Nas ava th
Hippo
Tabarka
Carthage
Tunis
Bagradas
Setif
Jemila
Tipasa
Mutchul
Orléansville
Aïn Tamda
Kerbet Bou-Addoufan
Maktar
Chylem ath
Batna
Timgad
Morsott
Ammaedara
Lambese
Tebessa
Sufetula
Feriana
Macomades
Minores

0   100   200 km
0   50   100 Miles

474. *North Africa.*

**E**  **F**  **G**  **H**

CARPATHIANS

Theiss

Dniestr

Dniepr

Don

PONTUS EUXINUS

• Odessos

Trapezus •

Konjuh •
• Stobi
Perushtitsa •

• Andrinople

• Amasia

Brindisi •

• Salonica

Constantinople
• Nicomedia

Dag Pazarli •

Euphrates

Ancyra •

Melitene •

Caesarea •

Sardis •

• Ephesus
Tralles •

Sagalassos •
• Daouleh
• Bin Bir Kilisseh
Kanytelideis

Anazarab •

Edessa •

Athens •

Corinth •

Perga •
Side •
Aspendos •
Alahan •
Seleucia

Korykos •
Meriamlik
Antioch •

Apamea •

RHODES

CYPRUS

Palmyra •

Paphos •

Berytus
(Beirut) •

Damascus •

CRETE

DITERRANEAN SEA

Tyre • Kabr Hiram

• Madaba

Cyrene •

Alexandria •

Petra •

EGYPT

Sakkara •
Fayum • Karanis •

Mt Sinai
▲

IA

Nile

Hermopolis •
• Antinoe

Bawit •

471. *The Mediterranean World*.

Capernaum
El Tabgha ●
*of Galilee*

*Yarmuk*

● El Hammeh

Beit Alpha

*Jordan*

▲

*Yabok*

● Gerasa

Jericho ●

Mt Nebo
▲
● Madaba

● 

**DEAD SEA**

*Arnon*

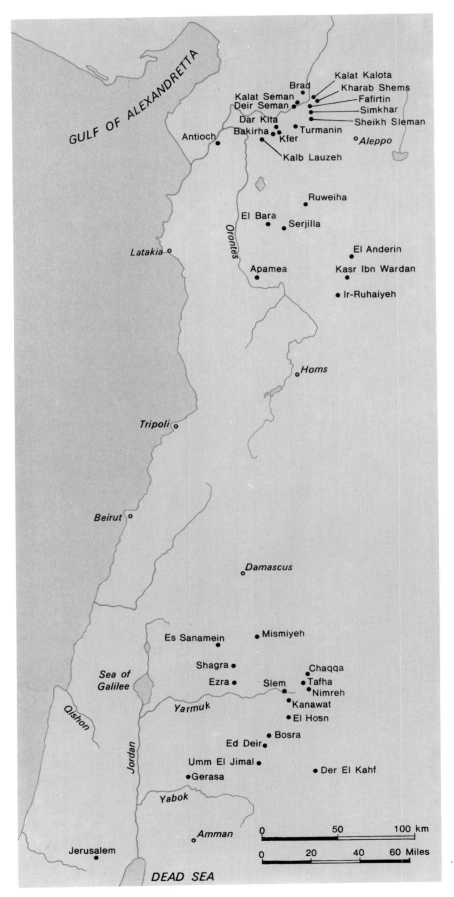

GULF OF ALEXANDRETTA

Kalat Kalota
Brad ● Kharab Shems
Kalat Seman ● Fafirtin
Deir Seman ● Simkhar
Dar Kita Sheikh Sleman
Bakirha ● Turmanin
Antioch ● Kfer ○ *Aleppo*
Kalb Lauzeh

Ruweiha ●

El Bara ●
Serjilla ●

Latakia ○

*Orontes*

El Anderin ●
Apamea ● Kasr Ibn Wardan ●

● Ir-Ruhaiyeh

● *Homs*

Tripoli ○

Beirut ○

*Damascus* ○

Es Sanamein ● ● Mismiyeh

Shagra ● Chaqqa ●
*Sea of* Tafha ●
*Galilee* Ezra ● Slem ● Nimreh ●
Kanawat ●
*Qishon* *Yarmuk* ● El Hosn
● Bosra
*Jordan* Ed Deir ●
Umm El Jimal ●
● Der El Kahf
● Gerasa
*Yabok*

*Amman* ○

Jerusalem ●

0          50          100 km
0     20        40      60 Miles

**DEAD SEA**

475. *Syria.*

THIS, THE TENTH VOLUME OF 'THE ARTS OF MANKIND' SERIES, EDITED BY ANDRÉ MALRAUX AND GEORGES SALLES, HAS BEEN PRODUCED UNDER THE SUPERVISION OF ALBERT BEURET, EDITOR-IN-CHARGE OF THE SERIES. THE BOOK WAS DESIGNED BY MICHEL MUGUET, ASSISTED BY SERGE ROMAIN. THE TEXT, THE PLATES IN BLACK AND WHITE AND IN SEPIA WERE PRINTED BY L'IMPRIMERIE GEORGES LANG, PARIS; PLATES IN COLOUR BY L'IMPRIMERIE DRAEGER FRÈRES, MONTROUGE. THE BINDING, DESIGNED BY MASSIN, WAS EXECUTED BY BABOUOT, GENTILLY.